Hawaii's Forgotten History

1900-1999

The good...the bad...the embarrassing

D1366578

by Rich Budnick

Hawaii's Forgotten History
1900-1999

The good...the bad...the embarrassing

Published by

Aloha Press
934 Wainiha
Honolulu, HI 96825
AlohaPress@ATT.net

Library of Congress Control Number: 2005930794
    Budnick, Rich
    ISBN No. 0-944081-04-5

Book Cover Design by Debra Castro

Photo credits:

Castle and Cooke Hawai'i, page 15; Hawaiian Dredging, page 16; Hawai'i
Hochi, page 29; © Don Love, attorney, page 34; Makiki Christian Church,
page 60; Finance Factors, page 163; City and County of Honolulu, page 172;
U.S. Congresswoman Patsy Mink, page 174; U.S. Senator Daniel Inouye, page
177; K. Russell Ho, page 180; Polynesian Voyaging Society, page 184; NASA,
page 200; K. Russell Ho, page 204; Small Business Hawai'i, page 205; David
Matthews, page 210; Hawai'i State AFL-CIO, page 214; Castle and Cooke
Hawai'i, page 220; State of Hawai'i, page 223; all other photos are from the
Hawai'i State Archives.

Table of Contents

Introduction

This book documents 2,001 important and little-known events in Hawai'i during the 20th century. Many events may have been forgotten, and others haven't been discussed in decades.

My title, **Hawaii's Forgotten History**, comes from a speech by U.S. Senator Daniel Inouye. He said: "We tend to forget the great events beyond our recent memory." This book is about people and events – the good...the bad...and the embarrassing.

I researched this book by reading 300 books and 8,000 newspapers, so you don't have to. Some events will make you laugh, and some will shock your senses. When "discovering" long-forgotten events I often said, "I didn't know that!" and you will too. Many popular words and deeds would be considered discriminatory or racist today.

You will discover a surprising history of contradictions. For example, in 1918, our leaders wanted to tell the world that Hawai'i was a melting pot of racial harmony. Yet our newspapers branded labor union leaders as "agitators," and many criticized our public schools and criminal justice system for having two separate standards – one for Caucasians and another for non-Caucasians. As Governor John Burns said in 1969, people who grew up in Hawai'i before WW II "know full-well what I mean."

The chart on page 242 shows how the "Big 5" corporations ruled Hawai'i for 50 years by keeping "power in the hands of a few." In fact, U.S. Labor Department officials criticized the plantations and Big 5 for acting like Fascists and treating workers like slaves.

To be fair, my criteria for including an event or statement was if it was "news worthy" – not if I personally agreed or disagreed with it.

This book covers diverse topics such as education, military, transportation, employment, business, economy, crime, immigration, ethnic history, Hawaiiana, land use, anti-war protests, internment, and much more.

You'll find my list of 100 important and little-known events on pages 7-9. Here's a tip: Don't miss the last chapter, "I Couldn't Resist."

You can learn more about many of these events by reading the front page of the Honolulu Advertiser and Honolulu Star-Bulletin.

Acknowledgments

Many people reviewed this book and gave me suggestions. First, I want to express a very special thanks to: Mel Ah Ching, Peter Apo, Duane Bartholomew, Judith Bowman, Dan Boylan, Debra Castro, Tom Coffman, Jim Dote, Sharla Hanaoka, Wally Inglis, Cliff Inn, Bob Katayama, Gaylord Kubota, Sabrina Kyi, Sybil Kyi, Alan Lloyd, Ah Quon McElrath, Jim Manke, Franklin Odo, Kalani Ogata, Bob Osgood, William Puette, Sonnie Rodrigues, Charlie Rose, Rae Shiraki, Bob Sigall, Sam Slom, Bill Souza, Ted Tsukiyama, Rich Ziegler...and many librarians at many libraries.

Also: Lyman Abbott, Melanie Abihai, Glennie Adams, Wanda Adams, Amy Agbayani, John Alamodin, Dean Alegado, Muriel Anderson, Chuck Anthony, Noe Arista, Jackie Aweau, Arlene Bally, Patty Lei Belcher, A. Duane Black, Jim Boersma, Marsha Bolson, Richard Borreca, Phil Bossert, Manu Boyd, Paul Breese, Paul Brewbaker, Boyce Brown, Keali'i Brown, Butch Bukes, Hayden Burgess, Burl Burlingame, Doc Buyers, David Callies, Laurie Carlson, Karee Carlucci, Norma Carr, Willetta Centeio, Doug Chang, Cheryl Chung, Christopher Chung, Karleen Chinen, Michaelyn Chou, Alice Clark, Delores Clark, Hugh Clark, Ashley Cobb, Chris Cook, Francisco Corpuz, Eddie Croom, Cathy Cruz, Zita Cup Choy.

Mary Daubert, Rick Daysog, Kevin Dayton, Denise De Costa, Gerald DeMello, Don Devaney, Jean De Ville, Steve Diamond, Paul A. Dolan, Marc Dixon, Kioni Dudley, Mark Dunkerley, Debbie Dunn, Harry Eager, Rick Egged, Hailama Farden, Derrick Farrar, John Henry Felix, Martti Fernandez, Elizabeth Fitzgerald, Reed Flickinger, Chuck Friedman, Sarah Fry, John Furman, Eunice Garcia, Laura Gallagher, Jim George, Laura Gerwitz, Stu Glauberman, Duke Gonzales, Chris Grandy, Pamela Gutara.

Dana Naone Hall, Stephanie Hall, Davin Hanaoka, Wayne Harada, Krislyn Hashimoto, Beverly Hayashi, Brad Hayes, Linda Hee, Mark Hellrung, Eileen Herring, Mark Hickman, Irma Hinazumi, Nancy Hiraoka, Barbara Ho, Russell Ho, Timothy Ho, John Hoag, Nathan Hokama, Evelyn Honda, Leonard Hoshijo, Gerald Hoswolt, Bruce Houghton, Linda Howe, Cindy Hunter, Laurel Bowers Husain, Jeong Ku Hwang, Rev. Wayne Ibara, Linda Iwamoto, Neal Iwamoto.

Kathy Jakuda, Donna Jung, Brande Kahalewai, Lowell Kalapa, Betty Kam, Chris Kam, Wes Kam, Keith Kamida, Bumpy Kanahele, Kanaʻi Kapeliela, Gwen Kashima, Scott Kawasaki, Beverly Keever, Gerry Keir, Shelly Kekuna, Joel Kennedy, Bruss Keppeler, Del Kleckner, Kalowena Komeiji, Judy Kono, Paul Kosasa, Bob Krauss, Kylee Kurita, Henry Kutsada, Sumner La Croix, Amber Ladera, Mardie Lane, Leroy Laney, Bill Langer, Antoinette Lee, Oliver Lee, Verna Lee, Becky Lennon, Patrick Leonard, Maggie Li, Maureen Lichter, Ian Lind, Chuck Little, Jim Loomis, Domingo Los Baños, Ray Lovell, Allen Lum, Francis Lum, Ryan Lum.

John McDermott, Holly McEldowing, Thom McGarvey, Davianna McGregor, Aven Wright-McIntosh, Bob McLaren, Tammy Maeda, Susan Maesato, Aaron Mahi, Dee Jay Mailer, TJ Malievsky, Lois Manin, Ann Marsteller, Daniel Martinez, Greg Matsumoto, Matt Mattice, Charlie Maxwell, Kristi Medeiros, Linda Menton, Barbara Mertz, Michael Miller, Claire Mitani, Abe Mitsuda, Wayne Miyahara, Sharon Miyashiro, Stephanie Monet, Darlene Morikawa, Jim Moulds, Joyce Murashige.

Joyce Nagahara, Pam Nakagawa, Cynthia Nakamura, Hiwa Namahoe, Kam Napier, Judy Neale, Sweetie Nelson, Joe O'Donnell, Ed Okubo, John Okumura, Gary Oliveira, Ricky Oshiro, Jon Osorio, Chris Oya, Fred Pascua, Agnes Paulian, Cheryl Percival, Colin Perry, Lauren Pippen, Dick Poirer, Aaron Pollock, Alfred Pratte, Anne Pulfrey, Diane Quitquit, Marilyn Rappun, Ken Redman, Tiffany Reed, Roxanne Rella, Sarah Richards, Muriel Roberts, Helen Rogers, David Rosenbrock, Randy Roth, Tony Rutledge, Nezette Rydell, Jeri Sato, James Scott, Melody Selvage, Sam Shenkus, Noe Noe Silva, Jessica Silverman, Yoshiko Sinoto, Mike Slackman, Donna Smith, Marion Smith, Joe Souki, Margaret Stafford, Thurston Twigg-Smith, Brynna Stankiewicz, Mary Steiner.

Ann Takiguchi, Ron Taketa, Carolyn Tanaka, Eric Tanaka, Carol Tang, Ed Tanji, Andre Tatibouet, Ann Takabuki, Allicyn Tasaka, Bill Tavares, Jan Tenbruggencate, Cynthia Thielen, Susie Thieman, Kim Thomas, Laura Thompson, Priscilla Thompson, Eugene Tian, Margaret Tippy, Michael Titterton, Ken Toguchi, Martha Tomey, Claire Tong, Lou Torraca, Murray Towill, Adele Tsukamoto, Ron Turner, Sonja Tyau, David Uchiyama, Sheila Uehara, Nancy Usui, Phil Vierra, Keoni Wagner, Debra Ward, Bob Watada, BJ Whitman, Puanani Wilhelm, Jeanne Williams-White, Jim Wilson, Nancy Wilson, Shannon Wilson, Karen Winpenny, Alyssa Wong, Milton Yamamoto, Janis Yee, Paul Yempuku, Martha Yent, Rev. Louis Yim, Brianne Yoshimoto, Dwight Yoshimura, Tinhu Young, Michelle Yu, Mike Yuen, Gerald Yuh, Glenn Zander, Janet Zisk, Jessica Zisk.

A very special thanks to my wife, Min-Tzu Hsiao Budnick, for patiently understanding that it takes zillions of hours to finish a book.

Top 50 Big Events by Year

1900   Hawai'i becomes a U.S. Territory and establishes a government
1900   Chinatown fire and bubonic plague
1909   7,000 sugar workers strike for 3 months
1912   Duke Kahanamoku wins Olympic gold medal
1918   American Factors (Amfac) is created when German-owned Hackfeld Co. is seized. A subsidiary is renamed Liberty House.
1920   5-month sugar strike
1920   U.S. Education Department report criticizes Hawai'i education
1920   First English standard school is established
1921   President Harding signs the Hawaiian Homes Commission Act
1924   8-month strike against half of Hawaii's sugar plantations
1924   Hanapēpē Massacre – 16 workers and 4 police are killed
1927   First airplane flight from the mainland (Oakland) to Hawai'i
1927 $25,000 Dole Derby – airplane race from Oakland to Hawai'i
1931-1932   Ala Moana "rape" case, Massie trial, and reaction
1935   Radio program, HAWAI'I CALLS begins
1938   Hilo Massacre – police shoot and stab 51 strikers in the back
1941   Pearl Harbor attack
1941   Martial law declared – 1946: U.S. Supreme Court rules it illegal
1942-1943   100th and 442nd military units are established for AJAs
1946   Hilo tsunami kills 173 people
1946   Police graft scandal – trials in 1947
1946   First territory-wide, industry-wide sugar strike
1948   School teachers John and Aiko Reinecke are fired, accused of being Communists
1949   6-month dock strike, "Broom Brigade," and "Dear Joe" letters
1950   "Reluctant 39" refuse to testify to Congress about Communism
1951   "Hawai'i 7" arrested for allegedly being Communists
1954   116,000 people sign a statehood petition
1954   Democratic "Revolution" – Democrats win the Legislature
1959   Statehood
1960   Hilo tsunami kills 61 people
1961   Chinn Ho is first Asian-American named to a Big 5 board
1967   Land Reform Act
1967   UH Professor Oliver Lee is denied tenure
1970   Hawai'i is the first state with a law to legalize abortion
1971   Kalama Valley farmers protest for their land rights
1974   Governor Ariyoshi signs the Prepaid Health Care Law
1976   Kaho'olawe is occupied secretly for the first time
1976   HŌKŪLE'A makes it's first voyage to Tahiti

1978 Voters establish the Office of Hawaiian Affairs
1988 Aloha Airlines' airplane roof rips off in flight – a stewardess dies
1992 Hurricane 'Iniki causes $2.5 billion damage
1993 100th anniversary of the overthrow is commemorated
1993 President Clinton signs apology resolution for 1893 overthrow
1994 Kaho'olawe is returned to Hawai'i jurisdiction
1998 UH scientists clone mice
1998 Photographic display of the 1897 petitions signed by 21,000 Hawaiians protesting annexation
1999 "Broken Trust" essay and several years of protests leads to the resignation of Bishop Estate trustees, and their selection process

Top 50 Little-Known Events by Year

1901-1917 Queen Lili'uokalani receives $130,000 from Territorial government, probably for Crown Land income
1901 Chamber of Commerce imposes a 50-year Wharf fee to control rats, promote public health programs, and support tourism
1907 Gov. George Carter says he wouldn't mind if his daughter married a Japanese man – legislators talk of inter-racial marriage ban
1913 Pearl Harbor drydock explosion costs $5 million to rebuild
1915 First U.S. submarine disaster – F-4 sub sinks, all 21 sailors die
1917 Typhoid germs are found in Honolulu water supply
1917 2 U.S. Navy sailors steal silver crown from Lunalilo tomb
1918 Legislature wants internment camps here for German aliens
1918 Selective Service classifies Hawaiians as "white" for WW I draft
1918 Hawai'i County Board of Supervisors is guilty of mismanagement
1918 German aliens are fired as school teachers and a UH instructor resigns under pressure
1921 Governor McCarthy signs anti-union law to restrict speech and press
1922 U.S. Supreme Court denies citizenship to a Japanese alien and rules that naturalization is only for Caucasians and African-Americans
1923 U.S. Army General Billy Mitchell predicts Japan will attack Hawai'i at 7:30 a.m. on a Sunday someday in the future
1927 Labor leader Pablo Manlapit gets parole only if he leaves Hawai'i
1929 Myles Fukunaga is hanged for kidnapping and murder
1930-1935 20% of new high school students are denied admission by Department of Public Instruction policy
1931 Hawai'i Supreme Court says it isn't cruel to whip a prisoner
1931 Prosser Report says schools should emphasize vocational education not academics because most jobs are on the plantations

1933	High school students pay $10 tuition to support teacher salaries
1935	5-year old actress Shirley Temple sings "Good Ship Lollipop" to 16,000 young fans at 'Iolani Palace
1936	U.S. Army Colonel George Patton prepares an internment plan
1937	Soichi Sakamoto trains swimmers in a Maui plantation ditch – they win 6 national championships and Olympic gold medals
1940	U.S. Labor Department report says Big 5 keep power in the hands of a few through "interlocking directorates"
1940	U.S. Labor official tells Congress that Hawaii's Big 5 are Fascist
1941-1943	Residents ordered to evacuate Iwilei, Liliha, and downtown
1942	A German alien is convicted of espionage in Pearl Harbor attack
1942	Japanese airplane drops 4 bombs near Roosevelt High School
1942	Special money is required in Hawai'i, and no one can have more than $200 cash. $200 million cash is burned at 'Aiea Sugar Mill
1943	U.S. Army makes a "Scorched Earth" plan to destroy industries and hotels in case of a Japan land invasion
1943	HSPA scientists make penicillin
1944	Pearl Harbor explosion kills 163 people
1945	Hawai'i submits a proposal to host United Nations at Waimānalo
1945	500 sailors riot and fight civilians at Damon Tract
1947	Translated documents reveal Japan's pre-war plot to kill President Roosevelt in Honolulu in 1941
1958	A raft deliberately drifts to Hawai'i from California to prove that ocean currents affected world population settlements
1958	Crew of GOLDEN RULE try to stop U.S. nuclear explosions
1959	4 airlines say Hawai'i lacks hotel rooms for tour groups
1959	Businessmen Henry Kaiser and Walter Dillingham argue in public
1960	Kahala residents vote 407-3 against a hotel in Kahala
1960	Hawai'i sends two delegations to the Electoral College because of a near tie in the presidential vote
1963	Realtors accuse Bishop Estate of housing discrimination
1964	Honolulu International Center (now Blaisdell) opens with 9 days of festivities, but no Hawaiian entertainers are invited to perform
1965	U.S. Navy accidentally bombs a Ni'ihau beach
1966	Housewives picket supermarkets to protest high food prices
1968	Pacific Club finally allows Asian-American members
1969	An unexploded U.S. Navy bomb is found near a Maui highway
1969	U.S. Army admits secret chemical and biological nerve gas tests
1975	Tsunami, earthquake and volcanic eruption on the same day
1976	Former Punahou President John Fox says eliminating the 10% quota of Asian students in the 1960s was his biggest problem
1977	Federal judge fines Hawai'i hotels $150,000 for price fixing
1982	A terrorist bomb kills a boy on a Pan Am flight before landing here

1900-1909

January 8, 1900: The first 26 Okinawans arrive in Hawai'i for 'Ewa Plantation. By 1924, 20,000 Okinawans arrive, but one-half leave Hawai'i for the U.S. mainland.

January 20, 1900: The quickest way to destroy the bubonic plague's dangerous bacteria" is to set small, controlled fires. Since December, the plague has been killing two people a day in Chinatown. Strong, sudden winds quickly spread today's fire, destroying nearly every building in Chinatown's 38 acres. No one dies in the fire. By January 26, 7,000 homeless are living in "detention camps" at Kawaiaha'o Church grounds – guarded by the U.S. Army to prevent violence. About 50% of the homeless people are Chinese, 30% are Japanese, and 20% are Hawaiian. The fire rids Chinatown's slum area of gamblers, prostitutes and gangsters, known as the "devil's den."

February 2, 1900: Pearl Harbor becomes a U.S. Navy coaling station.

February 10, 1900: The plague is declared on Maui when 6 people die in Kahului. On February 12, Kahului's 3-acre Chinatown is burned. 200 Chinese, Japanese and Hawaiians are quarantined until March at the horse-racing track.

February 17, 1900: The Maui News begins publication with editor G. Robertson. Maui Publishing Co. buys the newspaper on January 16, 1905. For 45 years, from February 11, 1905 to April 8, 1950, the editorial page masthead slogan proclaims it is "A Republican newspaper."

April 4, 1900: Hawaii's first successful strike begins. When three workers die in accidents, 2,000 Japanese workers strike at Maui's Pioneer and Olowalu Plantations until April 13.

The Chinatown Fire

A small crowd gathers to watch the fire when strong winds unexpectedly set Kaumakapili Church ablaze. The fire spreads quickly throughout Chinatown.

It's all gone.

April 24, 1900: William Howard Taft arrives in Hawai'i for 6 days, en-route to the Philippines where he will be the first U.S. territorial governor. As U.S. Secretary of War, he visits Hawai'i on January 16, 1904 and July 14, 1905. He is the first future U.S. president to visit Hawai'i.

April 24, 1900: 22 Austrians arrive in Hawai'i for Maui plantations.

April 30, 1900: The bubonic plague quarantine is lifted from all areas of Honolulu, including areas outside of Chinatown. The plague claims 61 lives since December.

April 30, 1900: President William McKinley signs the Hawaiian Organic Act to create the Territory of Hawai'i. The law also establishes English as the official language, prohibits any Chinese from entering the mainland from Hawai'i, and abolishes all plantation-labor contracts. The Organic Act also prohibits any new Hawai'i company from buying or owning more than 1,000 acres – which Congress repeals in July, 1921. After annexation, it took two years to finalize the Organic Act because many Hawai'i Republic laws, such as plantation labor laws, were inconsistent with the U.S. Constitution. The Organic Act takes effect on June 14, 1900, and lasts until Hawai'i becomes a state on August 21, 1959.

June, 1900: Chinese newspaper, HSIN CHUNG-KUO PAO (NEW CHINA PRESS) begins publication, and continues until March 13, 1941.

June 1, 1900: U.S. census begins. Hawai'i has 154,001 population, a 41% increase since 1890 – 24% Hawaiian, 19% Caucasian, 17% Chinese, 40% Japanese. There's only 4,284 Americans in Hawai'i – just 3% of the population.

June 2, 1900: President Theodore Roosevelt appoints Antonio Perry as Hawaii's first Portuguese on the Hawai'i Supreme Court. He is a Justice from 1900-1904, 1909-1914, 1922-1926, and Chief Justice from 1926-1934.

Governor Sanford Dole

June 14, 1900: Hawai'i officially becomes a U.S. territory because the Organic Act takes effect today. Thousands of Hawaiians are eligible to vote after being denied by the Republic of Hawai'i. Hawaii's first governor, Sanford Dole serves until November 23, 1903. He is appointed by President Theodore Roosevelt. Dole was a Supreme Court Justice during the monarchy, and president of the Republic of Hawai'i.

June 30, 1900: A&B incorporates as a Hawai'i company.

July 28, 1900: James Dole, the father of Hawaii's pineapple industry, pays $4,000 at an auction for 61 acres of government homestead land in Wahiawā. He arrived in Hawai'i on November 16, 1899. He is a second cousin to Governor Sanford Dole.

October 16, 1900: The 4 Young brothers arrive in Honolulu and establish a boat business, which becomes an interisland shipping company.

November 6, 1900: This is Hawaii's first election as an American Territory. Robert Wilcox, Home Rule Party candidate, is elected to Congress as Hawaii's first Delegate, a non-voting position. The Home Rule Party wins a majority control of the Hawai'i Legislature, but wins only a handful of seats from 1903-1913, and none after that.

November 12, 1900: Hawaii's first interisland message via Marconi wireless telegraphy is transmitted from Kaimukī to Moloka'i. Signals are transmitted from a kite at Wai'alae Beach.

November 23, 1900: 43 Japanese and Portuguese women strike at Kīlauea Plantation until December 3. Strikers win higher wages. It is one of Hawaii's first multi-racial strikes.

November 24, 1900: Mauna'olu College re-opens on Maui.

December 23, 1900: The first 56 Puerto Ricans arrive in Hawai'i, for Maui's Pioneer Mill. After the Spanish-American War, the U.S. acquired Puerto Rico in 1899 – the first U.S. Territory to send contract workers to Hawai'i Sugar Planters' Association (HSPA). By October 19, 1901, more than 5,200 Puerto Ricans arrive. Another 683 arrive in 1921-1922, when the HSPA threatens to stop importing Filipinos, due to Filipino labor strikes. 23 Italians from Louisiana arrive on the same 1900 boat, and they are sent to Spreckelsville Plantation.

January 2, 1901: The first 21 African-Americans, from Nashville, Tennessee, arrive in Hawai'i to work at C. Brewer's Wailuku Plantation. 200 Blacks arrive from the South in the next few years, but most don't stay. A 1903 Federal Labor Report says African-Americans leave Hawai'i because the cost of living is too high.

February 20, 1901: Hawaii's first Territorial Legislature convenes under American laws, with 15 Senators and 30 Representatives.

February 27, 1901: Territorial Rep. Jonah Kumalae introduces the first resolution in the Hawai'i Legislature to ask Congress for statehood. It does not pass.

March 1, 1901: Mutual Telegraph Company begins service as Hawaii's first interisland wireless telegraph business.

March 3, 1901: President Theodore Roosevelt approves spending $150,000 to excavate Pearl Harbor for large Navy ships. This is the first of several appropriations that will total millions of dollars for Pearl Harbor.

March 11, 1901: Waikiki's first major hotel, Moana, opens. The 200-room, $150,000 hotel has a 300-foot "Moana pier" with a pavilion (demolished in 1930 as unsafe), an elevator, and $1.50 rooms with a telephone and bath. The Sheraton Moana Surfrider, it is Waikiki's oldest surviving hotel.

April 30, 1901: Governor Sanford Dole signs a 2% income tax law. It is Hawaii's first tax. On August 26, the Hawai'i Supreme Court says the tax is constitutional.

May 1, 1901: Governor Sanford Dole pocket vetoes a bill to create county governments. The bill proposes to create Lili'uokalani (not Maui) County with the seat in Lahaina, and Lunalilo (not Kaua'i) County with the seat at Waimea. As a result, a U.S. Senate committee recommends that Congress pass a law creating county governments if Hawai'i doesn't. The ruling Caucasian Republicans object to creating county governments because they control the territory and fear losing patronage, and political and financial control over county governments.

May 1, 1901: Governor Sanford Dole pocket vetoes a bill to give $250,000 to Queen Lili'uokalani to satisfy her Crown Lands claim against the Republic and Territory.

July 18, 1901: Acting Governor Henry Cooper signs the budget into law, which pays Queen Lili'uokalani $15,000 for two years. The 1903 budget pays her $3,750, the 1904-1905 budget pays her $7,500, and the 1907-1909 budget pays her $15,000. On April 30, 1911, Governor Walter Frear signs a law to pay her $1,250 per month for the rest of her life. From 1901-1917, Lili'uokalani receives $130,000 from the Territory. The income may have been in lieu of rental income from Crown lands, which U.S. Senator John Mitchell recommends in a 1903 report prepared after visiting Hawai'i. Mitchell says his committee considers an allowance "an act of personal justice and national grace and wisdom...as the facts seem to justify..."

August 31, 1901: Honolulu Rapid Transit and Land (HRT&L) begins street car service with 10 overhead electric trolleys. It replaces street cars pulled by horses and mules. The new trolleys have 20,000 passengers the first day. By 1910, 9 million riders pay 5¢ fare to travel on 7 miles of track from Kalihi to Kaimukī, Waikīkī and Mānoa. Residential expansion to the "suburbs" of Kaimukī and Mānoa follows the trolley expansion. On January 1, 1903, HRT agrees to buy its competitor, Hawaiian Tramways. Electric street cars operate from 1901-1941, and trolley buses operate from 1938-1958.

November 16, 1901: The Honolulu Chamber of Commerce levies a 15¢ per ton "voluntary" fee on imports. The independent Shippers Wharf Committee is established on December 13, 1901 to manage the fund. By 1950, this tax has raised $2 million to support rat control at the wharf, plus tourism and many public health issues. Tourism promotion gets $571,000 and Palama Settlement gets $649,000. The Blood Bank gets $3,000 to begin operations on June 25, 1941.

November 18, 1901: Judge Abram Humphreys rules that Hawaiians can no longer give their children away for hānai adoption.

December 4, 1901: James Dole establishes Hawaiian Pineapple Company, which creates Hawaii's first large-scale pineapple industry. His first crop in 1903 is 1,900 cases of pineapples. When he needs money, the sugar companies ignore him because they don't think pineapple will succeed. The first record of pineapple in Hawai'i is on January 21, 1813. Don Francisco de Paula Marin wrote in his diary that he planted some pineapple.

James Dole, founder of Hawaiian Pineapple Company

December 7, 1901: Pioneer Inn is built in Lahaina by owner George Freeland. It is one of Hawaii's oldest hotels.

December 10, 1901: Hawai'i Judge Abram Humphreys rules that English, not Hawaiian must be spoken in court.

January 15, 1902: Native Hawaiian stevedores meet to establish a union to keep "cheap labor" Asians on the plantations where they won't compete for jobs.

January 29, 1902: Pu'unēnē Mill on Maui begins operation. It becomes the world's largest sugar cane factory in 1948.

February 22, 1902: MAUI NEWS reports 10 boys quit Lahainaluna School because of a rule that requires speaking only English.

March 3, 1902: Walter Dillingham establishes Hawaiian Dredging and Construction, which develops Honolulu Harbor and excavates Pearl Harbor. He builds many air bases in the Pacific, develops Pearl City in 1890, excavates the Ala Wai Canal in the 1920s, and builds Ala Moana Shopping Center in 1959. In 1961, Dillingham Corporation is created from a merger of Dillingham's two companies – O'ahu Railway and Land and Hawaiian Dredging and Construction. In 1982, a mainland investment company buys Dillingham for $348 million. Dillingham is considered as one of Hawaii's "Big 6" companies that control Hawai'i for more than a half-century.

May 13, 1902: The Order of Kamehameha is "re-established" by Jonah Kūhiō and Dr. George Huddy to preserve ancient customs. The first meeting is at Kuhio's home. It is re-established because the organization became a secret society after the monarchy overthrow.

May 14, 1902: Hawai'i begins tourism promotion. The Honolulu Chamber of Commerce and Merchants' Association agrees to send Honolulu businessman Walter Weedon on a 6-month tourism promotion to the mainland. He shows photos, gives lectures, and distributes pamphlets about Hawai'i. On July 19, 1902, the Merchants Association proposes a permanent tourism bureau.

September 8, 1902: A U.S. Senatorial Commission with 3 U.S. Senators from the Subcommittee on Pacific Islands and Puerto Rico begins the first Congressional hearings in Hawai'i until September 30. On September 23-24, their hearing about the monarchy overthrow receives more speakers than any other issue.

October 15, 1902: Carpenters union, Local 745 is chartered.

Fall, 1902: Charles Gay buys part of Lāna'i at an auction from W.H. Pain and Paul Neumann for $168,000 for a cattle and sheep ranch.

November 5, 1902: Prince Jonah Kūhiō Kalaniana'ole is elected to Congress as a Republican, defeating incumbent Robert Wilcox. The HAWAIIAN STAR newspaper has a huge headline, "Wilcox is dead." Kūhiō is Hawaii's 2nd Delegate, and remains in Congress until his death in 1922. He is persuaded to become a Republican by local politicians who want

**Prince Jonah Kūhiō
Kalaniana'ole**

to benefit from his popularity, and the fact that Hawaiians control about 2/3 of the vote. In exchange, he is assured that Hawaiians will be hired for government jobs. During his 20-year Congressional career, he wants to be appointed governor, but is passed over. He supports home rule of county governments.

December 5, 1902: The White Mechanics and Workingmen of Honolulu is established to stop Asian immigration. Mechanics complain that Chinese and Japanese will work for less pay than Caucasians, and take their jobs. A 1903 Federal Labor Report says "The presence of Orientals demoralizes some White mechanics."

December 28, 1902: A 2,100 mile underwater Pacific telegraph cable is laid, connecting Hawai'i and the mainland at Sans Souci beach. Pacific Commercial Cable Co. pays Hawai'i $8,000 cash for taxes for the last 3 miles of cable. The cable is extended to Asia on July 4, 1903.

1902: Sometaro Sheba establishes THE GARDEN ISLAND newspaper with separate Japanese and English editions. A 1911 fire destroys all of the early newspapers.

January 1, 1903: The first commercial cable message is sent to Hawai'i via underwater cable from San Francisco. On January 2, Henry Cooper, Secretary of Hawai'i, sends a message to President Theodore Roosevelt. Communication with the mainland now takes mere seconds instead of days.

January 13, 1903: The first 102 Korean plantation workers arrive in Hawai'i at the invitation of American missionaries in Korea. By 1907, about 7,000 Koreans immigrants arrive in Hawai'i when the U.S. passes a restrictive immigration law.

January 27, 1903: President Theodore Roosevelt signs into law $1 million to settle more than 6,700 claims of Chinatown fire victims, and allows the territory to raise $500,000 by selling bonds. Initial claims are $3 million, but only $1.3 million is awarded. Many claimants are broke and angry. On May 6, about 1,000 Chinese and Japanese agree to accept 75% in cash and 25% in bonds.

January 28, 1903: The Chamber of Commerce and Merchants' Association approve a plan to encourage tourism, advertise Hawai'i in magazines, hire tourist agents, and print 100,000 brochures.

January 29, 1903: Dengue fever reaches epidemic proportions with 10 new cases every day. It is described as "boohoo fever" because people cry from the nonfatal pain.

February 26, 1903: The Federal Report of the Commissioner of Labor on Hawai'i says the presence of Asians in Hawai'i is "no more felt than is that of the cattle upon the mountain range." The report also says "The 'white man' has always been sort of aristocrat in the islands...Permanent prosperity" depends on Caucasians moving to Hawai'i because "the future permanent population" will make "the islands practically Japanese."

March 6, 1903: For the first time, Governor Sanford Dole signs a joint resolution seeking statehood. The resolution seeks Congressional approval to allow Hawai'i voters to adopt a state constitution.

March 31, 1903: The Federation of Allied Trades is established in Hilo. 262 skilled workers petition the Legislature for higher wages for Caucasians and laws to require licensed contractors and skilled mechanics to be U.S. citizens. They oppose Asians who leave the plantations for skilled jobs in town.

April 9, 1903: Territorial Legislature overrides Governor Sanford Dole's veto of a joint resolution asking Congress to allow Hawaiian and English to be Hawaii's official languages. Legislators had been speaking and printing bills in both languages. Opponents of using the Hawaiian language point out that statehood has been delayed several decades for New Mexico and Arizona because they speak Spanish and English.

April 22, 1903: Governor Sanford Dole signs a questionable County Act to establish county governments, which Congress had urged. The law divides Hawai'i Island into two counties, east and west.

April 23, 1903: Governor Sanford Dole signs a law to exempt the pineapple industry from all taxes for 5 years.

April 23, 1903: Governor Sanford Dole signs a law to allow only U.S. citizens or people eligible for U.S. citizenship to work on government jobs as laborers or mechanics. This eliminates foreign born plantation workers from government jobs. Caucasians fear losing jobs to Asians.

April 25, 1903: Governor Sanford Dole signs a law to establish Hawaii's forest reserve system to protect our forests. This gives Hawai'i one of the few protected watersheds in the U.S.

April 28, 1903: Governor Sanford Dole signs a law to protect the Chinese Fund from embezzlement. Chinese immigrants working on plantations gave a part of their wages to the Hawai'i Republic for transportation home to China when their contracts end. About September 24, 1902, former Territorial Treasurer W. Wright left Hawai'i with $16,800 of Chinese Fund money. Wray Taylor, a former Agriculture Commissioner also ran away with some money. The new law protects $155,546 so it will be returned to the people it rightfully belongs to, but many Chinese don't collect their money.

May 2, 1903: Honolulu Symphony Society orchestra gives its first public performance at the Opera House.

July 31, 1903: Colonel Curtis I'aukea says he is switching from the Republican to Home Rule Party. He says Republicans oppose democracy for Hawaiians. During the monarchy, he was Minister of Foreign Affairs. In recent years he was an agent for Queen Lili'uokalani, O'ahu Sheriff, and a Territorial Senator.

July 31, 1903: Alexander Young Hotel opens with 2,000 guests. The $2 million, 6-story hotel has 192 rooms. It is Hawaii's largest building, sitting on a full downtown city block. This popular hotel is known as a great place for dining and weddings. Young tries to sell the hotel to the federal government in 1904, then buys the Moana Hotel in 1905, and gains a majority interest in the downtown Royal Hawaiian Hotel.

September 25, 1903: 500 Japanese workers strike at Honolulu Plantation after management rejects higher wages.

October 6, 1903: Mauna Loa erupts for 61 days.

October 17, 1903: The last of several thousand Gilbert Islanders leave Hawai'i and are happy to return home. They were brought to Hawai'i for plantation work in the 1880s.

October 20, 1903: PACIFIC COMMERCIAL ADVERTISER reports the Hawai'i government allows 6 California ranch families to buy 5,000 acres in South Kona. Hawai'i advertisements encourage white Americans to settle here as ranchers. An earlier "colony" is established in Wahiawā.

Governor George Carter

October 23, 1903: Former Congressional Delegate and Hawaiian royalist Robert Wilcox, age 48, dies while campaigning for Sheriff. He led the unsuccessful 1895 revolt to restore Queen Lili'uokalani, and was sentenced to death by a military court. President Dole commuted the sentence to 35 years and $10,000 fine. He gave Wilcox a conditional pardon, then a full pardon in 1898. In 1900, he was elected as Hawaii's first Congressional Delegate.

October 31, 1903: President Theodore Roosevelt appoints Governor Sanford Dole as a federal judge, a position he holds until he retires in 1916.

November 18, 1903: Daughters of Hawai'i is founded by 7 women who want to preserve Hawaiian culture, language, and historic sites. They will repair and operate Queen Emma Summer Palace, which opens in 1916, and Hulihe'e Palace, which opens in 1928.

November 23, 1903: Territory Secretary George Carter becomes Hawaii's second territorial governor. He serves until August 15, 1907.

November 24, 1903: The skeleton of a 55-foot sperm whale is displayed at the dedication of Bishop Museum's Hawaiian Hall. One side of the whale is a skeleton, the other side is paper mache.

December 12, 1903: PACIFIC COMMERCIAL ADVERTISER says the 1903 Legislature spent $20,000 to interpret, translate and print bills in Hawaiian, although federal law requires English only.

December 13, 1903: Former Hawai'i resident, Dr. Sun Yat-Sen speaks at the Chinese Theater about overthrowing China's "decaying" Manchu

Dynasty. During 4 visits to Hawai'i from 1894-1910, he raises perhaps $250,000 for his revolution. He becomes the first president of the
Republic of China on January 1, 1912. His brother, Sun Mei, is a Kula,
Maui resident. Sun Yat-Sen possessed a questionable American birth
certificate, issued by the Hawai'i Territory on March 4, 1904. It said
he is a Kula resident, born in Hawai'i on November 24, 1870. However he also signed a letter that "he waived his right to American citizenship and was...a subject of China" so maybe the false birth certificate was a mistake not of his own doing.

December 16, 1903: Possibly the first automobile trip around O'ahu is
completed in 11 hours, which includes nearly 5 hours in stops.

National News

December 17, 1903: Orville
Wright flies 120 feet in 12 seconds
at Kitty Hawk, North Carolina. He
is the first person to fly an airplane.

December 21, 1903: Dillingham Co. sells its 50-year lease of Kaho'olawe
to Christian Conradt for $15,000. The lease expires on January 1, 1913.
He will ranch sheep.

December 31, 1903: Today is the last day to exchange Hawaiian silver
coins for U.S. currency at the First National Bank. The Hawaiian coins
are sent to San Francisco. Only $185,000 of $1 million in coins –
mostly dimes – are unaccounted for, and probably kept as souvenirs
by tourists and collectors, made into jewelry, lost, or melted in the 1900
Chinatown fire. The coins with Kalakaua's profile were minted in 1883.

January 4, 1904: The first elected County Boards of Supervisors take
office, despite questionable constitutional status.

January 13, 1904: Hawai'i Supreme Court rules the 1903 law to establish
county government is unconstitutional because the legislation covers
more than one subject.

March 19, 1904: Waikīkī Aquarium opens. It is built by the Honolulu
Rapid Transit and Land Company, owned by James Castle and Charles
Cooke. It is America's 3rd aquarium, and 12th in the world.

April 8, 1904: Reverend Takie Okumura establishes Makiki Christian Church with 24 members. Rev. Okumura is warmly supported by Hawaii's Caucasian elite, yet many Japanese Buddhists reject him. He supports "Americanism" values, opposes the 1909 and 1920 Japanese plantation strikes because he fears they will incite a "racial clash." He also supports Hawaii's 1920 foreign language law because he wants to eliminate American distrust of Japanese. He established the first Japanese YMCA on April 28, 1900, Hawaii's first Japanese language school, Central Institute on April 6, 1896, and opened a Boy's Home.

September 27, 1904: Jose Miranda, age 23, an unemployed Puerto Rican, stabs and kills Edward Damon. The plantations consider unemployed Puerto Ricans to be vagrants, and had many arrested, receiving 3 months to 1-year jail sentences. Miranda could have been convicted of manslaughter, but he is hanged for first degree murder on October 26. The Hawai'i flag hangs at half-staff when Damon is buried.

November 8, 1904: Republicans win 42 of 45 seats in the Territorial Legislature, and dominate Hawai'i for most of the next 50 years. HONOLULU ADVERTISER headline calls the election a "Republican tidal wave." Republicans usually win 2/3's or more of the Senate until 1945, and House until 1953. A non-partisan wins a Senate seat in the 1936 and 1938 elections.

November 18, 1904: HSPA decides to hire only "American citizens, or those eligible for citizenship" for skilled plantation jobs.

February 28, 1905: Under mysterious circumstances, Mrs. Jane Stanford dies in her Moana Hotel room after drinking poison from a soda bottle she brought from San Francisco. She is the wealthy widow of U.S. Senator Leland Stanford, the founder of Stanford University. On March 9, the Honolulu coroner says she was murdered, but two San Francisco doctors say she wasn't. On April 3, San Francisco police declare that she died from natural causes, and drop the investigation.

March 31, 1905: Hawai'i Legislature overrides a veto by Governor George Carter to forbid work on Sunday, with some exceptions. Governor Lucius Pinkham signs a revised law on March 23, 1915 to exempt industries such as hotels, transportation, food service, utilities, and a few more. He signs another law on April 27, 1915 to allow educational or Biblical movies to be shown on Sunday, after 6:30 p.m. On April 16, 1935, Governor Joseph Poindexter signs a law to allow many specific stores to be open Sunday. An earlier law was passed in 1886. The law is repealed in 1949.

April 8, 1905: Police stop a riot by 300 Chinese workers at Oʻahu Sugar Company after 12 men are arrested for gambling. One worker dies.

April 14, 1905: Hawaiʻi Legislature overrides Governor George Carter's veto of a bill to establish 5 counties – Hawaiʻi, Kalawao, Kauaʻi, Maui, Oʻahu – and Kalawao County, governed by the Health Board.

April 18, 1905: Hilo High School is established when the Legislature overrides Governor George Carter's veto. Hawaii's first Neighbor Island public high school opens in September with 20 students. Up to now, Neighbor Island students were sent to Honolulu High School.

April 24, 1905: Governor George Carter signs a law to establish a Board of Immigration to encourage Europeans "desiring to make their home here." Europeans are not mentioned in the law.

April 25, 1905: Governor George Carter signs a law to require labor agents to pay a $500 annual license fee. This is intended to prevent employment brokers from taking plantation workers to the mainland, especially to higher-paying jobs in California.

April 26, 1905: Governor George Carter signs a 2% corporate income tax law.

April 26, 1905: Territorial Legislature overrides Governor George Carter's veto of a bill to require the territory to give each county half of the income, property, school and poll tax revenue collected in the county. On March 18, 1907, Governor George Carter signs a similar law.

May 20, 1905: When a luna beats a worker, 1,700 Japanese sugar workers strike 4 days at Lahaina Plantation. For the first time, the Hawaiʻi National Guard is sent to a strike scene. One worker is killed.

June 20, 1905: The first county elections are held under the new law.

June 25, 1905: ʻAhahui Kaʻahumanu is founded as a benevolent society for women to promote Hawaiiana and charities. The women are well-known for their black dress and yellow lei.

July 1, 1905: County governments begin at midnight when the first Board of Supervisors meets.

July 1, 1905: O'ahu County Board of Supervisors vote to bring the Royal Hawaiian Band under county jurisdiction because the Territorial Legislature refused to fund it.

October 3, 1905: Two-time presidential candidate William Jennings Bryan visits Hawai'i.

October 3, 1905: Board of Immigration votes to bring 10-15 Italian families to Hawai'i. It is not known if any came. Throughout the decade, Hawai'i leaders encourage Europeans and Americans to move here.

October 9, 1905: George Smith, chairman of the O'ahu Board of Supervisors, signs a gambling-enforcement law. The law prohibits anyone from blocking entrances or exits that make it difficult for police to enter or leave a place where there is gambling.

October 17, 1905: Secretary of Hawai'i Alatau Atkinson says Hawai'i will never be "Japanized" because Japanese "will not want American citizenship." He says Japanese are taking jobs from Americans, but a new Board of Immigration encourages white American settlers.

January 27, 1906: U.S. Army establishes Fort Ruger. It is named for Civil War General Thomas Ruger, Superintendent of West Point from 1871-1876. The fort includes 755 acres of Diamond Head. In December 1955, most of the land is transferred to the Territory for the National Guard.

February 19, 1906: The first 110 Russians arrive in Honolulu from California, en route to Kauai's Makee Plantation. They left Russia for religious freedom and want to buy land on Kaua'i, but they leave Hawai'i when they aren't allowed to buy land. The last ship of Russian plantation workers arrives on March 7, 1910. In all, nearly 1,800 Russians immigrate, but their experiment is considered a failure.

February 21, 1906: The Board of Health approves a plan by chairman Lucius Pinkham to drain the "unsanitary" and "dangerous" Waikīkī marsh. A 2-mile long lagoon will make it possible to create a beautiful city with "high price(d)" property near the ocean. Nothing happens until Pinkham becomes governor.

May 15, 1906: Governor George Carter establishes the Hawai'i National Guard with permission from the U.S. War Department. This action replaces the National Guard organization created by the Provisional Government in 1893.

June 8, 1906: O'ahu Country Club opens with 300 members. It is Hawaii's first country club. 25 sheep trim the greens.

June 11, 1906: The $600,000 Kohala Ditch opens on Hawai'i Island after 17 workers died during 18 months of construction. The 26-mile ditch

through 57 mountain tunnels brings water to allow large sugar plantations to prosper.

July 22, 1906: Hawaiian Islands Packing Co. is established in Wahiawā.
It joins the California Packing Corp. as part of Del Monte.

August 3, 1906: Hawai'i Attorney General rules that alien Japanese can't
buy public land, based on a March 2, 1897 federal law.

August 20, 1906: During a heavy rain, the ship, MANCHURIA, runs aground
between Waimānalo and Rabbit Island. All 257 passengers are removed
safely. This incident receives national publicity. Since 1888, several
ship captains had petitioned for a lighthouse to prevent a dangerous
accident. President Theodore Roosevelt issues an Executive Order on
January 12, 1907 to reserve 10 acres for Makapu'u Lighthouse, which
begins operation on October 1, 1909. It's light shines 28 miles from
the world's largest hyperradiant lens. On November 5, 1978, during
the organized crime trial of Wilford "Nappy" Pulawa, prosecutors hide
witnesses in the isolated Makapu'u Lighthouse for their safety.

August 23, 1906: The Territorial Archives Building is the first in the U.S.
built exclusively to preserve public records. A newer Archives building opens on July 31, 1953.

November 3, 1906: NIPPU JIJI begins publication as a daily newspaper. It is
one of Hawaii's two most influential Japanese language newspapers,
and is rumored to receive HSPA money. Yasutaro Soga is the editor
from 1906-1942. The newspaper began as NIPPON SHUHO in 1892 and
changes names several times until Soga buys it in 1905. An English
section is added in 1919. In 1927, NIPPU JIJI attains 11,000 circulation.
During World War II, the military governor suspends the newspaper
from December 12, 1941 to January 7, 1942. It is renamed the HAWAI'I
TIMES on November 2, 1942 when editor Soga is sent to an internment
camp. Publication ends on March 25, 1985.

December 20, 1906: The first 15 Filipino plantation workers arrive in Hawai'i. They earn $16 a month for three years, plus
free housing, water and medical care. Their pay is lower than
all other plantation workers. After the Spanish-American War,
the U.S. bought the Philippines from Spain for $20 million in
1899. Filipinos became American "Nationals," and the U.S.
did not prohibit their immigration. By 1935, 2/3 of the 125,000
Filipino immigrants return to the Philippines or move to the
U.S. mainland. About 85% of the Filipino plantation workers
are single men.

December 28, 1906: Christian Conradt sells his Kaho'olawe lease to Eben Low of Hawai'i Island's Parker family. Kaho'olawe has 3,200 sheep and 5,000 goats that eat the vegetation protecting the top soil, which is being destroyed by wind erosion and lack of rain.

January 9, 1907: Mauna Loa erupts for 15 days.

February 4, 1907: A&B's HC&S (Hawaiian Commercial and Sugar) and Maui Agricultural Company establish Nāhiku Rubber Plantation. It is the first rubber plantation on American soil. The need for automobile tires makes rubber a valuable product. It closes January 20, 1915.

February 14, 1907: PACIFIC COMMERCIAL ADVERTISER reports Chinese gamblers offer $1,400 a week in bribes to police to guarantee a monopoly.

February 20, 1907: President Theodore Roosevelt signs the U.S. Immigration Act of 1907, to prohibit Japanese contract laborers from entering the U.S. mainland from any American territory. On the same day, Hawai'i gets a telegram from Secretary of State Elihu Root, to prohibit Japanese immigrants to Hawai'i. Since the 1900 Organic Act nullified plantation contracts, 10,000 Japanese move to California by 1905. From 1907-1920, about 15,000 "picture brides" immigrate to Hawai'i as immediate family until 1920, when Japan stops giving passports to women without husbands. The U.S. stops Japanese immigration in 1924.

March 14, 1907: President Theodore Roosevelt issues Executive Order 589 to prohibit Japanese and Korean workers from leaving Hawai'i for the U.S. mainland. This is the first of several 1907-1908 orders which comprise the Gentlemen's Agreement between the U.S. and Japan.

April 5, 1907: Governor George Carter signs a law to require English as the basis of teaching in all public and private schools.

April 27, 1907: The first 2,287 Spanish plantation workers arrive in Hawai'i, including 500 children. By 1913, most of the 8,000 Spanish arrivals have moved to the mainland.

April 30, 1907: Governor George Carter signs a law to create the City and County of Honolulu, with a mayor and a Board of Supervisors with 7 members. They are elected in 1908 and take office on January 4, 1909.

May 7, 1907: Hawai'i hosts 23 U.S. Congressman and a U.S. Senator on a 3-week tour of the islands to encourage Congress to pass laws more favorable to Hawai'i. The Hawai'i Legislature invites the Congressmen, and pays the entire $15,000 cost for the trip. This is the second official visit of Congressmen – the first was in 1902. On May 29, Delegate Jonah Kūhiō hosts the visiting Congressmen and 2,000 guests, including Queen Lili'uokalani, at his Waikīkī home.

May 20, 1907: About midnight, a meteor falls 300 yards from a steamship near Hilo, with visiting U.S. Congressmen aboard.

May 20, 1907: Author Jack London arrives in Hawai'i, and stays until August 15. He returns in 1915 and 1916. He popularizes Hawai'i by writing more than a dozen stories. His most famous Hawai'i short stories are Ko'OLAU THE LEPER and ON A MAKALOA MAT.

June 24, 1907: The Hawaiian Pineapple Company opens its main office at the Iwilei Cannery, making Dole Cannery the world's largest fruit cannery. It's first cannery was located in Wahiawā in 1903.

June 24, 1907: Fort Shafter becomes Hawaii's first permanent military post. It is named for General William Shafter of the Spanish-American War.

July 20, 1907: Governor George Carter says Hawaii's minority Caucasian population fears "the islands will become 'orientalized' commercially and socially." On July 25, Federal Judge and former Governor Sanford Dole also complains that too many whites are moving away, and Hawai'i will become more Oriental and less American in education and culture.

August 15, 1907: Walter Frear becomes Hawaii's 3rd governor until November 29, 1913. He is appointed by President Theodore Roosevelt. Previously, Frear was a judge during the monarchy, a Supreme Court justice for the Republic, and from 1900-1907, the chief justice of the Territorial Supreme Court. He is the son-in-law of businessman Benjamin Dillingham.

September 2, 1907: U.S. Navy begins two weeks of war games in Hawai'i. A report says U.S. war games prove that Hawai'i is insufficiently protected because 50,000 Japanese can conquer Hawai'i in 3 weeks. America's military leaders see Japan as a potential threat, especially after Japan's victory over Russia in a 1905 war.

May 1, 1908: Alexander Ford establishes the Outrigger Canoe Club.

May 14, 1908: President Theodore Roosevelt signs a law to authorize up to $2 million to build the Pearl Harbor Naval Station with a dry dock to repair ships.

June 2, 1908: Prince David Kawānanakoa, heir to the throne, dies of pneumonia in San Francisco. He was the brother of Congressional Delegate and Prince Jonah Kūhiō Kalaniana'ole.

June 24, 1908: A&B establishes East Maui Irrigation (EMI) Company to provide water for A&B companies, and to replace Maui's Hāmākua Ditch Company. It is the largest privately-owned water company in the U.S., providing an average 160 million gallons a day, with a capacity of 450 million gallons a day. EMI now provides Maui County with up to 8 million gallons of water daily for domestic use.

July 16, 1908: A fleet of 16 white-painted American battleships and 14,000 sailors arrive in Honolulu. President Theodore Roosevelt sent the "Great White Fleet" around the world to showcase America's naval strength.

September 2, 1908: Photographer Ray Jerome Baker arrives in Honolulu. In 1910, he opens a photography business. He takes historic and candid photos of native Hawaiians because "no one had done it before." He also takes scenic photos and later makes films to promote Hawai'i on mainland tours. Thousands of his photos and negatives are at Hawai'i State Archives and Bishop Museum.

September 11, 1908: The new McKinley High School opens. The school began in 1865 as Fort Street English Day School. Tuition was 50¢ a week. In 1895, the school moved to the former home of Princess Luka Ke'elikolani, and is renamed Honolulu High School. The Board of Education paid $30,000 for the property. In 1907, the school moved to Beretania Street, and to its current King Street location in 1923. On March 5, 1908, the school was renamed to honor President William McKinley, who signed the resolution to annex Hawai'i. The $8,000, 8-ton McKinley statue is dedicated on February 23, 1911.

September 15, 1908: College of Agriculture and Mechanical Arts opens near Thomas Square with 5 full-time students and 12 faculty in a home behind Linekona School that had been the Chinese consulate. Legislative efforts from 1901-1907 tried to put the college at Mountain View, Hawai'i Island and Lahainaluna, Maui. The college is established when Governor George Carter signs a law on March 25, 1907. Four seniors are the first to graduate on June 3, 1912.

October 6, 1908: PACIFIC COMMERCIAL ADVERTISER says the O'ahu Board of Supervisors held a special Sunday meeting in Kāne'ohe on October 4 to exclude Chinese-American citizens from county jobs. However official county minutes say nothing about this.

October 10, 1908: Direct radio communication is made for the first time with the mainland from the Kahuku Station – 2,100 miles to San Francisco, a record for long distance radio communication.

November 12, 1908: U.S. Army establishes the Waikīkī Military Reservation on 74 acres the Army bought in 1904. The former fishponds, duck marshes and swamp land are filled with land excavated from Pearl Harbor. On January 28, 1909, it is named Fort DeRussy for General Rene DeRussy of the Corps of Engineers, and Superintendent of West Point from 1833-1838. Fort DeRussy is originally intended to protect Honolulu Harbor, and designated a subpost of Fort Ruger on March 19, 1913. In World War II, it is a headquarters for Military Police and a camouflage school.

December 11, 1908: Motoyuki Negoro and Fred Makino establish the Higher Wages Association to represent the interests of Japanese plantation workers. This is Hawaii's first plantation labor organization.

December 11, 1908: U.S. Secretary of War announces a $3.5 million contract to excavate Pearl Harbor so large ships can enter the harbor safely. The contract goes to San Francisco Bridge Company and its Hawai'i subcontractor, Hawaiian Dredging. It is the Navy's largest excavation contract.

December 20, 1908: Honolulu Advertiser publishes a November 30, 1908 letter from Mark Twain. He describes Hawai'i as "the loveliest fleet of islands that lie anchored in any ocean."

Fred Makino

December 31, 1908: Superintendent of Public Instruction Winfred Babbitt reports that overcrowding in Hawai'i public schools is "serious," with up to 60-80 students in a room. Classroom "congestion appears to be a prevailing practice."

January 4, 1909: New Honolulu city and county government officials are inaugurated. Joseph Fern is Honolulu's first mayor. He is a Democrat, Portuguese-Hawaiian, a stevedore worker, and a former member of the Board of Supervisors. A PACIFIC COMMERCIAL ADVERTISER headline ridicules him as representing unfit voters – "A day of official burlesque." Fern was elected by 7 votes on November 3, 1908. On December 29, 1908, the Hawai'i Supreme Court rules against requiring a recount.

January 12, 1909: The first soldiers arrive at Schofield Barracks, which is named for General John Schofield in April. He is the former West Point commander who arrived in Hawai'i in 1873 to spy for the U.S. on Pearl Harbor, while posing as a civilian on vacation. Schofield Barracks becomes America's largest permanent Army post, with 16,000 people in the 1930s, and up to 100,000 people during WW II. It is also called Castner Village, for Captain Castner who built the temporary Army post, or Leilehua Barracks, which is the name of the area.

March 22, 1909: Governor Walter Frear signs a law to impose a 2% tax on $4,000 or more income. Most of the money will support the immigration of plantation workers.

March 22, 1909: Governor Walter Frear signs a law to require all public employees to be U.S. citizens. This prohibits aliens, who may have participated in a recent sugar strike, from obtaining government jobs.

May 9, 1909: Hawaii's first major sugar plantation strike is led by Higher Wages Association leaders Yasutaro Soga and Fred Makino. 7,000 Japanese workers say their wages are "semi-slavery," and demand the same pay as Portuguese workers. The 3-month strike ends on August 4 with a victory for the plantations. The plantations pay Caucasian strike-breakers $1.50 a day compared with the striking Japanese workers who earn as low as 69¢ a day, and seek $1 a day. HSPA begins a 25-year policy of not recognizing worker unions and strikers. Neighbor Island plantations raise $2 million to help O'ahu plantations offset their losses.

May 22, 1909: For the first time, sugar plantations evict 5,000 strikers and families from plantation homes during the strike.

June 10, 1909: Lāna'i adopts Prohibition. No drunks are allowed on the island. Punishment is a $5 fine or "taken out in hide."

August 3, 1909: At the courthouse, Tamekichi Mori, a court interpreter and Higher Wages Association member, stabs Sometaro Sheba, editor of HAWAI'I SHIBA newspaper, which opposed the strike. Mori calls Sheba "a traitor to the Japanese people," and regrets that he didn't kill him. This attempted murder ends the 1909 sugar strike. A jury declares Mori guilty, and he is sentenced on October 27 to 5 years in prison.

September 2, 1909: On her 71st birthday, Queen Lili'uokalani welcomes thousands of visitors to Washington Place, including two dozen visiting U.S. Congressmen who are impressed when Native Hawaiians show respect by bowing their heads, kneeling, and kissing the queen's hand.

National News

October 1, 1909: Henry Ford introduces the Model T Ford. He sells it for $850. He says "Customers can have any color, as long as it is black."

September 24, 1909: A 20-minute meteor shower resembles a fireworks spectacle.

December 2, 1909: Queen Lili'uokalani creates the Lili'uokalani Trust to help orphaned and needy children.

1910-1919

January 14, 1910: Hawai'i historian William Alexander says native Hawaiians originated from North India before settling in Polynesia.

February 3, 1910: Hundreds of Russian plantation workers tell managers they want to go home. They want higher wages, complain about high prices at plantation stores, and desire free and furnished homes. On April 29, hundreds of Russians riot at Honolulu Police Station. Cops use clubs, whips and fire hoses to stop them. They want their leader, arrested for vagrancy, to be released.

February 8, 1910: Honolulu Mayor Joseph Fern signs a law to regulate jitneys or motor vehicles for hire that carry passengers.

February 17, 1910: Pablo Manlapit, age 19, arrives in Hawai'i with 280 Filipino sugar workers. On December 19, 1919, he becomes Hawaii's first Filipino to get a license to practice law. He will lead plantation workers on several strikes.

March 4, 1910: Hawai'i Supreme Court rules that Yasutaro Soga, Motoyuki Negoro and Fred Makino must serve 10 months in jail for "conspiracy" convictions for inciting violence. They were arrested on January 13, 1909, and pardoned on July 4, 1910.

April 8, 1910: Hawaii's first "permanent" astronomical observatory operated by the College of Hawai'i, opens in Kaimukī to view Halley's Comet. The Kaimukī Observatory is dismantled in 1958.

April 15, 1910: Federal census begins. Hawai'i has 191,874 population, a 25% increase since 1900 – 20% Hawaiian, 11% Caucasian, 11% Chinese, 41% Japanese, 1% Filipino, 2% Korean, 12% Portuguese.

May 18, 1910: A Washington, D.C. Court of Claims rules that Queen Lili'uokalani has no claim to "crown lands", now the property of the territory. In February, she failed in her last attempt to persuade Congress to compensate her for these lands, taken by the U.S. government after the 1893 overthrow.

July 1, 1910: A new 25-mile, cement lined $800,000 Hāmākua Ditch opens on Hawai'i Island, providing 45 million gallons of water daily for Hilo-

Hāmākua sugar plantations. The upper portion was completed in 1907.

July 2, 1910: A news story in the WASHINGTON TIMES quotes American Federation of Labor leader Samuel Gompers charge that Russians from Siberia are suffering in "conditions akin to slavery" on Hawai'i sugar plantations. He says 1,000 Siberians were brought to Hawai'i under the false pretenses of a comfortable life.

July 4, 1910: Acting Governor Ernest Mott-Smitt commutes the prison sentence of four newspaper and labor leaders including Yasutaro Soga, Motoyuki Negoro, and Fred Makino.

July 26, 1910: Hawai'i voters vote 3-1 against prohibition. Federal law required a public vote.

August 25, 1910: Governor Walter Frear proclaims Kaho'olawe as a Territorial Forest Reserve, which is cancelled on April 20, 1918. Governor Frear visits the island in September 1911, and hunts goats.

November 16, 1910: Libby McNeill and Libby buys half of Hawaiian Cannery Co., and enters the Hawai'i pineapple industry on 4 islands.

November 28, 1910: The first of 951 Korean picture brides arrives.

December 31, 1910: "Bud" Mars pilots Hawaii's first airplane flight. His P-18 biplane reaches 1,500 feet above Moanalua Polo Field. He makes several flights, up to 10 minutes each, during 3 days. 8,000 people pay $1 admission to watch.

February 4, 1911: Mun Lun School opens. It is the first Chinese school outside China or Japan. By 1916, it is Hawaii's largest school.

February 17, 1911: Territorial House votes not to receive bills from the Senate unless they are translated into Hawaiian.

February 18, 1911: Territorial House adjourns early to pay its respect to Queen Lili'uokalani at Washington Place. Every two years, the House makes it a custom to pay a "courtesy" visit to the queen. Each legislator is introduced, bows, and shakes her hand.

February 20, 1911: The first Pan Pacific Travel Congress opens with 50 delegates to attract attention to the Pacific region for tourism.

March 21, 1911: When 25% of Honolulu's dairy cows are discovered to have tuberculosis, Honolulu Mayor Joseph Fern signs a city law to require dairies to test all dairy cows, prohibit selling milk from infected cows, and get a permit to sell milk.

March 31, 1911: College of Agriculture and Mechanical Arts is renamed the College of Hawai'i.

April 4, 1911: Governor Walter Frear signs a law to impose a fine or prison for anyone who recruits a contract plantation worker. Recruiters from other states try to lure workers from Hawaiʻi with offers of higher wages. From 1/3 to 1/2 of Hawaii's plantation workers go to the mainland or return to their homeland.

June 25, 1911: A new Kaumakapili Church is dedicated. The old church burned in the 1900 Chinatown fire.

July 11, 1911: Henry Ginaca invents the Ginaca Automatic Pineapple Machine to mass produce canned pineapple. By 1925, the machine cuts, cores and slices up to 105 pineapples a minute. He receives a patent on November 1, 1912, and gets 11 more patents from 1912-1914. He happily gave his royalty rights to Hawaiian Pineapple Co.

July 24, 1911: Hiram Bingham, grandson of Hawaii's missionary, discovers the Inca ruins of the lost city of Machu Picchu in a Peru jungle, elevation 8,000 feet. He is guided by Peruvians. 200 buildings were built about 1400 A.D. for 1,200 people.

July 30, 1911: First recorded temperature of a Kīlauea lava lake is 1,832° F.

October 5, 1911: The Hawaiʻi Volcano Research Association is established to support the observatory at Kīlauea. The first director, Dr. Thomas Jaggar begins work on January 17, 1912.

October 11, 1911: Board of Health says Honolulu Hale is unsanitary. It is sold in 1917 at a public auction for $10 and demolished. It was built with coral blocks in 1843 as Hawaii's first executive building, located next to the Merchant Street Post Office.

November 7, 1911: Board of Health orders all banana plants in Honolulu to be cut to prevent mosquitoes from spreading yellow fever.

December 14, 1911: USS CALIFORNIA is the first large U.S. Navy war ship to enter the newly-excavated Pearl Harbor. Queen Liliʻuokalani and Judge Sanford Dole meet aboard the ship, possibly their first public meeting since the 1893 overthrow. A small gunboat, PETREL, was the first warship to enter Pearl Harbor in January 1911.

January 5, 1912: HSPA announces that higher wages and bonus payments will be based on higher sugar prices in New York, and there will be no more race distinction in earnings.

February 23, 1912: PACIFIC COMMERCIAL ADVERTISER announces that it has received the first complete wireless news stories from the west coast. It takes only 10 minutes to receive news from San Francisco by wire

Duke Kahanamoku

less instead of cable. The newspaper will "publish much more of the world's news as it occurs."

February 24, 1912: 60,000 Japanese Buddhists plan to raise $100,000 to build the Honpa Hongwanji Hawai'i Betsuin Buddhist temple, which opens on August 14, 1921.

July 1, 1912: Two newspapers, HAWAIIAN STAR and EVENING BULLETIN merge to become the HONOLULU STAR-BULLETIN with Riley Allen as the editor. The "Star" symbolizes U.S. annexation.

July 6, 1912: Duke Kahanamoku wins the first of two gold medals at the Sweden Olympic Games. His victories bring favorable publicity to himself and Hawai'i. Thousands of people welcome him home on October 1. To recognize his accomplishments, money is raised through public donations to buy him a house and lot in Waikīkī, where the Hilton Hawaiian Village now stands. The fund began on July 10, when two Hāna residents send $15 to the HONOLULU STAR-BULLETIN for Duke.

July 27, 1912: The Federal Telegraph Co. opens a wireless station. The HONOLULU ADVERTISER sends a news story to a San Francisco newspaper via an antenna atop two 480-foot wooden platform masts in He'eia.

August 1, 1912: For the first time, a seismometer records a Hawai'i earthquake at Kīlauea.

December 7, 1912: Fred Kinzaburo Makino publishes HAWAI'I HOCHI as a daily Japanese newspaper until he dies on February 17, 1953. It is Hawaii's 4th oldest newspaper that is still in business. Makino pays all his bills in cash because no bank gives him credit. By 1927, the newspaper attains 12,000 circulation. The newspaper pursues justice not obedience, and urges Japanese to demand their rights. The first newspaper criticizes U.S. immigration requirements for "assembly line" Christian weddings of arriving Buddhist Japanese picture brides at the wharf. The 1909 and 1920 plantation worker strikes are vigorously supported. In later years, HAWAI'I HOCHI supports equal rights for Japanese and Japanese language schools, and criticizes the court decisions of the Fukunaga and Massie cases. During WW II, the military governor suspends the newspaper from December 12, 1941 to January 8, 1942. Makino was born in Japan of British and Japanese parents. He

arrived in Hawai'i on April 19, 1899 and worked at Nā'ālehu Plantation. In 1901 he opened Makino Drugstore in Honolulu.

January 14, 1913: Soldiers arrive at U.S. Army Fort Kamehameha. The
fort is transferred to the U.S. Air Force on November 1, 1991. War
Department names the fort based on a local petition.

February 1, 1913: Hawaii's first public library opens in downtown Honolulu. On November 29, 1909 the Andrew Carnegie fund donated
$100,000 for construction.

February 17, 1913: The foundation of the 1,000 foot long, 35 feet deep,
$4 million Pearl Harbor naval drydock collapses after 4 years of con-
struction. No one dies. The collapse is caused by external water pressure, and the Navy takes responsibility for poor design. It costs $5
million to clean up the mess and rebuild on December 14, 1914. The
project is completed in 1919.

March 19, 1913: U.S. Army designates Fort Armstrong as a subpost of
Fort Ruger. On June 11, it is named for General Samuel Armstrong, a
founder of Hampton Institute in Virginia.

April 2, 1913: Governor Wallace Frear signs a law to fine and imprison
vagrants and disorderly people.

April 4, 1913: Governor Walter Frear signs a law to create a county civil
service system.

April 30, 1913: Governor Walter Frear signs a law to add a 1% tax on

**Pearl Harbor Dry Dock Explosion – $5 million and 1 year to
clean the mess. Most of the damage is underwater.**

income over $4,000 − on top of the 2% tax up to $4,000. About 1/2 of the revenue will support the Board of Immigration, 1/2 will support forestry conservation, and the Board of Agriculture.

June 4, 1913: The last 1,283 Portuguese contract workers arrive. From 1878-1913, 20,000 Portuguese came to Hawai'i, mostly from Madeira and Azores Islands. Unlike single male Chinese and Japanese contract workers, the Portuguese could bring their families, encouraged to obtain U.S. citizenship, and vote.

July 13, 1913: The first military airplanes, Curtiss seaplanes, arrive in Hawai'i on a ship. The airplane unit is commanded by Lt. Harold Geiger at Fort Kamehameha, but is disbanded in November and the aircraft are returned to the mainland.

October 2, 1913: Hawai'i Board of Immigration decides not to recruit Europeans for plantation work because there is a lack of money, and European workers aren't satisfactory.

October 3, 1913: 14 people, including a one year old baby, arrive in Honolulu after sailing 1,100 miles in two small, open lifeboats. Their ocean liner ran aground on August 4 near Jarvis Island.

November 29, 1913: Lucius Pinkham becomes Hawaii's 4th governor until June 22, 1918. He is appointed by President Woodrow Wilson. He entered business after moving to Hawai'i in 1892.

April 29, 1914: New Chamber of Commerce of Hawai'i is established when the Chamber of Commerce and the Merchants' Association agree to merge. Established in 1850, the Chamber is Hawaii's oldest business organization.

June 2, 1914: Governor Lucius Pinkham is nearly killed when a car strikes his, and stops one foot from a Waimānalo cliff of several hundred feet.

October 24, 1914: While Germany and Japan are at war, a small German gunboat, GEIER, ports at Honolulu Harbor for repairs, and a Japanese battleship, HIZEN, waits to sink the GEIER when it leaves the harbor.

November 13, 1914: 200 Hawaiians establish 'Ahahui Pu'uhonua 'O Na Hawai'i to improve the political and social position of Hawaiians through education, business and employment. They establish a plan to "rehabilitate" Hawaiians for what becomes the Hawaiian Homes Commission Act.

November 25, 1914: Mauna Loa erupts for 48 days, with 600 foot fountains that are visible for 80 miles.

December 29, 1914: Congressional Delegate Jonah Kūhiō introduces a bill to allow women in Hawai'i to vote. The bill doesn't pass.

February 3, 1915: Future President Warren Harding arrives in Honolulu to speak to the Ad Club. He is introduced by his friend Wallace Farrington, whom he will appoint as governor in 1921.

March 25, 1915: America's first submarine disaster occurs here. U.S. Navy F-4 Submarine sinks a mile from Honolulu Harbor, to 300 feet depth, killing the entire 21-man crew. Leaking battery acid corrodes rivet holes, causing the sub to sink. The sub is raised on August 29, 1915, and deliberately sunk in 1940, a mile from the USS ARIZONA.

April 15, 1915: Governor Lucius Pinkham issues an Executive Order to allow the Daughters of Hawai'i to repair and operate the Queen Emma Summer Palace, which opens on October 18, 1916.

June 7, 1915: Charles Bishop, age 92, dies in Berkeley, where he lived his last 20 years. A week later, an urn with his ashes is placed near his wife's casket at the Mauna Ala Royal Mausoleum, and the Kamehameha vault is sealed. His trust had financed the construction of the Mausoleum. His wife, Bernice Pauahi Bishop, left a $3 million estate.

August 2, 1915: John Balch of Mutual Telephone Company receives the first Marconi Wireless message sent from Asia to Hawai'i. On July 30, Balch sent a wireless message to Wichi Torikata of Tokio, reminding him of a 1909 visit to Hawai'i, when Torikata said it would take 25 years for technology to allow such a message to be transmitted.

November 10, 1915: "Hawaiian Pineapple Day." To promote the "King of Fruits," Hawai'i pineapples are served in the White House to President Woodrow Wilson, and in many mainland restaurants.

January 13, 1916: 500 Black 9th Cavalry soldiers on leave create a disturbance when Iwilei prostitutes refuse some of them. Iwilei homes are looted, women are attacked, and martial law is declared.

January 18, 1916: Maui's 'Iao Valley flood kills 14 people.

April 12, 1916: U.S. Secretary of Labor submits a report on labor conditions in Hawai'i – "The plantation interests form a benevolent industrial oligarchy. The relations between the plantation manager and his laborers are semi-feudal (and)...paternal."

May 5, 1916: International opera tenor, Tandy MacKenzie, a Hāna-born native Hawaiian, sings at the White House for President Woodrow Wilson. On June 9, 1922, he sings at the Princess Theatre. He also gives a free outdoor concert for the Hawaiian Civic Club at 'Iolani Palace.

May 19, 1916: Mauna Loa erupts for 12 days. Steam and smoke rise to 20,000 feet.

May 27, 1916: Waiāhole Ditch opens, taking up to 32 million gallons of water daily from Waiāhole and Kahana Valley streams on windward O'ahu through the Ko'olau mountains to serve Amfac's O'ahu Sugar Plantation on the leeward side. The 25-mile, $2.3 million tunnel took two years to build.

August 1, 1916: President Woodrow Wilson signs a law to create Hawai'i National Park, which includes the volcanoes on Maui and Hawai'i Island. The legislation is introduced by Congressional Delegate Jonah Kūhiō. The Hawai'i park is America's 12th national park. The park is renamed Hawai'i Volcanoes National Park in 1961.

September 6, 1916: The African elephant, Daisy arrives in Honolulu. City Parks Director Ben Hollinger raises Daisy's $3,000 purchase price from donations in one week. Daisy is one of the first animals for the Kapi'olani Park Zoo. The elephant is a very popular attraction at many public events. The facility is named the Honolulu Zoo in 1947.

September 18, 1916: 1,600 Hawaiian and Japanese workers of a new union, International Longshoremen Association, strike for nearly a month until October 11.

October 2, 1916: 1,000 multi-racial dock workers strike. They derail a train car with strikebreakers inside, and overwhelm the police.

October 2, 1916: Sumitomo Bank of Hawai'i opens. It is owned by Japanese millionaire Kichizayemon Sumitomo.

November 6, 1916: The first soldiers occupy Kīlauea Military Camp on 50 acres inside the Hawai'i Volcano National Park. During WW II, the camp serves as an internment camp and holds war prisoners.

November 16, 1916: First-ever Kalākaua Day is celebrated with a parade and festivities. It isn't a holiday, but many businesses close and city workers get a half-day off.

December 1, 1916: Hawaii's Territorial Teacher Association approves a resolution demanding higher pay to meet the high cost of living.

December 2, 1916: 103 Iwilei prostitutes plead guilty to a "disorderly" charge. Each woman gets a 13-month suspended sentence.

January 25, 1917: 'Āinahau, the former 12-acre Waikīkī home of Archibald Cleghorn, Princess Likelike and Princess Ka'iulani is sold to James

Pratt, and divided into house lots. The house burns to the ground on August 2, 1921, but the famous banyan tree saves adjacent homes. The land is later sold to Matson and Sheraton, for the current site of the Sheraton Ka'iulani Hotel.

February 4, 1917: 90 German sailors are arrested for attempting to injure people and for attempting to destroy their German ships. The crew of a German gunship GEIER sets fire to their ship to avoid capture by a bigger Japanese warship, HIZEN, which is just outside the 3-mile limit. The HIZEN sinks a small German ship with a loud gun noise that awakens Honolulu. The U.S. declares war on Germany April 7, and the ship and crew of the GEIER are seized. On June 8, 1917, the MAUI NEWS reports 5 German sailors are working at Kīpahulu Plantation. On September 3, 180 German sailors of the GEIER in Honolulu and the ALBUS in Hilo are sent to Utah internment camps. From 1914-1917, many German naval ships took refuge in a neutral Honolulu Harbor.

February 5, 1917: Congress overrides President Woodrow Wilson's veto and adopts an immigration law, the Barred Zone Act. This law prohibits U.S. immigration from a large geographic area that includes India, South East Asia and Polynesia. The law is repealed in 1965.

March 1, 1917: Frank and Harry Baldwin buy Lāna'i from Cecil Brown and others for $588,000. Lāna'i Ranch Co. is established.

March 2, 1917: U.S. Congress passes the Jones Act, which gives U.S. citizenship to Puerto Ricans. However all county clerks in Hawai'i refuse to allow Puerto Ricans to register to vote. Some Puerto Ricans refuse to register for the WW I draft if they can't vote. The Hawai'i Supreme Court rules that Puerto Ricans are U.S. citizens, and can vote.

March 24, 1917: Governor Lucius Pinkham signs a law to spend $5,000 to compile and publish a Hawaiian dictionary. On April 26, 1921, Governor McCarthy signs a law giving Bishop Museum $4,500 to print 500 copies. The Public Archives publishes the 15,000 word, A DICTIONARY OF THE HAWAIIAN LANGUAGE, updated by Rev. Henry Parker from Lorrin Andrews' 6,000-word dictionary of 1836 and 1865.

March 27, 1917: Queen Lili'uokalani receives Hawai'i legislators at Washington Place for the last time. She had been hosting official visits of the Territorial Legislature for many years.

April 3, 1917: Queen Lili'uokalani agrees to fly the U.S. flag at Washington Place for the first time to honor Hawaiian soldiers fighting in WW I.

April 6, 1917: President Woodrow Wilson signs a resolution to decare war on Germany and enter World War I. He also signs a proclamation to prohibit German aliens from possessing a gun or signaling device.

May 2, 1917: Governor Lucius Pinkham signs a law to create a Territorial

Food Commission to urge people to conserve food, grow food at home and in school gardens, and to make Hawai'i self-sufficient. This may have been the nation's first Food Commission. The slogans are "Grow your own food" and "Food will win the war." By 1918, there is a near shortage of rice and taro. From January 14 to November 15, 1918, the Federal Food Administration urges people to obey "porkless Tuesday" and "meatless Monday." These efforts reduce Hawaii's food imports by 31,000 tons, saving $2.4 million.

Curtis I'aukea

May 3, 1917: Curtis I'aukea becomes Secretary of Hawai'i. This is Hawaii's #2 Territorial position, under the governor. President Woodrow Wilson appointed him on January 10, 1917.

May 15, 1917: To keep plantation workers at their jobs, the Territorial Food Commission asks U.S. War Secretary Franklin Lane not to send National Guardsmen to WW I. Until now, the plantations had encouraged their workers to join the National Guard.

July 22, 1917: Federal officials find dynamite under an Outrigger Club dancing pavilion in Waikīkī after a dance attended by U.S. sailors.

July 31, 1917: More than 26,000 men register today for the military draft.

August 3, 1917: A citizens group buys the downtown Royal Hawaiian Hotel from Arthur Young for $275,000. They convert the hotel to an Army and Navy YMCA, which opens on November 25, 1917. In 1987 the building is sold for $11 million to developer Chris Hemmeter, then sold to a Japanese company, BIGI Corp. in 1990. In 1999, the State of Hawai'i prepares to pay $22 million for offices and an art gallery.

August 6, 1917: Governor Lucius Pinkham announces that an all-AJA company of the Hawai'i National Guard will be established. On August 17, General Enoch Crowder says Japanese aliens are "friendly aliens" and eligible for the National Guard. On October 2, 1918, Captain H. Gooding says Selective Service classifies Hawaiians as white.

October 1, 1917: Clifford and Juliet Kimball open the Halekūlani Hotel, once the home of Robert Lewers, and the 1907 site of the Hau Tree Hotel.

October 7, 1917: Rev. Henry Parker resigns after 54 years at Kawaiahaʻo Church, effective when the year ends. He became the church's 4th pastor in 1865.

October 11, 1917: HONOLULU STAR-BULLETIN reports that Conrad Schirman, a German spy living in San Francisco, has been arrested there for plotting to bomb cargo ships between Honolulu and San Francisco.

October 11, 1917: Typhoid germs are found in the city water supply at Nuʻuanu Reservoir – perhaps caused by filthy conditions at the reservoir or by sabotage during World War I.

October 30, 1917: A silver crown and silver lei atop King Lunalilo's casket are stolen from the Lunalilo tomb by two U.S. Navy sailors, and melted into a silver bar. The silver is returned to Hawaiʻi on May 23, 1918 by Hawaiʻi Deputy Sheriff J. Asch. It was found in a Key West, Florida pawnshop. On April 19, 1918 sailors Albert Gergbode and Paul Payne are arrested and confess in Florida. Payne is court martialed on June 13, 1919 and convicted of "disobeying a law." He is fined $180 and demoted in rank. There is no record of a court martial for Gergbode. The two sailors pulled the old, worn padlock from the tomb door, but didn't open the casket. They thought all Hawaiians were buried with jewelry.

November 11, 1917: Queen Liliʻuokalani, age 78, dies at Washington Place. On November 18, a funeral procession takes the body to the Royal Mausoleum. 40,000 people watch the procession.

November 11, 1917: It is discovered that Queen Liliʻuokalani had two wills, prepared in 1909 and 1917. Her estate is valued at $280,000, mostly for her home.

December 5, 1917: George Rodiek and Heinrich Schroeder plead guilty to charges of conspiracy to start a revolution in British-ruled India. Rodiek is HSPA president, a Hackfeld Co. vice

Queen Liliʻuokalani

president and the former German consul. Schroeder is a Hackfeld clerk. On December 22, Rodiek is fined $10,000, and both men lose their U.S. citizenship. They were arrested on July 28.

December 27, 1917: Maria Heur, a German language teacher at UH resigns because she is a German citizen and a pacifist "not loyal to any country." The UH Regents want to fire her, but UH President Arthur Dean defends her. During war hysteria, PACIFIC COMMERCIAL ADVERTISER editorials complain that a nation at war shouldn't allow a teacher to be disloyal to the U.S.

January 3, 1918: The Department of Public Instruction (DPI) asks all 1,000 public school teachers if they are loyal to America and if they have pro-German opinions. The first to be questioned have German names. In December, 1917, a DPI letter informed teachers that less than "absolutely American" values won't be tolerated.

January 11, 1918: A Grand Jury reports "Honolulu is foul with prostitution," liquor and opium. Also "Honolulu tenements are crime centers and fire traps." On January 22, U.S. Army General John Sisser reacts. He tells Honolulu Mayor Joseph Fern that soldiers will be forbidden to enter Honolulu town unless the city cleans up its vice problems – and a war of words continues.

January 25, 1918: HONOLULU ADVERTISER reports a translated document taken from the German ship, GEIER, reveals the German crew had intended to burn Honolulu Harbor and the city.

February 23, 1918: Kīlauea erupts for 14 days.

April 7, 1918: Hale 'O Na Ali'i 'O Hawai'i is re-organized. Originally established in 1886, it went underground after the monarchy overthrow. It is a fraternal and benevolent organization.

April 11, 1918: President Woodrow Wilson issues an Executive order banning the sale or service of alcohol on O'ahu, which takes effect today. All saloons are closed. Private homes are not affected by the order, requested by Governor Lucius Pinkham and Hawai'i business leaders.

April 30, 1918: A jury takes just 4 minutes to acquit retired Navy sailor Henry Allen for shooting and killing his housemate, John Walker, who made a pro-German speech on April 14 at 'A'ala Park. Allen says he is a patriot and Walker was a traitor.

May 9, 1918: Army Major Harold Clark makes Hawaii's first interisland flight. He flies from Fort Kamehameha to Maui then Hilo, but clouds, fog and darkness at Mauna Kea make him crash into trees near Kaiwiki, Hawai'i Island. He walks two days before reaching a road.

May 22, 1918: 70 Hawai'i organizations agree that Hawai'i should be a "melting pot of the world," and all the world's races should meet in Hawai'i to spread goodwill and better understand each other. On October 26, 1922, the Pan Pacific Commercial Conference opens. A dozen nations attend to discuss peace, prosperity and friendship.

May 23, 1918: President Woodrow Wilson signs a law to prohibit the sale of intoxicating liquor in Hawai'i during WW I.

May 27, 1918: Hawai'i Legislature approves a resolution, asking President Wilson to establish a federal internment camp in Hawai'i to imprison alien enemies. On June 1, the U.S. Attorney General says Hawai'i is "without power" to enact a law to establish a Hawai'i internment camp, even though a similar law is passed in Texas. Some aliens, mostly German sailors on U.S. ships stranded in Hawai'i, are sent to Kīpahulu Maui Plantation to work until 1919.

May 29, 1918: Governor Lucius Pinkham signs a law to drain and fill Waikīkī marsh, and build a canal. On May 2, 1917, he signed a law to create a Commission to plan for the draining and filling.

June 3, 1918: Governor Lucius Pinkham signs a law to create a felony crime for anyone who criticizes, uses abusive or disloyal language about the U.S. government, military or flag during war time.

June 22, 1918: Charles McCarthy becomes Hawaii's 5th governor until July 5, 1921. He is appointed by President Woodrow Wilson. During the 1893 overthrow, he supported the monarchy. Prior to his appointment, he was a Territorial legislator and treasurer.

June 24, 1918: U.S. government acquires 334-acre Ford Island for $235,000, to be used by the Army

Governor Charles McCarthy

and Navy for aviation. The island is named for Dr. Seth Ford, a Honolulu physician.

June 26, 1918: President Woodrow Wilson approves the 15-year hard labor prison sentence of Ft. Shafter Army Chaplain Captain Franz Feinler. On January 10, Feinler made pro-German remarks. He was arrested on March 2 and a court martial found him guilty on May 10.

June 29, 1918: "Princess" Theresa Belliveau and James Kealoha are sentenced to 3 years in prison for making a fake "last will" of Queen Lili'uokalani. A 3rd defendant turned evidence and wasn't prosecuted.

July 6, 1918: Governor Charles McCarthy says he wants Waikīkī to be a beautiful residential area, without cheaply-built stores and homes.

July 20, 1918: A new locally-owned company, American Factors (the name changes to Amfac on April 30, 1966) is created when the German company, H. Hackfeld & Co. is seized by the U.S. government and transferred to a new company. A 1917 U.S. Trading with the Enemy Law, passed during WW I prohibits German-owned companies in America. Hackfeld Company complains the $7.5 million compensation it gets is far less than the company is worth, but eventually loses its plea after many years of court battles. Hawaii's Big 5 companies eagerly take advantage of the federal law and buy stock in Amfac. On January 11, 1918, Hackfeld removes all aliens from its Board of Directors, and new ownership is dominated by Americans.

August 2, 1918: A German company, B.F. Ehlers and Company, owned by Hackfeld, is renamed Liberty House, which is considered a patriotic name during WW I.

August 27, 1918: A grand jury indicts the entire Hawai'i County Board of Supervisors and several business leaders for wasteful practices, keeping inauditable books, and awarding contracts illegally. They are found guilty of most charges on January 20, 1919. Four supervisors are fined $200 on February 5.

September 25, 1918: A public school teacher and principal are fired for being pro-German or pacifist. On October 1, the School Board asks 4 "enemy" alien teachers to resign, and they do by October 16.

September 27, 1918: A new Japanese hospital opens on Kuakini Street.

The $100,000 hospital is built with donations from Japan's royal family and from American donations. The original hospital, which opened on July 15, 1900, was known as Japanese Charity Hospital because it gave free medical care.

October 16, 1918: Hawai'i Supreme Court rules that a teacher can whip a misbehaving student. The principal of Kalihiwaena School gave a student 15 lashes with a belt that left temporary welts on the boy's body.

December 6, 1918: The first Hawaiian Civic Club is established by Jonah Kūhiō Kalaniana'ole to promote education for Hawaiians, preserve Hawaiian cultural traditions, and encourage members to participate in civic activities. The Association of Hawaiian Civic Clubs is established in 1959. There are now 51 civic clubs nationwide.

December 23, 1918: Maui rancher Angus McPhee pays $600 a year for a 21-year lease to Kaho'olawe. He must remove all goats and sheep.

January 10, 1919: Federal Judge Horace Vaughn revokes Dr. Frank Schurmann's U.S. citizenship for disloyalty. His 1916 book was pro-German, and he never fully renounced his allegiance to Germany.

February 11, 1919: Congressional Delegate Jonah Kūhiō introduces the first bill in Congress for Hawai'i statehood.

April 19, 1919: Hawai'i Senate rejects a bill to let the people vote on whether to give women the right to vote.

April 29, 1919: Luke Field on Ford Island is dedicated to honor Lt. Frank Luke, a Congressional Medal of Honor winner who shot down 18 enemy aircraft in 17 days. He died in France in air combat on September 28, 1918. The Navy takes control of Ford Island on October 31, 1935.

April 29, 1919: Governor Charles McCarthy signs a law to make it a felony crime to advocate sabotage or violence," or participate in a group that commits such acts for "industrial or political ends."

April 30, 1919: Governor Charles McCarthy signs a law to rename the College of Hawai'i as the University of Hawai'i on July 1, 1920.

June 26, 1919: Hawai'i Promotion Committee, established in 1903, is renamed the Hawai'i Tourist Bureau, and will get government funds.

July 3, 1919: Two Army seaplanes make the first interisland air mail flight, from Luke Field on Ford Island to Hilo.

August 21, 1919: U.S. Navy Secretary Josephus Daniels dedicates the $5 million Pearl Harbor Naval Station drydock "to the God of Commerce, the God of Civilization, and the God of Christianity."

August 31, 1919: Pablo Manlapit establishes the Filipino Labor Union at an 'A'ala Park meeting.

National News

September 26, 1919: President Woodrow Wilson suffers a stroke during a 3 week, 8,000 mile speaking tour to rally public support for the League of Nations. The U.S. Senate fails to ratify the Treaty of Versailles, which ends WW I.

September 26, 1919: Territorial Attorney General Harry Irwin issues a report, written by a plantation manager, that Puerto Rican plantation workers are "comfortably housed" and don't experience discrimination. Puerto Rican workers had complained to the U.S. government.

September 26, 1919: Mauna Loa erupts for 42 days. Lava overflows onto the caldera floor and becomes a popular tourist attraction.

November 1, 1919: Hawaii's first plantation newspaper, MAKAWELI PLANTATION NEWS is founded, and continues until June 1, 1923. The 4-page monthly is written in English, Japanese and Filipino. It is followed by dozens more publications, owned and written by sugar and pineapple management to promote enthusiasm among workers, reduce worker complaints, and make management look good.

> **November 27, 1919**: Mormon Temple at Lā'ie is dedicated. The $200,000 temple is built on a former 6,000 acre Kahuku Plantation. It is the first building outside the continental U.S for sacred Mormon religious ceremonies for the living and the dead. Four years earlier, on June 1, 1915, LDS Church President and former Hawai'i missionary, Joseph F. Smith dedicated the land.

December 1, 1919: Japanese Federation of Labor is established to unify Japanese plantation workers for higher wages. On December 4, the Federation submits worker demands for $1.25 a day wages and an 8-hour work day to HSPA, which HSPA rejects on December 11. This rejection leads to the January 19, 1920 strike.

December 21, 1919: Kīlauea erupts for 7 months.

December 30, 1919: Secretary of Hawai'i Curtis I'aukea becomes Acting Governor while Governor Charles McCarthy goes to Washington, D.C. He is the Territory's first "Acting" Hawaiian Governor.

1920-1929

January 2, 1920: Federal census begins. Hawai'i has 255,881 population, a 33% increase since 1910 – 16% Hawaiian, 11% Caucasian, 9% Chinese, 43% Japanese, 8% Filipino, 11% Portuguese, 2% Korean.

January 2, 1920: HONOLULU STAR-BULLETIN story describes overcrowded, filthy tenement slums. One building with 430 residents had just 5 small kitchens and 7 bath tubs.

January 19, 1920: 2,600 Filipino sugar plantation workers, led by Pablo Manlapit, strike 5 O'ahu sugar plantations for 165 days until June 30.

February 1, 1920: 5,800 Japanese plantation workers join Filipino strikers in Hawaii's first large multi-racial strike. Workers earning 77¢ a day want a $1.25 that other nationalities get, and criticize the unfair "bonus" pay. Plantation owners try to divide strikers by race. When plantations evict 12,000 strikers and families from their plantation homes, the Federation of Japanese Labor builds "tent cities" to house the homeless. A flu epidemic kills 1,200 people, including many homeless workers and their families. There are "orders given" to deny striker's children from attending public schools. To end the strike, more than 2,000 Hawaiian, Portuguese, Puerto Rican, Chinese and Korean strikebreakers are hired at $3 a day.

February 4, 1920: U.S. Congressman Charles Curry, chair of the Territories Committee says Hawai'i statehood means Japanese control.

February 11, 1920: In dramatic "old west" style, a gun-totting masked man named Kaimiola Hali or Hale, commits Hawaii's first train robbery. He stops a Kekaha Sugar Company train, taking $10,000. Most of the money is recovered in a few days.

February 25, 1920: John Wilson (D) is elected Honolulu mayor by the

Board of Supervisors, after Mayor Joe Fern dies of diabetes on February 20. Wilson is Honolulu's second-longest serving mayor, with 17 years, from 1920-1926, 1929-1930, and 1947-1954.

April 3, 1920: 3,000 plantation strikers march in Honolulu. Some carry banners, "Can you live on 77¢ per day?"

April 20, 1920: Japanese Federation of Labor is renamed Hawaiian Federation of Labor, and union leaders seek affiliation with the American Federation of Labor (AFL). Union members vote to expel any members "tainted with Communism, radicalism or anarchy."

May 8, 1920: Two Army seaplanes make the longest non-stop inter-island flight, Honolulu to Kaua'i, 100 miles. It is the first airplane to land on Kaua'i. Previous flights from Honolulu to Hilo refueled on Maui.

June 8, 1920: Angus McPhee partners with Maui rancher and Territorial Senator Harry Baldwin, to establish Kaho'olawe Ranch.

June 11, 1920: The HONOLULU STAR-BULLETIN reports a national Russell Sage Foundation study that Hawai'i is 23rd of 52 states and territories in the percentage of school efficiency.

June 11, 1920: Republican National Convention endorses home rule, "the rehabilitation of the Hawaiian race," and federal spending to Americanize Hawaii's "greatly disproportionate foreign population."

June 30, 1920: Workers end the longest sugar strike in Territorial history, which began January 19. Strikers return to work at 77¢ a day, which is later raised to $1.15 a day, and other benefits. Plantations lost $12 million during the strike, but they are insured for $20 million crop losses.

July 15, 1920: A U.S. Commission on Education Survey criticizes Hawaii's school system. The report says Hawai'i has too few schools and too few classrooms. The schools are underfunded, poorly maintained, and overcrowded. There are too few teachers, who are underpaid, which is why most teachers quit. The report also says Hawai'i spends "a small fraction" of what mainland communities spend on education. The report says Hawai'i has the nation's smallest proportion of students in public high schools. The report suggests providing educational opportunities for all students, adding more academic classes, including foreign language classes, and abolishing private foreign language schools. The report urges opening more high schools and junior high schools. At the time, secondary education is generally left to the private and parochial schools, because Hawai'i has only 4 public high schools – one on each major island. A majority of public high school students are Asians, and most first graders speak pidgin English or no English. The report says non-English speaking Asians should learn "the ideals, customs and language of the American Nation" in public schools. Many

Caucasian leaders resent paying taxes for public schools having a majority of Asian students. An advance report is published in the HONOLULU ADVERTISER beginning June 2, 1920. By 1930, Hawai'i has 9 high schools and 16 junior high schools.

August 20, 1920: Board of Education votes to abolish teaching German, and says, "There are few, if any original ideas in German books..."

September 7, 1920: School Board votes to open Central Grammar School – later renamed Lincoln School – for students who pass a verbal English test. English standard schools are for students who speak good English rather than pidgin or limited English, and to promote high educational standards and "Americanism." Parents of 400 English-speaking students had submitted a petition for an English-speaking school. On September 8, DPI Superintendent Vaughan MacCaughey says, "no discrimination by reason of race, color, parentage or social condition will govern..." standard schools. In 1927 and 1931 two governors sign laws for English standard schools.

September 17, 1920: MAUI NEWS reports Bishop Museum scientists and Hawaiian advisor Pua Wei, find man-made stone terraces, 3-5 feet high, in Haleakalā, similar to terraces of New Mexico cliff dwellings.

November 20, 1920: Kamehameha Schools holds the first inter-class song contest on an outdoor stage lit by car headlights.

November 24, 1920: Governor Charles McCarthy signs a law to require the Department of Public Instruction to regulate private foreign language schools, limit instruction to one hour per day, and to issue licenses to such schools and their teachers. All foreign language school teachers must pass an English test and possess "the ideals of democracy...promote Americanism." There are 163 such schools – 9 Korean, 7 Chinese and 147 Japanese – with 300 teachers and 20,000 students. Many schools file a lawsuit to protest the law.

January 1, 1921: Dr. George Straub and other doctors are partners in "The Clinic," which becomes Straub Clinic in 1952. Dr. Straub left Germany in 1903 to avoid court martial charges for hitting a drunk officer.

January 27, 1921: Rev. Takie Okumura begins meeting on Kaua'i with Japanese workers. This leads to meetings with 1,452 Japanese workers at 75 plantations throughout Hawai'i. He says the Japanese are "losing the confidence of the American people...We must forget the idea 'Japanese' and always think and act from the point of view of the American people..." We must be "good and loyal American citizens." Adopting American customs is not disloyal to the forefathers in Japan. He wants to eliminate American distrust of Japanese.

March 18, 1921: Kīlauea erupts for 7 days.

April 6, 1921: Governor Charles McCarthy signs a law to create a Hawaiian Legend and Folklore Commission to publish legends and folklore. On April 19, another law adds songs and mele.

April 18, 1921: Governor Charles McCarthy signs a law to create an Historical Commission to publish Hawai'i history. In 1922, the Commission hires Ralph Kuykendall, a University of California history professor. He begins teaching at UH in 1932. He writes a high school history textbook and authors the 3-volume HAWAIIAN KINGDOM.

April 27, 1921: Governor Charles McCarthy signs a law to require foreign language newspapers to submit an English translation to the Attorney General. The law is never enforced.

April 27, 1921: Governor Charles McCarthy signs two laws to create the Waikīkī Improvement Commission, and provides $600,000 for a canal to provide "proper drainage and sanitation." This will eliminate the duckponds, wetlands, rice and taro farms, and create an urban district for hotels. Draining and excavating the two mile, Ala Wai Canal begins in 1921 and finishes in 1928.

April 27, 1921: As a result of the 1920 sugar strike, Governor Charles McCarthy signs a Conspiracy Law to restrict freedom of speech and the press. This anti-union law prohibits unions from distributing flyers against a plantation, and prohibits union newspapers from publishing complaints about the sugar industry.

April 27, 1921: Governor Charles McCarthy signs an Emergency Labor Commission Law to send 3 people to urge Congress to declare a "labor shortage" to allow Chinese immigration to replace Japanese workers. On August 13, a U.S. Senate committee begins hearings on this issue. Hawai'i Commission Chairman Walter Dillingham tells the Senate – "If the agricultural interests of Hawai'i are taken over by the Japanese, the territory itself will press rapidly into Japanese control." The proposal fails in Congress.

May 14, 1921: Washington Place, the former home of Queen Lili'uokalani, is purchased for $55,000 by the Territory as the governor's official residence.

July 5, 1921: Wallace Farrington becomes Hawaii's 6th governor until July 5, 1929. His friend, President Warren Harding, appoints him, and President Calvin Coolidge reappoints him. In 1894, he moved to

Hawai'i to be editor of the PACIFIC COMMERCIAL ADVERTISER. After his governorship, he is publisher of the HONOLULU STAR-BULLETIN.

Governor Wallace Farrington

July 9, 1921: President Warren Harding signs the Hawaiian Homes Commission Act, also known as the Rehabilitation Act, authored by Congressional Delegate Jonah Kūhiō. It sets aside 203,000 acres of territorial agricultural lands so Hawaiians with 50% or more Hawaiian ancestry can obtain a low-cost, 99-year leasehold home ownership. The first "experiments" will be on Moloka'i. An optimistic Kūhiō says, "It marks an epoch in our history," however only a small portion of land is provided to Hawaiians for homesteading.

July 9, 1921: President Warren Harding repeals the "1,000 acres clause" of the Organic Act so new companies can have 1,000 acres of land. This provision is included in the Hawaiian Homes Commission Act.

July 9, 1921: President Warren Harding signs a law to require a citizen or an alien eligible for citizenship after living in Hawai'i for 3 years to qualify for most territorial and federal jobs. This law eliminates most Japanese and Filipinos from jobs.

August 2, 1921: Congressional Delegate Jonah Kūhiō tells a Congressional hearing that Hawai'i is slipping from American to Japanese business control, and he supports a law to allow Chinese immigration. American Federation of Labor President Samuel Gompers replies that importing plantation labor is "an act of shame and disgrace for any American to advocate peonage, bonded labor or slave labor..."

August 28, 1921: HSPA brings 342 Puerto Ricans to Hawai'i to work on sugar plantations during a strike. Another 341 arrive on November 10, but they receive less wages than promised.

September 1, 1921: Kamehameha School begins with a 10th grade. Grade 11 begins in 1922, and grade 12 in 1923.

October 10, 1921: Hawai'i hosts the 2nd World Press Congress at the Moana Hotel. 100 news reporters from 8 nations attend.

January 7, 1922: Prince Jonah Kūhiō Kalaniana'ole, age 50, dies of a heart attack in Waikīkī. He was the last Prince of the monarchy and a

Congressional Delegate from 1902-1922. More than 50,000 people watched his January 15 funeral procession. This is the last state funeral for Hawaiian royalty.

March 27, 1922: U.S. Army establishes Fort Weaver, honoring General Erasmus Weaver. It is designated a subpost of Fort Kamehameha on November 1, 1923, and inactivated after WW II. On May 10, 1929, Hawai'i Territory asks the U.S. War Department to rename the fort for King Kalākaua, but the rejection letter says it would be an "injustice" to General Weaver's memory.

April 1, 1922: The $1 million Federal Building opens. It is known as the U.S. Post Office, Custom House and Court House, located on the former site of the Opera House, which was demolished in 1917. The downtown Post Office opens on May 1.

April 17, 1922: Board of Education restores Central Grammar School as an English standard school, provided there is no racial discrimination.

May 11, 1922: Today is Hawaii's first commercial radio broadcast. Marion Mulrony of the HONOLULU ADVERTISER says a few "hellos" on 50-watt KGU, owned by the newspaper. Fifteen minutes later, Governor Wallace Farrington offers aloha greetings on KDYX (later KGMB and now KSSK), owned by the STAR-BULLETIN. KGU is the 32nd radio station licensed in the U.S.

June 27, 1922: David Kamai is the first Hawaiian homesteader to move to Molokai's Kalaniana'ole Settlement.

August 26, 1922: A&B executive John Guild pleads guilty to stealing $500,000 to $1 million from his company and his church, and is sentenced to prison for 5-10 years. He says he lost the money in the stock market.

September 6, 1922: Hawai'i Theatre opens in Honolulu. It closes on May 27, 1984.

September 14, 1922: The $250,000 Aloha Amusement Park opens on 5 acres next to Fort DeRussy. 10,000 people visit the first day. The park closes in the 1930s.

September 15, 1922: President Warren Harding signs a law to allow women in Hawai'i to be candidates for the Territorial Legislature and Congress.

October 12, 1922: The ship, CITY OF HONOLULU, catches fire en route to Hawai'i, 600 miles from California. All 217 passengers and crew are rescued by nearby ships before it sinks.

October 13, 1922: Governor Wallace Farrington says Hawaii's AJAs who "erect a little Japan" with foreign language schools will be confronted with "an increasing feeling of suspicion and distrust, born of the fact that the Americans feel that their confidence and good will have been abused."

October 14, 1922: Governor Wallace Farrington escapes from a burning seaplane that lands in Pearl Harbor. Wearing a lifejacket, he swims to safety to a waiting seaplane piloted by Commander John Rodgers. On September 1, 1924, Governor Farrington's fishing boat nearly crashes on Wai'anae rocks, so he and others swim ashore.

November 11, 1922: Wheeler Field is named for Major Sheldon Wheeler. He died in a July 13, 1921 flying exhibition at Ford Island.

November 13, 1922: U.S. Supreme Court rules that Takao Ozawa, a Japanese-born Hawai'i resident is not eligible for U.S. citizenship because of his race. The court says a 1790 U.S. law gives citizenship to free whites, and the 14th Amendment, adopted on July 28, 1868, gives citizenship to African descendants. This ruling prevents thousands of aliens living in Hawai'i from becoming U.S. citizens.

November 15, 1922: James Dole of Hawaiian Pineapple Co. buys Lāna'i from Harry and Frank Baldwin for $1.1 million. Dole invests more than $4 million on Lāna'i for roads and a water reservoir, and begins large-scale planting of pineapple. In 1929 he builds a $1.5 million Iwilei Cannery, and buys canning equipment. These investments use the cash he needs to get out of debt in 1932, and he loses his company.

January 1, 1923: Libby gets a 17-year lease to plant 5,000 acres of pineapple on Molokai's Mauna Loa plantation. At the time, Molokai's population is only 700 people.

February 3, 1923: Seven tidal waves create $1.5 million damage in Kahului and Hilo. The highest wave is 19 feet, killing one person.

February 19, 1923: The HONOLULU STAR-BULLETIN buys the HILO TRIBUNE, which merges with two other Hilo newspapers and the name changes to the HILO TRIBUNE-HERALD, a daily.

March 31, 1923: Governor Wallace Farrington signs a law to require all teachers and government workers to be U.S. citizens. This prevents Asians and Filipinos from such jobs.

April 10, 1923: Pablo Manlapit give HSPA a petition with 6,000 signatures, seeking $2 a day, an 8-hour work day, time-and-a-half for overtime, and equal pay for men and women. HSPA ignores the petition.

April 21, 1923: Governor Wallace Farrington signs a law to require students from age 6-14 to attend school.

April 26, 1923: Governor Wallace Farrington signs a "Bill of Rights" law that asks Congress to treat Hawai'i as if it were a state. This would qualify Hawai'i for more federal funds for education, farms, roads, etc.

April 27, 1923: Cayetano Ligot arrives in Hawai'i as the Philippines' Resident Labor Commissioner. He is supposed to investigate Filipino labor complaints, but often supports HSPA positions for fear of being recalled. The Philippines is a U.S. Territory, and the U.S. Governor-General of the Philippines appointed Ligot with HSPA support.

May 2, 1923: Governor Wallace Farrington signs a law to increase the poll, school, and road taxes from $1 to $2 for men and women ages 20-60. The original 1896 law required only males to pay these taxes.

May 2, 1923: Governor Wallace Farrington signs a law to eliminate the most popular grades, K-2, from Japanese language schools. All such schools must get a permit from the Department of Public Instruction (DPI), which will charge $1 per pupil at every language school. DPI must approve all textbooks and receive all income from textbook sales.

May 2, 1923: Governor Wallace Farrington signs an Anti-Picketing law to discourage union activities. The law makes picketing illegal if it tries to prevent people from doing business with another person. The law is repealed by Governor Ingram Stainback on April 9, 1945.

May 2, 1923: Governor Wallace Farrington signs a law to make Lahainaluna a public high school. It is the oldest public school west of the Rocky Mountains, established by missionaries in 1831.

August 25, 1923: Kīlauea erupts for one day. 700 feet of lava is drained out of the crater.

December 10, 1923: U.S. Army General Billy Mitchell inspects Hawai'i aviation, and writes a report that predicts a Japanese air attack on Pearl Harbor on a Sunday morning at 7:30 a.m. He says Hawai'i would be "helpless" in a war.

March 10, 1924: President Calvin Coolidge signs an appropriation law, commonly known in Hawai'i as the "Hawai'i Bill of Rights." This law treats Hawai'i as if it is a state, for purposes of receiving more federal funds for education, farms, roads, etc.

March 25, 1924: Jewelry of Queen Lili'uokalani are auctioned for $12,192 to support the Lili'uokalani Home for Orphans, according to her will.

April 1, 1924: Pablo Manlapit leads an 8-month strike of 12,000 Filipino plantation workers at 23 of 45 Hawai'i sugar plantations. Strikers seek an 8-hour work day, $2 a day in wages, an end to the bonus system, and better housing. It is known as the "Filipino Piecemeal Strike" because non-striking workers do little work. On April 7, many O'ahu strikers are evicted from their plantation homes.

April 11, 1924: KGU radio station makes the first broadcast to the entire U.S. featuring all Hawaiian music. Conductor Johnny Noble, who popularizes hapa haole music, leads the orchestra.

April 23, 1924: An earthquake shakes Kapoho, Puna, and splits the road 12 feet.

May 10, 1924: Kīlauea erupts for 17 days. Falling rocks from violent explosions at Halema'uma'u kill one person.

May 26, 1924: President Calvin Coolidge signs the 1924 Immigration Act, known as the Oriental Exclusion Act. This federal law allows tens of thousands of northern and western Europeans to immigrate each year, but limits Asians to 100 a year from each nation because they are "ineligible for U.S. citizenship." Japan calls the law an insult. From 1885-1924, 220,000 Japanese immigrated to Hawai'i.

June 6, 1924: HSPA Executive Secretary John Butler sends a memo to plantation managers about Pablo Manlapit – "In spite of surveillance, we have not been able to get a good case against him." Planters work with police and county officials, spy on union leaders, and try to pin "conspiracy" charges against them.

September 2, 1924: Miles Cary begins 24 years as principal of McKinley High School, commonly known as "Tokyo High." He encourages many non-Caucasian students to get an academic education and seek professional careers, which ultimately changes the social, political and economic fabric of Hawai'i. This angers the Caucasian elite who demand vocational education skills for plantation workers. Cary writes in his 1930 M.A. thesis at the University of Hawai'i – "Those in more favored positions are apparently not interested in seeing their circle entered by young people of the immigrant laboring class."

September 9, 1924: The "Hanapēpē Massacre." A Filipino sugar worker strike in Hanapēpē, Kaua'i turns violent. 16 workers and 4 police are killed, a deputy sheriff and 9 strikers are wounded. Governor Farrington sends the National Guard to Kaua'i. 130 strikers are arrested on September 9-10. 60 strikers get 4-year prison sentences for assault and battery, and some are deported. HSPA pays for extra police who arrested the strikers, and government legal costs too.

October 11, 1924: Pablo Manlapit is sentenced to 2-10 years for perjury in his testimony related to the Hanapēpē, Kauaʻi sugar strike, even though he wasn't on Kauaʻi at the time. HSPA paid witnesses to testify against Manlapit, and they are returned to the Philippines after the trial. They later admit that they "framed" Manlapit. On May 29, 1925, the Hawaiʻi Supreme Court approves Manlapit's conviction. After serving the minimum 2-year sentence, Governor Wallace Farrington signs Manlapit's parole on July 27, 1927 with a handwritten condition that he leave Hawaiʻi. In February, the Prison Board had offered a parole if he returns to the Philippines and never comes back to Hawaiʻi, but the Hawaiʻi Legislature said the Prison Board exceeded its authority. Manlapit leaves prison on August 13 and is escorted under guard to a ship departing for Los Angeles. He is met at the pier by the Attorney General, who gives Manlapit a one-way ticket. On November 12, 1931, the Prison Board rejects Manlapit's petition to spend Christmas with his family in Hawaiʻi because his probation in California doesn't expire until February 13, 1932. Manlapit says he was "railroaded to prison" by a system of industrial exploitation, and the governor is under instructions of a "little group of sugar planters." On May 20 the Prison Board denies a request for a full pardon.

November 4, 1924: Rosalie Kiliʻinoi (R) of Kauaʻi is the first woman elected to the Hawaiʻi Legislature. Her legislation to allow women to sell property without their husband's approval is signed into law by Governor Wallace Farrington on May 5, 1925. She also introduces legislation to establish community property and to allow women to make their own contracts – which become laws decades later.

April 25, 1925: Army-Navy war games attempt to "recapture" Pearl Harbor and Molokaʻi from "enemy hands" during 3-day exercises. The Oʻahu "invasion" is led by 127 ships.

April 27, 1925: Governor Wallace Farrington signs a law to allow schools to charge students $1 for textbooks, except needy students.

April 29, 1925: Governor Wallace Farrington signs a law asking Congress to prevent the U.S. Immigration Bureau from discriminating against Hawaiʻi citizens when they travel to the mainland. While Chinese and Japanese nationals can't enter the mainland from Hawaiʻi, many U.S. citizens are having a difficult time entering the mainland.

September 10, 1925: First mainland-to-Hawaiʻi flight is unsuccessful, but it establishes a new flying record. John Rodgers and a 4-man crew leave San Francisco in a two-engine Navy seaplane that runs out of fuel in 28 hours, about 450 miles from Hawaiʻi. The flying distance of 1,870 miles is a new seaplane distance record, and proves the seaplane worthy of long distance flight. After floating on the ocean 10 days, the

Lava from a Mauna Loa eruption will destroy Hoʻōpūloa Village

near-starvation crew is rescued by a Pearl Harbor submarine about 15 miles from Nāwiliwili, Kauaʻi.

March 4, 1926: Two U.S. Army seaplanes complete Hawaii's first interisland round-trip flight in one day – Honolulu to Kauaʻi and Honolulu to Hilo. The flight proves the feasibility of interisland air travel.

April 10, 1926: Mauna Loa erupts for two weeks. On the Kona coast, Hoʻōpūloa Village is destroyed on April 18. The eruption is shown worldwide in movie newsreels.

June 8, 1926: The 184-foot tall, $830,000, Aloha Tower opens. It is Hawaii's tallest building for 30 years. A siren sounds 3 times a day, but it is discontinued because it is too loud. The tower light is visible 19 miles at sea. For decades, Aloha Tower wharf is abuzz with "boat day" activities when luxury liners arrive and depart amidst parties, music by the Royal Hawaiian Band, lei-giving, and Hawaiian boys diving for coins that passengers toss overboard. During WW II, Aloha Tower is painted in Army camouflage colors. On December 7, 1941, a Japanese airplane shoots a hole in the 10th floor window.

June 9, 1926: A tornado hits Hawaiʻi briefly, and causes minor damage. It is the first tornado ever recorded in Hawaiʻi.

June 9, 1926: Sanford Dole, age 82, dies. He was president of the Provisional Government, Hawaiʻi Republic, territorial governor, and federal judge.

June 22, 1926: Governor Wallace Farrington commutes the sentences of 48 workers from the Hanapēpē massacre if they return to the Philippines. On November 7, 1925, the judge gave them 4-5 years in prison.

November 11, 1926: Honolulu Stadium opens in Mōʻiliʻili. 12,000 people attend the first event, a football game. Town defeats the Deans, 14-7. The termite-ridden stadium is demolished on October 4, 1976.

December 18, 1926: Hāna Highway opens. Since 1909, $1.5 million is spent to pave the entire 125 miles around Maui, with 44 miles left.

December 31, 1926: Superintendent of Public Instruction reports that a majority of Hawaii's 29,546 Asian students attending foreign language schools are U.S. citizens, not aliens.

February 1, 1927: The $4 million, 400-room Royal Hawaiian Hotel in Waikīkī, opens on 15 beachfront acres. The Spanish and Moorish style hotel is known as the "Pink Palace." The opening is described as Hawaii's "greatest social event" with 1,200 black-tie guests paying $10 for dinner. During construction, the hotel partially sinks. In 1942, the U.S. Navy leases the hotel for $17,500 monthly, and 200,000 sailors stay there during WW II. The Seaside Hotel formerly occupied the site with cottages, where author Jack London wrote a novel. The hotel is built on land formerly known as the Helumoa coconut grove.

February 21, 1927: The U.S. Supreme Court rules unanimously that Hawaii's 1920, 1923 and 1925 laws regulating Japanese language schools are unconstitutional. The Territory refunds $20,000 in fees paid by language schools.

March 21, 1927: John Rodgers Airport is dedicated as Hawaii's first territorial airport. At the dedication, carrier pigeons are released to fly to Wheeler and Luke Fields. In 1942, the Navy controls the airport and names it Honolulu Naval Air Station. In 1947, it is renamed the Honolulu International Airport.

March 23, 1927: Hail stones as large as one inch fall during a storm.

April 8, 1927: Honolulu Academy of Arts opens on the site of the former Spanish-style home of Charles Cooke and Anna Rice Cooke. The museum is established to house their large art collection.

April 23, 1927: Governor Wallace Farrington signs a law to allow the Department of Public Instruction to establish English standard schools after they were established by DPI. Governor Lawrence Judd signs a similar law on April 30, 1931. Hawaii's controversial dual school system is phased out from 1949-1960, when the last class graduates. Throughout its controversial history, only 10% of Hawaii's public school students attend English standard schools. By 1947, a majority of the standard school students are AJAs.

Welcome to Hawai'i. Lt. Maitland and Lt. Hegenberger pilot the first successful airplane flight from the mainland.

April 27, 1927: Governor Wallace Farrington signs a law to eliminate billboard advertising, which is considered a blight to Hawaii's scenery. This new law is a huge victory for the Outdoor Circle, which paid $4,000 in 1926 to buy Hawaii's last billboard company, then closed the company. Today, Hawai'i is the only state with such a law.

May 3, 1927: Governor Wallace Farrington signs a law to spend $50,000 to add sand for the first time to restore Waikīkī beach. A HONOLULU ADVERTISER story of October 17, 1928 blames sea walls for the loss of sand. In the decades since, the state has added many tons of sand to Waikīkī beach. As recent as June 7, 1989, Governor John Waihe'e signs a law to spend $1 million to restore Waikīkī Beach sand with "periodic sand replenishment."

May 14, 1927: Bishop Museum receives a royal feather cape known as the "Starbuck Cape" as a donation from Priscilla Starbuck. It belonged to King Kamehameha I and Kamehameha II, who took it to London, where he died in 1824.

June 29, 1927: Navy Lt. Lester Maitland and Lt. Albert Hegenberger complete the first successful Pacific air flight from the mainland (Oakland) to Hawai'i (Wheeler Field). 10,000 people welcome the pilots.

July 7, 1927: Kīlauea erupts for 13 days.

July 15, 1927: Ernest Smith and Emory Bronte are the first civilians to fly from the mainland to Hawai'i. 25 hours after leaving Oakland, their airplane runs out of gas and crash lands on Moloka'i. The pilots are not injured.

Reverend Takie Okumura

August 8, 1927: Assistant Secretary of State William Castle Jr. of Hawaii's missionary family, becomes America's acting head of state for one day when President Calvin Coolidge, the vice president, and the entire cabinet are away from Washington, D.C.

August 17, 1927: The Dole Air Derby is the first trans-Pacific flight race – 2,400-miles from Oakland to Hawai'i. Art Goebel wins a $25,000 prize for piloting the winning monoplane to Wheeler Field in 26 hours. He lands with 4 gallons of gas. He is welcomed by 20,000 people. Eight airplanes leave Oakland, but two crash on takeoff, two return to Oakland, two disappear, and only two land in Honolulu. A search airplane disappears too. In all, 10 people die in 4 airplanes. The Dole Derby air race was inspired by Charles Lindbergh's famous 3,600 mile flight from New York to Paris on May 20-21, just 3 months earlier.

August 21, 1927: From 1927-1941, Reverend Takie Okumura, a Japanese Christian minister organizes annual "New Americans" conferences to promote American values, and eliminate Japanese distrust of Americans. 900 delegates attend the 15 conferences.

August 24, 1927: The $250,000 War Memorial Natatorium at Waikīkī opens. It is built to honor Hawaii's World War I casualties. Duke Kahanomoku, Johnny Weismuller (champion swimmer and future Tarzan movie actor) and Hawai'i Olympic swimmer Buster Crabbe compete in a national swimming championship. Several world swimming records are broken during the opening days.

September 30, 1927: Sheriff David Desha resigns amidst charges of helping Chinatown gamblers. Patrick Gleason is appointed Sheriff after changing from a Democrat to a Republican. On September 1, 1928, Desha is acquitted of taking bribes, but another man is found guilty.

November 21, 1927: 50,000 people welcome Matson's first luxury cruise ship, MALOLO, on its first voyage. It is the most expensive and fastest luxury liner built in the U.S. The voyage from San Francisco takes just 4 1/2 days, the fastest ever to date, but it arrives 9 months after the Matson-owned Royal Hawaiian Hotel opens. The hotel was built by the Territorial Hotel Company for passengers of Matson liners.

December 25, 1927: Hawaiian language newspaper, Kuokoa, founded in 1861 and bought by the Advertiser in 1898, ends publication.

February 4, 1928: Hawaii's first mainland chain supermarket opens. 5,000 people arrive at 7:30 a.m. for the Piggly Wiggly store on Beretania St.

February 11, 1928: Major Clarence Young, the U.S. Director of Aeronautics dedicates Hilo Airport when 4 Navy seaplanes and an Army airplane arrive. The completed airport is dedicated on May 1, 1941, during Hilo's first Lei Day celebration. On April 19, 1943, Hilo Airport is re-named General Lyman Field, for Albert Lyman, the first native Hawaiian to serve the U.S. Army as a brigadier general.

February 22, 1928: A new Lunalilo Home for aged Hawaiians opens near Koko Head after relocating from a termite-ridden facility in Makiki. The home first opened on April 9, 1881, based on King Lunalilo's will.

February 23, 1928: Dole builds a giant pineapple water tank for $16,500 at the Iwilei Cannery. The tank holds 100,000 gallons of water for a fire sprinkler system. The 30-ton water tank stands 195 feet above ground. The giant pineapple is 40 feet tall with a 22 foot crown.

February 28, 1928: Hawai'i plays a role in one of America's most famous corruption scandals known as Teapot Dome. The U.S. Supreme Court rules unanimously that $9.3 million in Pearl Harbor improvements must be returned to the U.S. government. On May 31, 1921, President Warren Harding issued Executive Order 3474 to transfer Naval oil reserves to Secretary of the Interior Albert Fall. Fall took $100,000 in bribes to lease oil fields to two oil companies. He issued contracts for California and Wyoming oil, and to build oil storage tanks, including one in Hawai'i. Secretary Fall resigns and goes to jail.

April 15, 1928: The original 7-mile Chain of Craters Road opens. It is Hawaii's first federally-financed road.

May 1, 1928: Hawai'i celebrates the first official Lei Day. The event is proposed by Don Blanding of the HONOLULU STAR-BULLETIN.

May 10, 1928: A Hawaiian language weekly newspaper is established, KE ALAKAI O HAWAI'I. It continues until 1939.

June 11, 1928: Hulihe'e Palace at Kailua-Kona opens after restoration by the Daughters of Hawai'i.

July, 1928: Maui author Armine Von Tempski, who spent time on Kaho'olawe, writes a novel, DUST, about the island. On July 2, 1922, the NEW YORK TIMES published a von Tempski story about how goats are destroying Kaho'olawe.

August 13, 1928: The U.S. Post Office overprints "Hawaii 1778-1928" on 2¢ George Washington stamps and 5¢ Theodore Roosevelt stamps. The stamps commemorate the 150th anniversary of Captain James Cook's arrival in Hawai'i.

September 18, 1928: Myles Fukunaga, age 19, kidnaps and murders 10-year old Gill Jamieson from Punahou School. The boy is the son of a Hawaiian Trust Company executive. Fukunaga hurriedly accepts $4,000 of the $10,000 ransom, then kills the boy. He confesses, and says he needed the money to pay his family's overdue rent or they'd be tossed out of their home by Hawaiian Trust Company. When Fukunaga is arrested on September 22, about 250 bayoneted National Guardsmen control a mob of 20,000 people at the Police Station. He is found guilty, and on October 4, he is sentenced to hang. Governor Lawrence Judd refuses appeals for life imprisonment. Japanese language newspapers say if Fukunaga was Caucasian, his punishment would be different. On January 3, 1929 the Hawai'i Supreme Court approves his death sentence, agrees that he was sane during the murder, and that he got a fair trial. He is hanged at O'ahu Prison on November 19, 1929. Jamieson was a cousin of James Barrie, the famous author of PETER PAN.

October 17, 1928: HONOLULU ADVERTISER reports that an important international treaty, the Kellogg-Briand Pact, was drafted in Hawai'i by the man who had the idea for the treaty, Professor James Shotwell of Columbia University. Shotwell came here to attend a conference of the Institute of Public Relations, and he discussed his draft with the conference. 62 nations sign this symbolic treaty, which makes war illegal, because they agree not to use war to settle a conflict. On November 27, 1930, U.S. Secretary of State Frank Kellogg receives the Nobel Peace Prize for negotiating the treaty.

November 6, 1928: Nolle Smith (R) is the first African-American elected to the Hawai'i Legislature.

March 26, 1929: New Kapi'olani Maternity Home opens.

April 6, 1929: In response to a recent gang assault of a teenage girl, some prominent Honolulu women declare war on gangs. They suggest a public whipping and tougher penalties for certain crimes. On April 13, legislators introduce a much-publicized bill to provide 5-20 lashes as an additional punishment for rape or assault. The Legislature passes a bill, but Governor Wallace Farrington vetoes it.

April 23, 1929: John Clarke is the first native Hawaiian appointed as a Bishop Estate trustee. He is the 14th appointment to the Trusteeship since it was established in 1884. All previous trustees were Caucasian. He serves as a trustee until 1951.

April 30, 1929: Governor Wallace Farrington signs a law to exempt leased coffee land from taxes for 5 years, to encourage the industry.

April 30, 1929: Governor Wallace Farrington signs a law to allow public school students to receive one hour of weekly religious lessons from a private religious organization, which counts as public school attendance.

May 15, 1929: Governor Wallace Farrington signs an Unlawful Assembly and Riot law to punish people who assemble or riot, with up to 20 years of hard labor. This law intends to restrict basic rights and discourage labor union activities.

July 5, 1929: Lawrence Judd becomes Hawaii's 7th governor until March 1, 1934. He is appointed by President Herbert Hoover. He is a descendent of the missionary Judd family.

November 4, 1929: Machu Picchu explorer Hiram Bingham, grandson of the Hawai'i missionary, is now a U.S. Senator from Connecticut. The Senate censures him for morals and ethics violations for having a lobbyist on his payroll. In two days in January 1925, he went from Connecticut's Lt. Governor to Governor to U.S. Senator.

November 11, 1929: Inter-Island Airways (now Hawaiian Airlines) begins commercial service. Governor Lawrence Judd proclaims "Air Day" as the first flight goes from Honolulu to Maui and Hilo. The airline is founded by Stanley Kennedy, a former WW I pilot, whose father owns the parent company, Inter-Island Steam Navigation. 10,000 people welcome the arrival at Maui's Mā'alaea field. As many as 49 Army and Navy airplanes escort the first flight.

November 24, 1929: Governor Lawrence Judd visits Kaho'olawe. He is considering a reclamation project, but is disappointed that the island is so barren. It is described as "the island that is blowing away."

December 17, 1929: New $750,000 City Hall, initially called Honolulu Municipal Building, and later re-named Honolulu Hale, opens at King and Punchbowl. The building has an attractive Moorish design.

1929: Hawai'i residents lost $10 million in the stock market crash.

1930-1939

March 15, 1930: KGMB radio makes its first broadcast, with 6 hours of music.

March 26, 1930: The 95-foot tall Alexander Dam at Kauai's McBryde Sugar Company collapses in a heavy rain just before completion. Mudslides kill 6 people. The rebuilt dam is completed on December 22, 1932.

April 1, 1930: Federal census begins. Hawai'i has 368,300 population, a 44% increase since 1920 – 14% Hawaiian, 14% Caucasian, 7% Chinese, 38% Japanese, 17% Filipino, 8% Portuguese, 2% Korean. For the first time, there are more part-Hawaiians than full-blooded native Hawaiians.

May 28, 1930: More than 100 earthquakes shake the Kīlauea area for several days.

July 6, 1930: Arson-caused fire burns many Lower Pā'ia, Maui stores, creating $150,000 damage, and making 150 people homeless.

July 23, 1930: Maui Sheriff John Lane suggests using Kaho'olawe as a prison for tough inmates.

October 4, 1930: Noburi Miyake (R) is elected in the primary to the Kaua'i County Board of Supervisors. He is the first AJA elected to public office in Hawai'i. On November 4, 1930, Andrew Yamashiro (D) is the first AJA elected to the Territorial House. On November 5, 1940, Sanji Abe (R) is the first AJA elected to the Territorial Senate. Abe is sent to an internment camp in 1942.

November 18, 1930: Honolulu rain storm and floods kill 12 people.

November 19, 1930: Kīlauea erupts for 19 days. A 70-foot deep crater lava lake begins filling.

December 25, 1930: Hawaii's first international radio broadcast from KGMB on NBC is a 10-minute Christmas program.

January 19, 1931: The Japan consul says 121,131 of Hawaii's 139,903 Japanese are citizens of Japan. The Japanese government automatically gives dual citizenship to all Hawai'i Japanese born before December 1, 1924, whether they want it or not.

February 9, 1931: Governor's Advisory Committee on Education issues the Prosser Report, emphasizing vocational rather than academic education, and urging limits on financial support for high schools. This would keep non-Caucasians in plantation jobs. The committee was created in 1929 at HSPA's recommendation.

April 25, 1931: Governor Lawrence Judd signs a law to put Kalawao County under control of the Board of Leper Hospitals and Settlement.

Governor Lawrence Judd

April 29, 1931: Governor Lawrence Judd signs a law to allow public schools to "rent" textbooks for $1-$5, depending on grade level.

April 30, 1931: Governor Lawrence Judd vetoes a joint resolution asking Congress for statehood. He says, "The time is not opportune...unwise." He thinks Congress is unhappy with Hawai'i.

June 2, 1931: Japan's Prince and Princess Takamatsu visit Honolulu. Their ship is escorted into Honolulu by 72 U.S. Army and Navy airplanes.

June 20, 1931: Lyman Museum opens in Hilo for the 100th anniversary of David and Sarah Lyman's arrival with the 5th missionary company. It was originally built by the Lyman's in 1839 as their home.

September 13, 1931: The $1.3 million Kamehameha School for Girls opens on Kapālama campus.

October 28, 1931: A federal report says Hawai'i spends about one-half the money that other states spend for education.

November 2, 1931: Mutual Telephone Company begins interisland telephone service.

November 30, 1931: Foster Gardens opens on the 6-acre property that Mary Foster gave to the city in her will. Tom and Mary Foster bought the property in 1880 from Dr. William Hillebrand who had established a unique gardens from 1851-1871. Foster imported monkeys, and a giant tortoise carried children on its shell.

The crimes that changed Hawai'i

September 12, 1931: Thalia Massie, a 20-year old mainland socialite wife of a Navy Lieutenant, is beaten, and claims to be raped by 5 "Hawaiian boys" after she leaves a Waikīkī party. This becomes known as the "Ala Moana case" because newspapers refuse to reveal her name. The crime incites racial arguments and receives substantial national publicity. After sloppy police work, 5 youth are arrested, but witnesses at the trial testify that the youth were in another part of town at the time. The November 16 to December 2 trial ends in a mistrial on December 6. The jury fails to reach a verdict after 97 hours and 100 ballots, so the suspects are released on bail.

December 12, 1931: One of the Massie defendants, Horace Ida is kidnapped and beaten by 20 men. He says Navy sailors beat him, but he can't identify them. U.S. Navy Admiral George Pettengill says Honolulu is not safe for military families and wives.

January 8, 1932: This Massie case is America's #9 Associated Press news story for 1932. One of the alleged rape suspects, Joe Kahahawai is kidnapped and murdered by Lt. Thomas Massie and three others — Thalia's mother Grace Fortescue, and two Navy sailors, Edward Lord and Albert Jones. They wrap Kahahawai's naked body in a bed sheet on the car floor, but they are caught by police in a high-speed chase before they can dump him near Koko Head Blow Hole. 2,000 people attend Kahahawai's funeral. On January 12, the crime is discussed at President Calvin Coolidge's Cabinet meeting, and as a result, Assistant U.S. Attorney Seth Richardson is sent to Hawai'i to investigate. A grand jury rejects first degree murder and indicts the accused of 2nd degree murder only when Judge Albert Cristy urges them to do so. America's most famous attorney, Clarence Darrow represents the defense at the April 4-27 trial. The accused admit killing Kahahawai. On April 29, a jury approves a manslaughter guilty verdict. On May 3 they are sentenced to 10 years in prison. On May 4, Governor Lawrence Judd commutes the sentences to a mere one-hour in the governor's office. On May 7, while in Navy custody, the Navy sneaks the Massies out of Hawai'i and prevent a policeman from giving Thalia a subpoena for a retrial of the rape case. 30 years later, on February 13, 1967, former Governor Lawrence Judd tells the HONOLULU STAR-BULLETIN, "I acted under the heaviest Congressional pressure against my better judgment." Judd says if he didn't commute the sentences, Congress was considering "punitive legislation" to change Hawai'i to a commission form of government, and we "might not be a state."

Public Reaction in Hawai'i and on the mainland

Throughout the trial, there is intense protest from the mainland public, the sensationalistic news media, military leaders, and U.S. Congress. For example, on January 18, Congressman Charles Curry introduces a bill to impose the "full power of Congress" over Hawai'i police. A U.S. Senate committee orders an investigation of Hawaii's law enforcement, and recommends keeping thousands of Navy sailors from shore leave until reforms are made. This angers Honolulu business owners who profit from money-spending sailors. Other Congressmen want to remove Hawaii's territorial status, deny self-government, impose martial law, or establish a commission government. 120 Congressmen petition Governor Judd to pardon Massie, and others call the conviction a "miscarriage of justice."

January 22, 1932: Governor Lawrence Judd signs a law to reorganize the Honolulu Police Department, establish a Police Commission that appoints a Police Chief, and prohibit police from political activities.

January 29, 1932: Governor Lawrence Judd signs a law to make the crime of rape punishable with death or up to life in prison.

February 9, 1932: Governor Lawrence Judd signs a law to create a Honolulu Public Prosecutor, to be appointed by the mayor.

March 29, 1932: Governor Lawrence Judd signs a law to establish a Prison Board that appoints a warden to administer the prison.

April 4, 1932: The U.S. Attorney General issues the Seth Richardson Report. This report says there's no serious crime problem or racial prejudice in Hawai'i. The report criticizes the lax "undisciplined" police, and their excessive political activities. The report urges the U.S. president to appoint a police chief, and the Attorney General should be responsible for all criminal prosecutions.

May 2, 1932: U.S. Senate passes a bill to overrule a Hawai'i law that says two mistrials automatically result in an acquittal. This would allow the prosecution of the 4 surviving, accused rapists of Thalia Massie.

February 13, 1933: Judge Charles Davis frees the 4 surviving youth accused of raping Thalia Massie, and the case is officially closed. The Pinkerton Detective Agency, hired by Governor Lawrence Judd to investigate the facts, files a 279-page report with the Honolulu City Clerk. The report concludes that the 5 accused youth were innocent – they were elsewhere at the time, and the medical report of the doctor and nurse who examined Thalia Massie said no rape was committed. Governor Judd received the report on October 3, 1932.

December 23, 1931: Mutual Telephone Company begins telephone service to the mainland.. The first call with a "human voice" takes place in 'Iolani Palace with a phone call to Washington, D.C. Later that day, the HONOLULU STAR-BULLETIN publishes news it receives via radio phone from New York.

December 23, 1931: Kīlauea erupts for two weeks.

February 6, 1932: U.S. Army and Navy aerial war games successfully "attack" Pearl Harbor at dawn with more than 100 airplanes, proving that an aggressor can seize Oʻahu.

March 1, 1932: A Governor's committee opens Hawaii's first unemployment office to help the 8% unemployed find jobs. The office is partially funded by the Tourist Bureau. During the Great Depression, unemployment in Hawaiʻi is less severe than the mainland due to a prosperous sugar industry.

April 29, 1932: Labor leader Pablo Manlapit returns to Hawaiʻi from California to build a Filipino labor organization here. Sugar plantation spies follow him, and he is arrested on July 9, 1934 for overcharging a veteran soldier seeking a federal loan. Manlapit says the charges are false. The first trial reaches no decision, but he is convicted at a second trial on October 3, 1934. The jury recommends leniency, but the judge sentences him to one-year in prison or 5 years probation outside Hawaiʻi. On October 8, Manlapit says he has no money to appeal his case. On October 10, 1934, Manlapit leaves for the Philippines. On October 26, 1935, the Prison Board rejects his request for a full pardon, but on November 18, recommends to the governor a lifetime ban from Hawaiʻi in exchange for a pardon. Hawaiʻi Governor Oren Long pardons Manlapit on November 6, 1952.

May 21, 1932: Thomas Thrum, age 90, dies. In 1875 he began publishing a 50-page HAWAIIAN ANNUAL AND ALMANAC, later known as THRUM'S ANNUAL to answer frequent questions about Hawaiʻi. He wrote hundreds of articles about Hawaiʻi history, edited Fornander's COLLECTION OF HAWAIIAN ANTIQUITIES, co-founded PARADISE OF THE PACIFIC in 1888, and helped to found the Hawaiian Historic Society.

July 1, 1932: Honolulu Police Detective Chang Apana retires after 34 years. He inspired author Earl Biggers to write the best-selling, but racially stereotyped CHARLIE CHAN novels, which first appeared in 1925 – and 48 movies from 1926-1942. Apana joined the HPD in 1898 and carried a whip instead of a gun. He couldn't read or write English or Chinese. Biggers first read about Apana in a HONOLULU STAR-BULLETIN story about how he risked his life to capture drug sellers. Biggers was impressed that Honolulu has a Chinese detective. The books are intended to honor Chan Apana, but the movies insult Chinese by using Caucasians who stereotype Chinese.

August 30, 1932: Pineapple Producers Co-Operative Association is established to promote pineapples and to prevent its overproduction. It is renamed the Pineapple Growers Association in 1943. From the 1920s to early 1940s, colorful, attractive national ads urge people to "insist on HAWAIIAN pineapple."

November 6, 1932: Democrats win most county elections, but not the Legislature. After losing 9 previous elections to Congress, Lincoln McCandless (D) is elected as Hawaii's second democratic Congressional Delegate.

December 29, 1932: Castle and Cooke gains control of Hawaiian Pineapple Co. James Dole is removed from management of the company he founded, and advised to "take a long vacation..." Hawai'i banks lend Dole's company the money it needs only if he resigns as president. Dole's financial problems began when he borrowed money to build a larger plant, and he grew and canned more pineapple than he could sell during the Great Depression. Dole also angered Hawaii's Big 5 by shipping pineapples to the mainland with a freighter that offers a lower rate than Matson. Waialua Agricultural Company, owned by Castle and Cooke, had obtained a 1/3 ownership of Dole's Hawaiian Pineapple Co. in 1922.

January 5, 1933: The Public Utilities Commission (PUC) approves rules to regulate jitneys – private autos and buses that carry passengers, and compete with Honolulu Rapid Transit (HRT) bus service. On May 6, 1940, after years of court hearings and protests from HRT, the PUC rules the "jitney menace" must end on December 31, 1940.

February 1, 1933: Schofield Barracks, with 14,000 soldiers, is America's largest Army base.

March 3, 1933: Police shoot and kill "Miss Daisy," the popular Kapi'olani Zoo elephant, after the elephant kills her keeper.

March 10, 1933: Governor Lawrence Judd signs a law to give the governor the authority to declare a "bank holiday" anytime until April 8 if too many people demand their money. Banks can give "scrip" as money if they lack cash. President Franklin Roosevelt closes all mainland banks for several days, and re-opens only the sound banks. Hawai'i gets an exemption because we are "able to meet our own situation."

March 29, 1933: Governor Lawrence Judd signs a law to establish a gasoline tax to support public roads.

March 29, 1933: Honolulu Taxpayers' Association demands cuts in government to erase a deficit. 2,000 people attend a meeting to oppose a 1% income tax to help the unemployed, and to end duplication of government services. At a November 2 meeting, a proposal by John Balch of Mutual Telephone Co. asks for a federal investigation of Hawaii's government, but people are so rowdy, the meeting is adjourned before a vote is taken. This organization has many prominent members.

April 6, 1933: Governor Lawrence Judd signs a law to increase the poll tax to $5. All employers deduct $5 from workers age 20-60. The poll tax is abolished by Governor Joseph Poindexter on April 30, 1943.

May 15, 1933: A bill by Congressman John Rankin (D-Mississippi) to allow the president to appoint a non-Hawai'i resident as territorial governor, is defeated by a Senate filibuster after passing the House of Representatives. A week later, on May 22, President Franklin Roosevelt asks Congress for a law to allow the president to appoint an "absolutely impartial" non-Hawai'i resident as governor. Federal law requires the nominee to be a 3-year Hawai'i resident. On May 23, a front-page HONOLULU STAR-BULLETIN story calls the president "Roosevelt the wrecker."

May 23, 1933: Kaho'olawe Ranch Co. renews its lease for 21 years at a public auction. It is the only bidder.

June 1, 1933: To cope with a financial deficit during the Great Depression, Governor Lawrence Judd signs a law requiring public high school students to pay $10 tuition to help fund the salary of high school teachers. Attendance falls at some schools. The fee is repealed by Governor Joseph Poindexter on May 10, 1937.

June 2, 1933: Governor Lawrence Judd signs a law to require all government workers to take a 10% pay cut.

June 2, 1933: Governor Lawrence Judd signs the Old Age Pension Act, that pays up to $15 a month to people age 65 who are 15-year residents and citizens. Several states have enacted pension laws, which precedes federal Social Security.

June 2, 1933: Governor Lawrence Judd signs the Hawai'i Unemployment Relief Act to impose a 1/2% tax to raise money to pay unemployed people hired to work on government projects.

October 23, 1933: Baseball great Babe Ruth plays to a sold-out crowd at Honolulu Stadium. He was greeted by 10,000 fans when he arrived in Honolulu on October 19.

November 2, 1933: Cayetano Ligot, the controversial Filipino Resident Labor Commissioner is replaced because he accepted $150 a month from HSPA to publish a newspaper, TI SILAW. Since Ligot's arrival in 1923, Filipino sugar workers had been criticizing him for representing the interests of sugar planters rather than sugar workers.

December 2, 1933: Mauna Loa erupts until December 18.

February 3, 1934: Hawaii's first bank robbery. David and George Wong rob $970 from the Bank of Hawai'i in Pā'ia. On February 10, they plead guilty, and Judge Daniel Case sentences them to 20 years in prison.

March 1, 1934: Joseph Poindexter becomes Hawaii's 8th territorial governor until August 24, 1942. He is appointed by President Franklin Roosevelt. Previously he was Montana Attorney General, and in 1917 a Hawai'i federal judge. After his governorship, he is a Bishop Estate trustee from 1943-1951.

March 24, 1934: President Franklin Roosevelt signs the Tydings-McDuffie Act to give independence to the Philippines in 10 years. The law denies Filipino aliens from entering the mainland, but gives HSPA an exemption for Hawai'i, which has a shortage of plantation workers. The law also establishes a quota of only 50 Filipinos to immigrate annually to the U.S., except for Hawai'i.

May 1, 1934: Lualualei Navy Magazine is commissioned to store military weapons and ammunition. The Navy bought 7,900 acres of a former cattle ranch owned by the McCandless estate.

May 9, 1934: President Franklin Roosevelt signs the Jones-Costigan Act to protect mainland sugar cane growers and make Hawai'i a "foreign area." Hawai'i sugar growers protest by filing a lawsuit in a Washington D. C. court, which results in a U.S. Supreme Court ruling in January 1936, that the sugar tax and benefit payments are unconstitutional. As a result, the U.S. Secretary of Agriculture agrees to a compromise to give Hawai'i more favorable treatment. Hawaii's economy is based on sugar and pineapple, which accounts for 40% of Hawaii's employment. Hawaii's leaders decide to push for statehood to avoid future problems like this.

July 24, 1934: President Franklin Roosevelt is the first U.S. president to visit Hawai'i while in office. He stays 5 days and is welcomed by 60,000 people. Fort Armstrong Army airplanes fly overhead in a "FR" formation. He fishes at Kona, dedicates Ala Moana Park, speaks to the public at 'Iolani Palace, visits Shriners Hospital, reviews a Schofield Barracks military parade, and tours O'ahu. He plants a kukui tree at 'Iolani Palace that is still growing.

Governor Joseph Poindexter

August 15, 1934: The world's largest known supply of chemical weapons is stored on O'ahu – 854 tons of chemical poisons plus mortars and shells to deliver the poison, according to a report by Colonel Walter Krueger, War Plans Division.

September 6, 1934: Kīlauea erupts for 33 days.

October 8, 1934: Inter-Island Airways begins business as an interisland air mail service with a federal government contract. The sound of the airplane taking off on a flight from Honolulu to Maui is broadcast by CBS national radio, and locally on KGMB and KGU radio.

November 6, 1934: Duke Kahanamoku is elected Honolulu Sheriff. He is a Democrat from 1934-1938, then a Republican from 1940 until January 2, 1961 when the office is abolished by the 1959 City Charter.

November 23, 1934: U.S. Army establishes Fort Barrette in Kapolei. On August 11, it was named for General John Barrette, who commanded the Hawaiian Division in the 1920s. The fort is built to house cannon that can shoot 26 miles. The land is returned to the Territory in 1956, and is now an archery range at a city park.

January 11, 1935: Amelia Earhart completes the first solo airplane flight from Hawai'i to the mainland (Oakland), in 18 hours and 17 minutes.

February 23, 1935: Haleakalā Highway is dedicated at the summit with a 15-minute national NBC radio broadcast via KGU. The MAUI NEWS prints a 116-page souvenir supplement. The $500,000 road is called the "highway to the house of the sun." It is America's only road that takes motorists from sea level to 10,000 feet in less than two hours.

February 25, 1935: Department of Public Instruction (DPI) abolishes a 1928 policy that took effect in 1930 – to exclude 20% of all 8th and 9th grade graduates from attending high school. The minutes of DPI's 1928-1935 meetings do not mention the 20% rule, but it is mentioned in one sentence in its 1935 Annual Report. The 1935 rule is adopted in Executive Session, not in a public meeting. A committee of teachers will decide which students will "work or continue in school."

April 17, 1935: Pan American Clipper makes the first commercial flight from the mainland – Alameda, California to Ford Island.

May 12, 1935: During secret Army-Navy war games, 250 airplanes may have "attacked" O'ahu. Two Navy destroyers, USS LEA and USS SICARD, collide at night in Pearl Harbor. One sailor dies.

May 13, 1935: Governor Joseph Poindexter signs a 1.25% excise tax, also known as a "consumption" tax for personal property and business.

May 20, 1935: Governor Joseph Poindexter signs a law to create the Hawai'i Equal Rights Commission, to obtain equal treatment in federal laws, and support statehood in Congress. On September 27, the governor appoints 5 members to the new Commission. As a result of the Commission's efforts, Congress holds the first of 22 statehood hearings.

May 30, 1935: Retired Major General Briant Wells, now the HSPA executive secretary, says Hawaii's 148,000 AJAs would be "loyal" to the U.S. if there is war with Japan.

July 3, 1935: To promote Hawai'i, the Hawai'i Tourist Bureau debuts the radio program, HAWAI'I CALLS, created by Webley Edwards, featuring Harry Owens as musical director. It is the first Hawai'i radio program to air nationally and internationally with live Hawaiian music, broadcast by NBC and KGMB radio from the Moana Hotel. Hawaiian music and celebrity interviews go to 750 radio stations worldwide. The program assembles the largest collection of Hawaiian songs, numbering 3,000 by 1965. HAWAI'I CALLS ends on August 16, 1975 when the HVB and Legislature stop their financial support.

September 5, 1935: Honolulu Longshoremen's Association is established because the AFL refuses Asian members. It is chartered on October 5, 1937 by the ILWU as Local 1-37. On September 1, 1952,

ILWU Local 142 is established to consolidate dock, sugar, pineapple, general grades, and tourism workers.

October 7, 1935: The first-ever U.S. Congressional hearing on Hawai'i statehood is held in Hawai'i by the House Committee on Territories until October 18. The committee says further study is needed.

October 28, 1935: Union organizer Jack Hall arrives in Hawai'i. For the next 34 years, he will successfully organize ILWU workers, lead labor strikes, and gain union contracts from employers. In 1950 and 1951 he is arrested and put on trial for being a Communist, but he is acquitted in 1951 and 1958, respectively.

November 4, 1935: "Hawaii's only working-class newspaper," VOICE OF LABOR, edited by Corby Paxton, is published weekly until July 6, 1939.

November 21, 1935: Mauna Loa erupts for 40 days, and is seen in Honolulu for the first-recorded time. Lava covers 14 square miles. There is a double eruption at 10,000 and 14,000 feet. Vulcanologist Dr. Thomas Jaggar predicted the eruption 10 days earlier.

November 23, 1935: Pan Am's CHINA CLIPPER brings the first air mail from the mainland to Hawai'i, but no passengers – from Oakland to Pearl Harbor, then continues to the Philippines.

December 8, 1935: U.S. Vice President John Garner visits Hawai'i.

December 27, 1935: When lava is about 12 miles from Hilo, and moving a mile a day, the U.S. Army Air Corps drops 20 bombs with 6 tons of TNT that break a lava tube, and cool the lava. At the time, scientists thought the bombing saved Hilo, but that is considered doubtful today. Upon returning to Luke Field, one of the bombers crashes, killing one person. Some say it was Pele's revenge.

January 24, 1936: Two Army aircraft bombers collide 500 feet in the air, and explode over Luke Field. Six die and two survive.

January 27, 1936: Father Damien's remains are sent "home" to Antwerp, Belgium, where he is re-buried on May 6, 73 years after his death.

July 1, 1936: Pacific anthropologist Peter Buck (Maori name is Te Rangi Hiroa) becomes director of Bishop Museum for 15 years.

September 12, 1936: This is the first newspaper acknowledgment of the Hawaiian Government Employees' Association (HGEA), which was quietly established in 1934 to protest 10% pay cuts in 1933. The exact founding date is unknown. HGEA intends to be "nonpolitical" with 5,000 territorial and county workers, and 2,800 teachers.

October 22, 1936: Pan American Airways arrives in Hawai'i from Manila and Midway. It is the first passenger flight from Asia to the U.S. mainland, via Hawai'i.

In the 1930s, the Health Department investigates living conditions here at Hilo Plantation. A 1939 U.S. Labor Department report says 20% of plantation housing is "slum" and some homes are "entirely lacking in modern sanitation."

October 30, 1936: 1,000 maritime union warehouse workers strike for 3 months until February 8, 1937.

December 30, 1936: Rev. Takie Okumura dedicates a new Makiki Christian Church. The church looks like Otakasaka Castle in Okumura's home town. Okumura unites Japanese and Caucasian Christians, and gains prominent Caucasian friends who give money to his efforts.

1936: U.S. Army Colonel George Patton submits an undated "Orange Plan" that recommends arresting and interning 126 Japanese and 2 Caucasians in Hawai'i, closing Japanese language schools, and declaring martial law if there is war with Japan. Patton serves in Hawai'i from 1934-1936, and becomes a famous general in WW II.

March 4, 1937: The first Kodak Hula Show, near the Waikīkī Natatorium lets visitors photograph hula performers in daylight hours. It is created by Kodak executive Fritz Herman to sell film and promote tourism. Kodak ends the Waikīkī Shell show in May, 1999, but in July, the Hogan

Family Foundation of Pleasant Hawaiian Holidays becomes new sponsors. Since 1937, 20 million people have watched the show.

March 7, 1937: Joseph Tatibouet and Eric deBisschop are the first people to sail a catamaran from Hawaiʻi to France. They arrive in Cannes, France on May 21, 1938 with their catamaran, KAMILOA.

March 18, 1937: Amelia Earhart sets a new flying record from Alameda, California to Hawaiʻi in less than 16 hours. Her arrival is the first part of her 27,000 mile around-the-world flight. On March 20, she damages her airplane during take off at Ford Island, and sends her airplane to California for repair.

March 25, 1937: The movie, WAIKĪKĪ WEDDING, has its world premiere in Honolulu. The movie features the Academy Award-winning song, SWEET LEILANI, sung by Bing Crosby, and also the song BLUE HAWAIʻI. Harry Owens wrote SWEET LEILANI on October 20, 1934 to honor his one-day old baby daughter, Leilani. The song stays on the national "Hit Parade" for a then-record 28 weeks, and becomes the biggest-selling Hawaiian song, with 26 million sales. BLUE HAWAIʻI is recorded a second time in a 1961 movie of the same name, sung by Elvis Presley. In all, Owens writes 300 songs.

April 5, 1937: The first National Labor Relations Board (NLRB) hearing in Honolulu reviews ILWU complaints about unfair labor practices

Songwriter Harry Owens (l) with his daughter, "Sweet Leilani." (r)

during a dock strike, and the firing of 54 workers. Labor unions consider this NLRB hearing an "historic event."

April 6, 1937: Helen Keller addresses a joint session of the Hawai'i Legislature, through her interpreter. Although she is deaf, blind and unable to speak, she hears the applause through the floor vibrations. When she smells the fragrant lei, she says, "For the first time, I know the full meaning of Hawai'i."

April 20, 1937: Hawaii's last plantation strike by a "single race" group is supported by the union known as "Vibora Luvimindo." 3,000 Filipino workers strike HC&S in Pu'unēnē to protest low wages, and many are evicted from their plantation homes. The 86-day strike ends on July 16 when workers win recognition of their union, and a 15¢ wage hike. It is Hawaii's first successful major strike because a plantation officially recognizes the union.

April 22, 1937: ILWU dock workers strike at Pt. Allen, Kaua'i for 6 months until October 22.

April 23, 1937: Hilo is "destroyed" by 35 "enemy" aircraft in annual Army-Navy war games.

April 29, 1937: After a trial, the Hawai'i Legislature "severely reprimands" Rep. Thomas Sakakihara for misconduct. He required a legislative clerk to give half her salary to pay another clerk.

June, 1937: Maui's Soichi Sakamoto establishes the "3 Year Swim Club." Despite having no training as a swimming coach, Sakamoto promises his swimmers that they will be Olympic champions. Sakamoto trains young Maui swimmers for the 1940 Olympics in a Pu'unēnē irrigation ditch because the plantation pool had an unwritten "whites only" policy. The 1940 and 1944 Olympics are cancelled, so his Maui swimmers win 6 national team titles. One of his Hawaiian swimmers, Bill Smith wins two gold medals in the 1948 Olympics.

July 2, 1937: Amelia Earhart disappears during her second attempt to fly around the world. She is never seen again. While flying from New Guinea to Hawai'i, she disappears 100 miles from Howland Island, which is 1,500 miles from Hawai'i.

August 14, 1937: Federal NLRB examiner George Pratt reports that Caucasians control Hawaii's mostly-Asian plantation workforce. He reports, "It (is) far from surprising that an attitude of feudal paternalism on the part of the employers has developed toward the working peoples of the islands."

August 25, 1937: President Franklin Roosevelt vetoes an immigration bill by Hawai'i Congressional Delegate Sam King. The bill would have prevented continuing Filipino immigration to Hawai'i because, King says, Hawai'i doesn't need Filipino labor for sugar plantations.

October 8, 1937: The first Joint Committee on Hawai'i of the U.S. House and Senate holds statehood hearings in Hawai'i until October 22. On October 19, several witnesses such as DPI Superintendent and future Governor Oren Long support statehood and say Japanese are loyal to America. On February 15, 1938, the joint committee reports, "Hawai'i has fulfilled every requirement for statehood..." but does not recommend statehood until there is a public vote by Hawai'i voters. The report also says annexation was by "voluntary action of the people and government of Hawai'i."

October 18, 1937: U.S. Post Office issues a 3¢ stamp to honor the Hawai'i Territory, with a picture of the King Kamehameha statue.

October 26, 1937: Ellery Chun, "Father of the Aloha Shirt" registers the name with the Territory. He created the aloha shirt in 1931 and sells it from his store, King-Smith Clothiers. His sister, artist Ethel Chun designs the shirts. Hollywood movies make the shirt popular in the 1940s and 1950s. President Harry Truman is photographed wearing an aloha shirt on the cover of LIFE MAGAZINE on December 10, 1951.

November 12, 1937: HAWAI'I CHINESE JOURNAL begins publication, edited by William Lee. The 6-page weekly terminates on December 31, 1957.

January 1, 1938: Hotel, Restaurant and Bar Caterers Association of Honolulu, Local 5 is organized. On February 10, bartender Art Rutledge joins the union, and will soon lead the union for several decades.

January 14, 1938: The 530,000 gallon, octagonal water tower is built on Hickam Field. This landmark is 171 feet tall, with 8 one-ton sculptured eagles near the top.

February 10, 1938: Honolulu's first permanent Unemployment Office opens to help people find jobs.

May 12, 1938: NLRB rules that plantation workers who work with machinery are covered by the Wagner Act – about 1/4 of the workers.

May 26, 1938: 500 ILWU and International Boatman's Union workers strike the Inter-Island Steamship Co., demanding equal pay with west coast workers. The 80-day strike ends on August 15. The strike hurts the shipping industry, so many tourists fly to Hilo, giving Inter-Island Airways its best year to date.

The Hilo Massacre. Workers run for their lives and jump into the water as police shoot and stab 51 people in the back.

June 1, 1938: HMSA is the first to write group health insurance with a monthly fee. The plan is considered better than any on the mainland. The first subscribers are nurses, social workers and school teachers, who pay 10¢ a day, per person.

July 9, 1938: U.S. Agriculture Department says HSPA agrees to retroactively pay plantation workers $1 million in back wages owed for several months of 1937. This represents a 5%-20% wage increase for the workers. As a result, sugar plantations will receive $4 million in federal sugar subsidies.

July 21, 1938: Hawai'i Judge Louis LeBaron upholds Hawaii's 1923 Anti-Picketing Law.

July 22, 1938: Hilo Police use tear gas to stop 100 ILWU picketers when the ship WAI'ALE'ALE arrives.

August 1, 1938: The "Hilo Massacre" is also known as "Bloody Monday." During a 98-day Hilo dock worker strike, 500 picketers protest when strikebreakers try to unload cargo from the WAI'ALE'ALE. Police fire tear gas, water hoses, and guns loaded with "birdshot" and "buckshot" into the crowd, and use their rifle bayonets to injure 51 strikers, many in the back as they flee. The strike is broken, but union solidarity gains in Hawai'i. On September 20, Judge Delbert Metzger is angry that the Grand Jury indicts no one. Some collective bargaining agents make August 1 a worker holiday to commemorate the event.

National News

June 25, 1938: President Franklin Roosevelt signs the Wage and Hour Act to raise the minimum wage from 25¢ to 40¢ an hour. The 44 hour work week drops to 40 hours in 1939.

August 1, 1938: The Central Labor Council of Honolulu is founded. It is the predecessor to the Hawai'i State Federation of Labor, AFL-CIO, established on January 9, 1966, and renamed Hawai'i State AFL-CIO on July 17, 1980.

August 16, 1938: In a remarkable display of accuracy, Ft. Weaver's 16 inch canon shoots 2,100 lb. shells 20 miles to sea, accurately hitting the target 6 of 10 times.

September 15, 1938: The $15 million, 2,225-acre Hickam Field is activated. It is named for Lt. Colonel Horace Hickam who died in a November 5, 1934 Texas airplane crash. On April 6, 1940, a HONOLULU ADVERTISER story says Hickam is the Army's largest Air Corps base. It is renamed Hickam Air Force Base on March 26, 1948.

September 16, 1938: HONOLULU ADVERTISER reports a federal survey that food costs 23% more in Honolulu than 50 mainland cities.

September 30, 1938: A federal program known as AAA abolishes the bonus wage system that plantation workers had tried to abolish in their 1920 and 1924 strikes. Bonus pay, which was 8% of total wages in 1937, was determined by the number of workdays and the price of raw sugar in New York.

October 17, 1938: Hawaii's first woman Supervisor, Mrs. Jessie Crowell is elected by the Maui County Board of Supervisors to fill her late husband's unexpired term.

May 6, 1939: Governor Joseph Poindexter signs a law to establish a Territorial Civil Service Commission that will create a civil service system. A county civil service system was established in 1913.

May 16, 1939: Governor Joseph Poindexter signs a law to establish a Department of Labor and Industrial Relations to administer labor laws and investigate wage complaints by plantation workers.

August 26, 1939: William Pai, age 30, is the first person to swim the Kaiwi Channel, from Moloka'i to Sandy Beach, O'ahu.

Hawai'i Prepares for War

May 18, 1939: Honolulu's first evening blackout drill lasts 19 minutes. Hawai'i prepares for war.

May 23, 1939: U.S. Navy holds its biggest Hawai'i war games to date. For two days, O'ahu is "attacked" from the sea by Navy ships, on land by the Army, and in the air by 49 "enemy" Army bombers. Radio broadcasts and plantation sirens signal the "attack."

May 31, 1939: To prevent sabotage, President Franklin Roosevelt declares a 3-mile area around Pearl Harbor as a restricted naval area.

August 1, 1939: FBI opens a Honolulu office under the direction of Agent Robert Shivers, to investigate potential sabotage, spying and Japanese loyalty. In 1941, Honolulu Police Lt. John Burns leads a Police Counter-Espionage Unit which cooperates with the FBI and military, and investigates 6,000 Japanese. Burns and Shivers gain the confidence of the Japanese, and vice versa. In contrast to mass arrests of mainland Japanese that led to the internment of 120,000, Shivers and Burns work to prevent internment, and identify loyal Japanese here. The FBI taps the telephones of the Japan Consul and some Japanese companies. The only Hawai'i person convicted of spying is a German alien in 1942. Honolulu's FBI office had closed in May, 1938 due a lack of funds.

1940-1949

January 5, 1940: HONOLULU ADVERTISER says a U.S. Labor survey reports that Hawai'i sugar plantation workers earned twice the salary as the average migrant mainland farm worker who worked 7 months in 1938. Hawai'i workers also got free housing, medical care, water, etc.

January 13, 1940: 3,000 Pearl Harbor workers sign a loyalty oath and pledge to report any subversive activities.

March 4, 1940: U.S. Army Chief of Staff General George Marshall arrives in Hawai'i for 9 days to review the military defense of Pearl Harbor. Two months later, President Franklin Roosevelt orders Hawaii's military increased to 50,000 personnel, and aircraft increased to 500 war airplanes as part of a "limited emergency." This increased strength is intended to give the U.S. superiority on land, air and sea.

April 1, 1940: Federal census begins. Hawai'i has 422,770 population, a 15% increase since 1930 – 15% Hawaiian, 26% Caucasian, 7% Chinese, 37% Japanese, 12% Filipino, 2% Korean.

April 7, 1940: Mauna Loa erupts for 134 days, threatening Hilo twice.

April 25, 1940: 98 U.S. warships arrive with 42,000 sailors for May war games. More than 100,000 people watch the ships arrive at night, sailing past Diamond Head, illuminated by 300 search lights.

May 3, 1940: FBI and Navy discover a plot to dynamite Pearl Harbor oil tanks. To protect the oil supply, a top secret, $42 million underground fuel storage project is built on 400 acres at Red Hill. It is 200 feet underground, with 20 vertical tanks, each 20 stories tall, holding 250 million gallons of fuel. 4,000 people are employed, and 16 are killed during construction. The 3-year construction began in January, 1941, and completed on October 1, 1943, 9 months ahead of schedule.

May 23, 1940: The entire Territory participates in a 12-minute blackout drill. It is the nation's biggest blackout drill, as "enemy" war airplanes "attack" Hawai'i.

July 1, 1940: Honolulu city government allows men to wear aloha shirts to work during the summer. On July 11, 1951, Governor Oren Long says Territorial workers can wear Aloha shirts during the summer. In 1966, the Bank of Hawai'i may have been the first major company to inaugurate Aloha Friday to encourage men to wear aloha shirts.

July 16, 1940: The Democratic National Convention votes to "favor a larger measure of self-government leading to (Hawai'i) statehood." On June 27, 1944, the Republican National Party Platform "looks toward" Hawai'i statehood. From 1944-1952, both political parties endorse statehood before making a "pledge" for it in 1956.

Fascism? Anti-Democratic?
Here's what U.S. Labor Officials say

May 3, 1940: Regional Director Elwyn Eagen of the National Labor Relations Board (NLRB) tells a U.S. House Labor Committee that Hawai'i plantations hold "absolute control and domination" over their workers by spying and blacklisting them. "A number of the laborers are more like slaves than free people." He says the Big 5 is "anti-labor...anti-democratic," and it owns or controls "virtually every business of any importance" to "keep out competition." He explains, "persons who do not comply with the wishes of the 'Big Five' are refused (bank) loans...and are forced out of business." Some Big 5 members "control the Police Department and use it for anti-union purposes." He concludes, "If there is any truer picture of Fascism anywhere in the world than in the Hawaiian Islands, then I do not know the definition of it."

June 5, 1940: The U.S. Department of Labor issues the 1939 James Shoemaker report, which says 101,000 people or one-fourth of Hawaii's population live on sugar plantations. Hawai'i plantations have improved pay and relations with workers, but about 20% of the housing is "slum" and some homes are "entirely lacking in modern sanitation." Employers are "paternalistic" and "antagonistic" to workers, believing that unionism is "dangerous radicalism." The report charts the influence of "interlocking directorates" which shows how power in the hands of a few people in a few companies control Hawaii's most important corporations. The report says, "the early history of the Hawaiian sugar industry is one of frank exploitation of contract labor at extremely low wages under conditions that were almost equivalent to slavery."

July 28, 1940: 'Ewa Marine Corps Air Station is established as a landing field for dirigibles, but none come. It closes on June 18, 1952.

July 29, 1940: ILWU dock worker strike begins at Kauai's Ahukini Terminal, an Amfac subsidiary. The 10-month, inter-racial strike ends on May 11, 1941. It is Hawaii's longest to date. Workers are told to choose their plantation job at Amfac's Līhu'e Plantation or a longshore job, not both. Before the strike, workers had to work both jobs.

August 27, 1940: HONOLULU STAR-BULLETIN reports FBI, police, plantations and utilities have been meeting to protect Hawai'i from sabotage.

August 28, 1940: Fingerprinting of all aliens begins under the federal Alien Registration Act, signed into law by President Franklin Roosevelt on June 29. Hawai'i has 45,000 aliens, including 35,000 Japanese aliens.

August 28, 1940: Maui-born author Armine von Tempski's latest book, BORN IN PARADISE, is announced as a national Literary Guild Selection.

September 2, 1940: Kamehameha School for Boys opens at Kapālama.

October 13, 1940: Rev. Yetatsu Takeda of Fort Street Hongwanji Temple says "American Buddhism" is separate from Japan.

October 14, 1940: President Franklin Roosevelt signs the U.S. Nationality Act. In part, the law says that any U.S. citizen with foreign parents will lose U.S. citizenship for living in a foreign nation for 6 months, voting in a foreign election, working for a foreign government, or joining a foreign military. Many AJAs quickly return home to Hawai'i.

October 15, 1940: The 1,600 member Hawai'i National Guard is called into active military service for one year.

October 24, 1940: Hawaii's first NLRB election victory for workers is won at Kauai's McBryde Plantation. United Cannery Agriculture Packing and Allied Workers of America is Hawaii's first union to win collective bargaining rights on a sugar plantation.

November 5, 1940: Hawai'i citizens get their first opportunity to vote for statehood. The general election vote is 46,174-22,438 or 2-1 for statehood. In 1897-1898, the people of Hawai'i were never given an opportunity to vote for or against annexation.

November 11, 1940: 30,000 AJAs prepare to send a petition to U.S. Secretary of State Cordell Hull, asking for an easier way to be free from Japan's required dual citizenship law. They don't want to be considered disloyal to America. Many European-Americans also have dual citizenship, but they get little if any criticism.

December 30, 1940: U.S. Navy Commander Claude Bloch reports of an "inability to meet hostile attack" because Hawai'i hasn't enough fighter airplanes, and the anti-aircraft warning system is insufficient.

January 24, 1941: U.S. Navy Secretary Frank Knox informs Secretary of War Henry Stimson that "If war eventuate with Japan, it is believed easily possible that hostilities would be initiated by a surprise attack" on Pearl Harbor. Knox adds that defense against an aerial bombing attack is not satisfactory.

February 1, 1941: The first HRT bus strike begins. 375 workers strike for 28 days until February 28. The strike affects 120,000 bus riders. As a result, a territorial law is passed to require a one-month mediation period before striking a public utility.

February 15, 1941: Kāne'ohe Bay Naval Air Station is commissioned. U.S. Navy buys the Mōkapu Peninsula site on August 5, 1939.

February 20, 1941: The Republican-dominated Territorial Legislature begins, and Democratic Governor Joseph Poindexter will veto 82 bills, a record that still stands. The Legislature overrides none. In 1955, Republican Governor Samuel King vetoes the second-most, 61 bills, and the Democratic-controlled Legislature overrides only one veto.

March 18, 1941: 26 Japanese nationals plead guilty to conspiracy charges for having falsely registered their fishing boats. In all, 71 were indicted by a federal grand jury on February 28.

March 27, 1941: Japanese spy, Takeo Yoshikawa, also known as Tadashi Morimura arrives in Hawai'i. He spends several months observing ships at Pearl Harbor and airplanes at Ford Island. His information aids the planning of the December 7 attack.

April 11, 1941: Governor Joseph Poindexter signs a law to prohibit advertising or selling any coffee as Kona coffee unless it is grown there.

April 23, 1941: Governor Joseph Poindexter signs a law to prevent sabotage, punishable with up to 20 years of prison for interfering with U.S. preparations "for defense or for war."

April 29, 1941: Governor Joseph Poindexter signs the "Hawai'i Loyalty Act." All government workers must sign a loyalty oath to the U.S., and declare that they don't belong to any group that advocates the government overthrow. For religious reasons, a person may omit the phrase, "So help me God."

May 10, 1941: U.S. Army subleases a small area of Kaho'olawe for target practice, for $1 a year until 1954, and shares it with the U.S. Navy.

May 12, 1941: U.S. Army practices a sunrise aerial bombing attack of Pearl Harbor and Hickam. The military war games end on May 24.

May 14, 1941: To strengthen U.S. military defense, 21 B-17 "Flying For-tresses" arrive at Hickam Field after a secret flight from San Francisco. It is the first mass flight of B-17 bombers to Hawai'i.

May 14, 1941: Governor Joseph Poindexter signs a law to require labor-management mediation to prevent strikes against public utilities.

May 20, 1941: Hawaii's 3rd blackout drill in three years is conducted from 9-9:30 p.m., during an air attack by "enemy planes."

June 12, 1941: ILWU and Castle & Cooke agree to the first written long-shore contract in Hawai'i.

June 15, 1941: U.S. Army plans to build a $750,000 bomb shelter and food storage tunnel near Fort Shafter. The shelter will be large enough to hold thousands of people and 15,000 tons of meat. The shelter is now closed.

July 1, 1941: Honolulu Rapid Transit replaces trolley street cars with elec-tric trolley buses powered by 600 volt overhead wires.

July 26, 1941: A Presidential Order freezes Japanese and Chinese assets in the U.S., resulting in a "bank run" in Hawai'i. $380,000 is withdrawn the next day from Japanese banks here.

August 9, 1941: To prevent "rent gouging" by landlords, Honolulu Mayor Lester Petrie appoints a rent control committee to arbitrate landlord-tenant complaints. This results from a complaint by U.S. Congress-man Melvin Mass, a Marine Colonel who says, "Honolulu property owners seem to be trying to pay for their property in one year." Thou-sands of defense workers move to Hawai'i before and during WW II. This creates a severe housing shortage, plus rent hikes of 40%-100%. On November 5, 1941, Governor Joseph Poindexter signs a law to give the counties the authority to regulate rents. Mayor Petrie signs a city law on December 13 to freeze rents back to May 27. On December 29, 1961, Honolulu is one of the last U.S. cities to repeal rent control.

August 11, 1941: University of Hawai'i President David Crawford says Hawai'i must be prepared for war.

September 26, 1941: Police Commissioner and former Hawai'i Congres-sional Delegate Victor Houston says prostitution is a $4-5 million an-nual business and "appear(s) to be tolerated" by police.

October 1, 1941: Inter-Island Airways takes control of the bankrupt Hawaiian Airways and is renamed Hawaiian Airlines.

October 3, 1941: Governor Joseph Poindexter signs the Hawai'i Defense Act, known as the "M-Day" law or the "civilian martial law." It gives the governor extensive authority in case of war. The M-Day law is patterned after President Franklin Roosevelt's May 27 declaration of an unlimited national emergency. The M-Day law says a "public emergency exists," that Hawai'i is in a "strategic military and naval area,." On December 7, Governor Poindexter ignores the M-Day law, and he voluntarily steps aside for military rule and martial law.

October 18, 1941: Governor Joseph Poindexter signs a law to establish a 20¢ an hour minimum wage for Neighbor Islands and 25¢ for O'ahu.

November 1, 1941: U.S. War Department opens a Military Intelligence Language School at San Francisco, which moves to Camp Savage, Minnesota on May 25, 1942. Volunteers, mostly Japanese, study the Japanese language to become interrogators, translators, and propaganda writers. Hundreds of Hawai'i soldiers apply. Later, Chinese and Korean languages are included.

November 4, 1941: U.S. War Department asks Congress to give the president the authority to declare martial law in Hawai'i and Puerto Rico. Hawai'i Congressional Delegate Sam King opposes the request as "unnecessary" and "an affront to the patriotism of Hawai'i." The next day, the HONOLULU ADVERTISER publishes a large, detailed map showing where O'ahu residents can go if they are injured or burned in a war attack.

November 7, 1941: President Franklin Roosevelt receives the State Department's Munson Report, which says AJAs are loyal Americans and not a threat – based on FBI and Navy information.

November 10, 1941: HONOLULU STAR-BULLETIN front-page headline says, "Threat of US-Japan War Emphasized by Spokesman."

November 18, 1941: HONOLULU STAR-BULLETIN publishes a letter signed by "JB" (for Honolulu Police Lt. John Burns), "Why Attack the People of Hawai'i?" Burns opposes martial law and says Hawaii's Japanese are loyal Americans.

November 30, 1941: HONOLULU ADVERTISER front-page headline reads "Japanese May Strike Over Weekend."

December 3, 1941: An FBI wire tap of telephones in the Honolulu office of the Japan Consul reveals that the consul is burning documents.

December 6, 1941: A front-page HONOLULU STAR-BULLETIN story reveals that the military has a new kind of radar to detect airplanes and ships at long distances.

December 7, 1941: A Japanese submarine near Pearl Harbor is first seen at 3:43 a.m., and it "should have been recognized as immediate basis for an all-out alert..." (From a 1946 Joint Congressional report that investigated the Pearl Harbor attack.)

December 7 Attack

3 Burning ships (l-r) USS WEST VIRGINIA, USS TENNESSEE and USS ARIZONA

Airplanes being bombed on Ford Island. To prevent sabotage, the airplanes were parked closely together, making it difficult to get the airplanes ready to fly.

December 7, 1941: About 6 a.m. Hawai'i time, Japan begins its war against America. The first of 350 Japanese airplanes take off from aircraft carriers 230 miles north of Hawai'i.

December 7, 1941: At 6:45 a.m., U.S. Destroyer WARD fires America's first shots of the Pacific, sinking a Japanese two-man, midget submarine near Pearl Harbor.

December 7, 1941: At 7:02 a.m., U.S. Army radar at Kahuku detects many airplanes 132 miles north of O'ahu. When radar personnel try to report it, the Army Information Center tells them to "forget it," because U.S. Army B-17s are scheduled to arrive that morning from the mainland. (From a 1946 Joint Congressional report about Pearl Harbor.)

December 7, 1941: About 8 a.m. Hawai'i time, a Japanese submarine sinks a U.S. ship, CYNTHIA OLSEN en route to Honolulu, about half-way from Washington State. The sinking is not made public until 1946.

December 7, 1941: Japan airplanes attack the U.S. Pacific Fleet at Pearl Harbor from 7:55-9:45 a.m. The surprise attack puts the United States in WW II. When the attack begins, 185 U.S. ships are in Pearl Harbor, 7 battleships are parked on "Battleship Row," and another is in drydock. Army airplanes at Bellows, Wheeler and Hickam airfields are parked closely in groups to prevent sabotage. Fortunately, 11 U.S. aircraft carriers are away at the time of the attack. Japanese airplanes fail to destroy U.S. submarines, repair facilities or fuel tanks. On December 8, President Franklin Roosevelt says December 7 is "a day that will live in infamy."

December 7, 1941: Soon after the Pearl Harbor attack begins, KGMB radio announcer and HAWAI'I CALLS host Webley Edwards tells listeners, "This is no test. This is the real McCoy. Pearl Harbor is being bombed by the Japanese."

Pearl Harbor Attack

Americans Killed	Injured		Japanese Killed	Injured
military 2,390	1,178		64	not known
civilians 57	35			
	U.S.		**Japan**	
aircraft destroyed	164		29	
aircraft damaged	159		74	
ships damaged	21		4 of 5 midget subs lost	

December 7, 1941: A two-man Japanese midget submarine runs aground near Bellows Army Air Base in Waimānalo. One sailor drowns and the other swims ashore. He is the only Japanese military man captured alive today. Of Japan's four other midget submarines – one is sunk in Pearl Harbor, and three others are lost at sea.

December 7, 1941: Governor Joseph Poindexter agrees to step aside and allow U.S. Army General Walter Short to assume control of civil courts and take over as military governor "until the danger of invasion is removed..." At General Short's request, Poindexter suspends the writ of habeas corpus and declares martial law, which lasts three years until October 24, 1944. (note: Suspending habeas corpus means a person can be arrested without charges and kept in jail for as long as necessary. Martial law means the military runs the government.) General Short's diary says he told Governor Poindexter that martial law "could be lifted in a reasonably short time" if Japanese military don't land in Hawai'i. Governor Poindexter assumes this means a month or so. The military governor controls nearly everything. He sets food prices, censors all personal mail and the news media, and everyone is fingerprinted and receives gas masks. There are night blackouts from 6 p.m. to 6 a.m. Anyone on a street, highway or beach without a pass can be arrested. Most businesses close by 4:30 p.m. People paint their home light bulbs blue. The FBI, military and civilian police arrest "potentially dangerous" Japanese, such as priests, teachers, fishermen, business and community leaders. Due to the communication blackout, few Neighbor Islanders know about the Japanese attack. General Short is Hawaii's military governor until December 16, 1941.

December 7, 1941: UH ROTC cadets are among the U.S. military called by radio to defend Hawai'i. They are ordered to defend St. Louis Heights against a false rumor of Japanese paratroopers. Hawaii's governor mobilizes UH ROTC cadets into the Territorial Guard.

December 7, 1941: At 7:15 p.m., U.S. military shoot down 4 of 6 approaching U.S. airplanes.

December 7, 1941: Public schools are closed until February 2, 1942. Schools are evacuation centers, hospitals and for defense activities.

December 8, 1941: HONOLULU ADVERTISER front-page headline mistakenly reports "Saboteurs Land Here!" and "Raiders Return in Dawn Attack" on the North Shore. The story falsely reports brief machine gun firing is "heard" downtown, and advises Kalihi residents to watch for parachuting invaders.

December 8, 1941: Bernard "Otto" Kuehn, a German alien living in Lanikai, is arrested for espionage as a Nazi spy. He may be the only Hawai'i resident to be convicted for espionage related to the Pearl Harbor attack. Kuehn gave military information to the Japanese consul in Honolulu. The FBI says the Japanese consulate paid him $14,000 cash and he put $70,000 in the bank over 3 years. The FBI says he confessed to his crime, and on February 21, 1942, a secret military court sentences him to be shot. The sentence is reduced to 50 years in Ft. Leavenworth, Kansas prison, but he is deported to Argentina, and returns to Germany. Kuehn's military trial is kept secret until June 1943. On July 24, 1962, his widow tries to sue the U.S. Government, claiming he wasn't a spy.

December 8, 1941: Hawai'i FBI arrests 430 aliens considered to be dangerous – 345 Japanese, 74 Germans and 11 Italians. They are confined to the Sand Island Detention Center from December 9 to February 20. Three months later, they are sent to Camp Honouliuli or mainland War Relocation Camps. One of two 15-foot tall fences surrounding Sand Island is electrified until the Army realizes it violates the Geneva Convention. Sand Island Detention Center closes on March 1, 1943.

December 8, 1941: U.S. assumes control of Kaho'olawe, and the military bombs the island until 1990. During WW II, the military uses Kaho'olawe to practice invasions, and as target practice for ships and airplanes. It is the most bombed island in the Pacific war.

December 9, 1941: President Franklin Roosevelt approves martial law and suspension of habeas corpus in Hawai'i.

December 10, 1941: President Franklin Roosevelt approves a military plan for the emergency evacuation of half of Oahu's 320,000 residents to move toward the mountains.

December 11, 1941: U.S. Navy Secretary Frank Knox arrives in Hawai'i to inspect Pearl Harbor damage and report his findings to President Franklin Roosevelt. On December 15, Knox says sabotage was committed here. "I think the most effective Fifth Column work of the entire war was done in Hawai'i with the possible exception of Norway." Knox is later proven wrong.

December 13, 1941: The "Battle of Ni'ihau." Ni'ihau residents don't know about the Pearl Harbor attack when Japanese pilot, Shigenori Nishikaichi, crash lands on Ni'ihau. A Ni'ihau AJA resident, Yoshio Harada fears for his safety, and agrees to translate for Nishikaichi. Nishikaichi and Harada threaten to kill island residents. Nishikaichi shoots Benehakaka Kanahele three times. Despite his wounds, Kanahele kills the pilot by knocking his head against a wall. This scares Harada, who shoots himself to death. On August 15, 1945, Kanahele receives a Purple Heart and Medal of Merit from the U.S. government.

December 15, 1941: A Japanese submarine fires 10 shells at Kahului, Maui about 6 p.m. Three shells hit the Maui Pineapple Company cannery, causing $700 damage.

December 15, 1941: Military Governor Walter Short limits all motor vehicles to 10 gallons of gas a month. Drivers pay with gas ration cards.

December 17, 1941: General Delos Emmons replaces General Walter Short as military governor until May 31, 1943. Admiral Chester Nimitz replaces Admiral Husband Kimmel as commander-in-chief of the Pacific Fleet. Kimmel is criticized for failing to act properly during the December 7 attack. U.S. Navy Secretary Frank Knox says our military leaders were "not on the alert" when Pearl Harbor was attacked.

December 18, 1941: The Office of Civil Defense establishes a 3-member Public Morale Committee, comprised of a Caucasian, Japanese and Chinese, to promote public harmony, fair and equal treatment for all residents. Committees are established on all islands.

December 19, 1941: U.S. Navy Secretary Frank Knox tells a presidential cabinet meeting that all of Hawaii's Japanese aliens should be put in internment camps on a Neighbor Island.

December 20, 1941: The U.S. military orders all 1,500 Iwilei residents to evacuate "in the interest of military necessity and public safety."

December 21, 1941: Survivors of the Matson freighter LAHAINA reach Maui's Spreckelsville Beach after sailing 800 miles in a 20-foot lifeboat. Their ship is sunk by a Japanese submarine on December 11. The entire crew of 34 get in a lifeboat, but two die at sea, and two jump overboard and die just 200 yards before landing on Maui.

December 21, 1941: One of the world's largest radio installations is built at the Naval Communications Station at Wahiawā. It is used to communicate with the Pacific fleet.

December 22, 1941: Military Governor Delos Emmons issues General Order 38 to suspend federal labor laws, freeze wages, prohibit many Hawai'i workers from changing jobs, and suspend labor contracts of employers and workers. The order affects 90,000 O'ahu workers considered essential for the war effort – such as hospitals, utilities, farms, laundries, and dock workers. Many Hawai'i workers resent the law because thousands of mainlanders work in higher paying defense jobs, while lower-paid plantation workers are "stuck" in their jobs.

December 23, 1941: U.S. War Department says Hawaii's Japanese population "has given no evidence of disloyalty." Hawaii's 425,000 population includes 160,000 Japanese – 125,000 AJAs and 35,000 aliens.

December 27, 1941: A dozen survivors of the Matson freighter MANINI are rescued near O'ahu after 10 days at sea. A Japanese torpedo sank their ship on December 17. Two days later, another 19 survivors are found.

December 28, 1941: 13 survivors of a New Orleans freighter arrive in Hawai'i after 10 days at sea. A Japanese submarine sank their ship on December 18 only 100 miles from Hawai'i Island. Another group took a second lifeboat, and traveled 2,500 miles to the Gilbert Islands.

December 30, 1941: Japanese submarines fire a few shots at Hilo, Nāwiliwili and Kahului, creating only $1,000-$2,000 damage.

December 31, 1941: All O'ahu civilians begin fingerprinting and registering with the military government. Aliens were fingerprinted in 1940.

January 2, 1942: President Franklin Roosevelt signs Executive Order 9006 to declare that Hawai'i is a Distressed Emergency Area. This qualifies farmers for larger government loans.

January 8, 1942: After a one-month suspension since December 12, 1941, Military Governor Delos Emmons orders HAWAI'I HOCHI and NIPPU JIJI newspapers to resume publication under military censorship – to keep Hawaii's Japanese population informed of news and events. On January 7, HAWAI'I HOCHI changes its name to HAWAI'I HERALD, but returns to HAWAI'I HOCHI after WW II. HAWAI'I HOCHI will publish a twice-weekly English newspaper, HAWAI'I HERALD on May 16, 1980.

January 10, 1942: Military Governor Delos Emmons issues orders to prohibit anyone from having $200 in cash, and no business can have more than $500 cash except for payrolls. Any excess funds will be confiscated. This is intended to prevent foreign agents and Japanese military invaders from obtaining U.S. cash. Many people who didn't trust banks during the Great Depression and kept cash at home, now bring their hidden or buried cash to the banks.

January 19, 1942: All AJA members of Hawai'i Territorial Guard are dismissed. They receive 4C draft status for "enemy alien."

January 21, 1942: All Hawai'i civilians begin to receive gas masks, which must be carried at all times. By April 13, about 400,000 gas masks are distributed at $1.5 million cost.

January 24, 1942: The first official report about Pearl Harbor, chaired by U.S. Supreme Court Justice Owen Roberts says there was no espionage by Hawai'i residents on December 7.

January 26, 1942: Japanese Education Association, Hawai'i Kyoiku Kai, closes all Japanese language schools until the war ends.

January 26, 1942: A report to President Franklin Roosevelt charges Admiral Husband Kimmel and General Walter Short with "dereliction of duty," failure to follow existing plans, and lack of military coordination to meet the Pearl Harbor attacks. They ignored two warnings on December 7 about hostile activities. They were warned throughout 1941 and on November 27 about possible hostilities and espionage. Kimmel and Short retire at reduced ranks without being court martialed. In all, 9 investigations are conducted.

January 27, 1942: Some civil courts reopen, but without jury trials, grand juries or habeas corpus.

January 28, 1942: A Japanese submarine torpedoes an Army transport ship ROYAL T. FRANK, which sinks in waters between Hāna and Kohala, killing 24. There are 36 survivors.

January 30, 1942: 160 AJA college students petition Military Governor Delos Emmons to "offer ourselves for whatever service you may see fit to use us." This offer leads to establishing the Varsity Victory Volunteers (VVV) to show their loyalty. The 169-member VVV does construction work for the U.S. Army Corps of Engineers, such as building barracks, operating the Kolekole rock quarry, stringing barbed wire, digging ditches, and building roads.

February 9, 1942: Military Governor Delos Emmons declares a labor shortage. On January 10, Emmons told U.S. Navy Secretary Frank Knox that a large evacuation would disrupt Hawaii's economy, which depends on skilled Japanese workers in construction, agriculture, and defense jobs.

February 12, 1942: The U.S. Army Chief of Staff advises the Joint Chiefs of Staff to consider a "Concentration Camp" on Moloka'i or on the mainland for 20,000 Japanese.

February 19, 1942: President Franklin Roosevelt signs Executive Order 9066 to allow the military to relocate people of Japanese ancestry to internment camps. 120,000 people, including 77,000 U.S. citizens, are evicted from their California, Oregon and Washington homes, and sent to 10 relocation centers in 7 inland states. Many are given just 24 hours notice to move. Violation of the Order may result in $5,000 fine and one-year in jail. Most are interned **after** America's June 4-6 victory at the Battle of Midway, which ends the threat of a Japanese invasion of Hawai'i or the west coast. Nationwide, AJAs and Japanese aliens lost more than $200 million in property and assets in 1945 dollars or $1-$4 billion in 1983 dollars. Unlike the mainland, there is no mass relocation from Hawaii – 2,100 Hawai'i Japanese are relocated.

February 21, 1942: The first U.S. Army ship takes about 200 Sand Island prisoners to mainland relocation camps. Also on the ship is the Japanese sailor who was captured at Bellows from the midget submarine.

February 21, 1942: Military Governor Delos Emmons orders Japanese people and naturalized citizens of German and Italian ancestry to turn in firearms and explosives.

February 23, 1942: U.S. Navy Secretary Frank Knox tells President Franklin Roosevelt that Honolulu is "enemy country," and 140,000 Japanese residents of O'ahu should be moved to the Neighbor Islands. President Roosevelt replies on February 26 – "I do not worry about the constitutional question – first because of my recent order (for internment camps) and second because Hawai'i is under martial law."

February 25, 1942: At 'Iolani Palace, Military Governor Delos Emmons welcomes 155 University of Hawai'i AJA students of the VVV.

February 27, 1942: A report by Congressman Martin Dies' House UnAmerican Activities Committee says Japanese fishermen committed sabotage by making secret maps of U.S. Navy ships and patrols in Pearl Harbor.

March 4, 1942: At 2:15 a.m., a Japanese seaplane drops 4-550 lb. bombs on lower Tantalus slopes, about 1,000 yards from Roosevelt High School. The noise wakens thousands of people. There is no damage or casualties, but this bombing increases fears of a Japanese invasion. The pilots couldn't see through overcast skies. The pilot of a second seaplane dropped his bombs in the ocean, near Wai'anae. Japan cancels plans for a March 7 attack on Pearl Harbor. At the time, it is the world's longest bombing raid for distance travelled from a ship at sea.

March 11, 1942: In Washington, D.C., the Joint Chiefs of Staff recommend sending all Japanese residents of Hawai'i to guarded concentration camps on the Mainland.

March 13, 1942: President Franklin Roosevelt approves a "slow evacuation of 20,000 potentially dangerous Japanese" from Hawai'i. Military Governor Delos Emmons disagrees, and says Hawai'i has no more than 1,500 dangerous Japanese aliens here.

March 30, 1942: Mandatory, mass vaccination begins against smallpox, diphtheria, typhoid and other diseases. During WW I in Europe, more people died of disease than in war battles.

March 31, 1942: Military Governor Delos Emmons issues General Order 91 to punish workers for being absent, and require workers to get their employer's approval to change jobs. This prevents plantation workers from taking better-paying defense industry jobs. Workers must work an 8-hour day, 6 days a week, with 56-hour maximum. From 1942-1944, hundreds of workers receive jail sentences for violating the law.

April 11, 1942: Ichiro Izuka, president of Kaua'i ILWU is arrested for distributing pamphlets and urging workers to slowdown at a military installation. The Civil Defense Board that sentenced him is comprised of 3 plantation managers and an Army officer. Four months later, he is released from jail on August 8 without ever being charged of a crime.

April 15, 1942: Barber's Point Naval Air Station is commissioned on 3,500 acres with 12,000 sailors. The site was intended for dirigibles in the 1930s, but none came. The base is named for Captain Henry Barber, whose ship that ran aground near Kalaeloa during on April 31, 1796.

April 20, 1942: U.S. Navy Secretary Frank Knox advises President Franklin Roosevelt to "tak(e) all of the Japs out of O'ahu and put them in a Concentration Camp on some other island." War Secretary Henry Stimson says Roosevelt agrees in an April 24 cabinet meeting. Stimson says, "Everybody agreed on the danger," but not the solution.

April 26, 1942: Military Governor Delos Emmons suggests transferring 1,400 AJA soldiers into an all-AJA battalion. General Dwight Eisenhower rejects the idea, then approves it.

April 26, 1942: Mauna Loa erupts for 13 days during a military blackout and people fear the volcano light could guide a Japanese attack. On May 10, flowing lava comes 8 miles of Hilo. 50 Army airplanes bomb the lava flow, and divert the lava.

May 13, 1942: Honolulu Police Captain John Burns says Japanese aliens and AJAs "will be good loyal Americans if given a little help and understanding." His Police Counter-Espionage Unit contacts 6,000 Japanese, with 60 volunteers at 121 meetings.

May 13, 1942: U.S. Secretary of War Henry Stimson is the first Cabinet official to tell Congress that there is no evidence of local sabotage on December 7, despite reports from many mainland newspapers.

May 13, 1942: Military Governor Delos Emmons announces that Hawai'i will comply with federal price freeze orders. Food products must sell at a price no higher than they were sold in March.

May 15, 1942: The first detailed criticism of Hawaii's martial law is presented by Honolulu attorney J. Garner Anthony in the University of California Law Review.

May 29, 1942: U.S. Secretary of War George Marshall establishes the all-AJA, Hawaiian Provisional Infantry Battalion of pre-war draftees.

June 3, 1942: Fearing another Japanese attack, Military Governor Delos Emmons orders all women and children to evacuate the area bordered by Punchbowl and Liliha. They return on June 6.

June 5, 1942: 1,432 AJA soldiers leave Hawai'i for Camp McCoy, Wisconsin, for war training. On June 12, the U.S. War Department activates the 100th Infantry Battalion, which the soldiers nickname "One Puka Puka."

June 6, 1942: Hawaii's fear of a Japanese invasion ends when U.S. military announces its defeat of Japan at the June 4-6 battle of Midway.

June 25, 1942: Special Hawai'i money replaces U.S. currency. The word "HAWAII" is printed on the front and back of all bills, with the seal and serial numbers printed in brown. Hawai'i residents must exchange their U.S. bills at a bank by July 15 – after that, old money can't be used. The new money is mandatory until October, 1944. Honolulu banks burn $200 million of regular money in the next 3 years at the 'Aiea Sugar Mill. It is the first time money is burned outside Washington, D.C.

July 13, 1942: The 1st Filipino Infantry Regiment is established with 300 Hawai'i volunteers and 7,000 from the mainland.

July 17, 1942: President Franklin Roosevelt approves sending up to 15,000 Hawai'i residents to the mainland that are considered "potentially dangerous to national security."

July 23, 1942: One-third of Hawaii's population, 138,000 men, register with Selective Service for the military draft, but AJAs are excluded because they are ineligible. Previous drafts were held in 1941, and a majority registering were AJAs.

August 24, 1942: Ingram Stainback becomes Hawaii's 9th governor until April 30, 1951. He is appointed by President Franklin Roosevelt. Governor Stainback has little authority in his first two years because the Military Governor rules under martial law. A former federal judge, Governor Stainback is critical of broad military rule. Stainback arrived in Hawai'i in 1912 as Territorial Attorney General, and was appointed a federal judge in 1940.

Governor Ingram Stainback

August 25, 1942: 40 Japanese aliens in Hawai'i are exchanged for Americans in Japan. On March 30, 1943, U.S. Secretary of War tells the Secretary of State there are 1,044 Japanese aliens from Hawai'i in mainland internment camps "available" for exchange with Japan.

September 2, 1942: Military Governor Delos Emmons allows Hawai'i civil courts to resume many normal functions, however martial law remains, and the writ of habeas corpus is still suspended.

September 30, 1942: Joseph Maxwell, a Līhu'e Plantation engineer is convicted of espionage and gets 5 years in prison. On April 27, he threw a cable over a transformer, cutting power for a half-hour. He wanted to show that it is easy to commit sabotage.

October 16, 1942: Territorial Representative Wallace Otsuka (R) of Kaua'i, is the last of 4 AJA elected officials to withdraw as a candidate for public office after winning the October 3 primary election. They withdraw to avoid aggravating the racial issue. Otsuka is unopposed and would have been re-elected. The other three are Kaua'i Supervisors.

October 29, 1942: U.S. War Secretary Henry Stimson tells President Franklin Roosevelt that all of Hawaii's dangerous Japanese aliens are in internment camps in Hawai'i or the mainland, and up to 5,000 more can be sent within 6 months when transportation is available. Stimson adds that Military Governor Delos Emmons is concerned about a worker shortage. President Roosevelt issues a blunt reply on November 2 – "I think that General Emmons should be told that the only consideration is that of the safety of the Islands and that the labor situation is not only a secondary matter but should not be given any consideration whatsoever...Military and naval safety is absolutely paramount."

October 31, 1942: To ease Hawaii's agricultural labor shortage, the Department of Public Instruction establishes a 4-day school week, so students can work one-day for the plantations.

November 5, 1942: To stop rumors, Military Governor Delos Emmons says that there will be no mass evacuation of Hawaii's 160,000 AJA and Japanese alien population to the mainland, but some will be moved. He repeats his announcement on January 23, 1943. During WW II, 875 Japanese aliens and AJAs, 100 Germans and 4 others are sent from Hawai'i to mainland internment camps, to be joined by 1,217 family members. In sum, about 1/3 of the 2,092 Hawai'i Japanese sent to internment camps are U.S. citizens. Governor Emmons succeeds in countering the War Department's desire to evacuate 100,000 then 15,000 Japanese to a Neighbor Island or the mainland. He says Hawaii's Japanese are loyal Americans, their labor is essential for the economy, and mass evacuation is too costly, "dangerous and impractical."

November 16, 1942: All females over age 16 begin to register for an employment survey so officials can identify the potential workforce.

November 23, 1942: The first group of 107 Hawai'i Japanese arrive at Jerome Relocation Center, Arkansas.

December 7, 1942: Honolulu Parks Department orders the Phoenix water fountain in Kapi'olani Park to be destroyed and used for metal scrap, "hopefully" as a bomb for Tokyo. The $10,000 fountain was seen to represent Japanese imperialism. It was a gift to Honolulu by Hawaii's Japanese population on March 16, 1919, to commemorate Japan Emperor Yoshito's 5th year on the throne.

December 27, 1942: Honolulu Chamber of Commerce sends a telegram to President Franklin Roosevelt, opposing the restoration of civilian government due to "military necessity." The Chamber also objects to suspending martial law. The "Big 5" companies benefit from frozen wages, government contracts, and prohibition of union strikes.

January 16, 1943: John Balch, former president of Mutual Telephone Company, distributes a brochure, "Shall the Japanese Be Allowed to Dominate Hawai'i?" The brochure recommends permanently sending 100,000 Japanese from Hawai'i to the mainland, and replacing them with Puerto Rican and California Filipino laborers. To prevent Hawai'i from being "a super Jap colony," Balch says Japanese shouldn't be allowed to own large amounts of property here. In Washington D.C. on June 23, Balch says Japanese will "achieve absolute dominance of the islands within 20 years" and recommends shipping 20,000 families to the Midwest. He says, "Hawai'i must be kept Caucasian." He adds that Admiral Chester Nimitz and General Delos Emmons gave him "the brush off."

January 28, 1943: Military Governor Delos Emmons calls for 1,500 AJA volunteers, and 9,500 respond by March 2. The volunteers include one-third of Hawaii's AJA population in the 18-38 age group.

January 30, 1943: The VVV de-activates because AJAs are allowed to volunteer for the 442nd Regimental Combat Team.

February 1, 1943: President Franklin Roosevelt approves creating an all-AJA voluntary combat unit despite objections by the Secretaries of War and Navy, among others. Roosevelt declares, "Americanism is a matter of the mind and heart. Americanism is not, and never was a matter of race or ancestry."

February 1, 1943: U.S. Army activates the 442nd Regimental Combat Team. All the officers are Caucasian, and all the soldiers are AJAs. 3,000 Hawai'i AJA volunteers and 1,500 mainlanders will be sent to Camp Shelby, Mississippi for training.

February 8, 1943: Military Governor Delos Emmons and Governor Ingram Stainback announce that civil authority will be restored on March 10. President Franklin Roosevelt signed a federal proclamation to do this on October 24, 1942.

February 27, 1943: One-half of Hawaii's AJAs at the Jerome, Arkansas Relocation Center answer "no" to a loyalty question for possible U.S. military service. Common reasons include not knowing why they are being interned on the mainland, and why their constitutional rights have been denied.

March 10, 1943: "Restoration Day." After 15 months of military rule, most functions of civil government are restored, and martial law is scaled down.

March 28, 1943: 15,000 people attend a program at 'Iolani Palace honoring 2,600 AJA volunteer Army soldiers. They leave Hawaii on April 5 for war training at Camp Shelby, Mississippi, where they are joined by 1,200 mainland AJA volunteers from relocation camps. The two groups of AJAs don't get along at first. They argue and fight each other. The Hawai'i AJAs are called "Budda Head" and the mainland AJAs are called "ktonk" because that is the sound of a coconut hitting the ground. The Hawai'i AJAs speak pidgin English and are more socially-oriented, while the mainland AJAs speak proper English and are more formal and individualistic.

April 13, 1943: General John DeWitt, head of the Western Defense Command tells a U.S. House Naval Affairs Subcommittee, "A Jap's a Jap.

**442nd Regimental Combat Team of AJAs is honored at
'Iolani Palace before leaving for Camp Shelby**

There is no way to determine their loyalty. You can't change him by giving him a piece of paper..." On June 29, the War Department destroys the original copy of DeWitt's written report that justifies the prosecution of AJAs who defy internment. DeWitt's records are put in a confidential file. In January 1944, the War Department distributes a falsified version of DeWitt's final report.

April 16, 1943: Bishop Estate trustees object to legislation by Territorial Senator David Trask to limit the commission of charitable trustees to 1/2%. Bishop Estate trustees were earning 5% commission. The bill doesn't pass.

April 17, 1943: A memo from U.S. Attorney General Francis Biddle to President Franklin Roosevelt says Executive Order 9066 for internment "was never intended to apply to Italians and Germans." Internment is not practical because there's too many living on the mainland.

April 30, 1943: Territorial Senate President Harold Rice of Maui resigns from the Republican Party and joins the Democrats. He says the Republicans represent "large interests and influential individuals" instead of the "rank and file" people.

May 1, 1943: Governor Ingram Stainback signs a law to prohibit the teaching of a foreign language below grade 5 because it "definitely detract(s)" from the ability to understand English, and can cause "serious emotional disturbances." On October 21, 1947, a 3-judge federal court rules the law unconstitutional, but this decision is overruled by the U.S. Supreme Court on March 14, 1949.

May 12, 1943: A confidential "Scorched Earth Policy" is completed for Iwilei, at military request, in case Japan invades Hawai'i. The military asks many companies to make a plan to destroy their hotels, warehouses, and industrial equipment by explosions, fires, and cannon shot. From 1943-1944, similar plans are prepared for other areas of Hawai'i.

May 18, 1943: 5,000 Koreans in Hawai'i petition to have their status changed from enemy to friendly aliens. On December 6, Military Governor Delos Emmons approves their petition and changes their status. During WW II, Korea is ruled by Japan.

June 1, 1943: General Robert Richardson replaces General Delos Emmons as military governor. He serves until martial law ends.

June 5, 1943: More than 1,700 AJAs protest Japan's murder of American prisoners of war by giving the U.S. government a $10,340 check to pay for "bombs on Tokyo."

National News

June 20, 1943: Detroit race riots leave 35 dead and 500 injured. Tension created by 300,000 whites and blacks working in war plants may have contributed to the violence.

July 1, 1943: Police cite 56 bus drivers for driving too slowly and blocking traffic. Bus drivers obey all rules strictly because a driver is disciplined on June 30 for not following a rule.

July 13, 1943: Blackout rules are eased to allow house lights until 10 p.m., except for rooms facing the ocean.

August 4, 1943: Honolulu FBI announces prostitution, controlled by ex-convicts, is so profitable that people are buying apartments with cash.

August 8, 1943: Dengue fever epidemic closes Waikīkī to soldiers. In July, two O'ahu soldiers returning from the South Pacific are the first to suffer from dengue fever. The first Hawai'i case was reported on August 3. 300 soldiers walk house to house, telling people about dengue fever, and 7,000 volunteers spray insecticide to kill mosquitoes that carry dengue. 1,500 people on O'ahu become ill with dengue, and two die. The ban is lifted on September 13.

August 16, 1943: Federal Judge Delbert Metzger upholds the March 10 restoration of civil authority, which he says ends martial law and restores habeas corpus.

August 18, 1943: Business leaders establish the Hawai'i Employers Council to eliminate conflict between management and workers, and to allow both groups to negotiate collective bargaining agreements. By 1946, the Council has 251 members, and the number of union labor contracts grows from 12 to 179, benefiting thousands of workers. About 800 companies are now associated with the Council.

August 25, 1943: Federal Judge Delbert Metzger spars with Military Governor Robert Richardson. Metzger fines Richardson $5,000, and holds him in contempt of court for ignoring a summons to explain why a writ of habeas corpus should not be restored. A few hours later, Richardson responds with General Order No. 31 that imposes a $5,000 fine and jail time for any federal judge or lawyer who tries to nullify martial law by seeking a writ of habeas corpus. In a compromise, the fine is reduced to $100 on October 25 when Richardson rescinds his order. A few months later, President Roosevelt pardons General Richardson. The case began in 1943, when two men, Walter Glockner and Edwin Seifert are jailed without being charged. The two defendants are sent to the mainland and released. In all, 5 court cases attempted to test the legality of martial law. Nowhere in America is martial law as extensive and long lasting as in Hawai'i.

September 20, 1943: First Lady Eleanor Roosevelt arrives in Hawai'i and visits Red Cross installations until September 22. She is America's first First Lady to visit Hawai'i. She is fingerprinted and receives an I.D. card, just like everyone else.

September 22, 1943: The 100th Infantry Battalion arrives in Salerno, Italy. Combat begins on September 29.

October 15, 1943: New regulations take effect today, freezing virtually all Hawai'i workers to their jobs. 85,000 workers can't change jobs without government approval.

October 17, 1943: A small Japanese reconnaissance airplane, launched from a submarine, flies to the Wai'anae coast, where it is spotted by search lights, then turns around. After the war, it is confirmed as a Japanese airplane.

October 19, 1943: After being arrested for violating the street blackout curfew, Navy Lt. Peter Alport is taken to the Bethel Street Police Station, where he shoots three military police and kills one.

November 4, 1943: At 10 a.m., the U.S. Army supervises Honolulu's first major evacuation drill. People vacate downtown in 15 minutes.

December, 1943: A Marine camp at Parker Ranch, Waimea, is named Camp Tarawa for the Pacific battle at Tarawa Island. It is used to train Marines for Iwo Jima combat. It becomes the largest Marine training camp in the Pacific, and closes in 1945.

December 17, 1943: President Franklin Roosevelt signs a law to repeal the 1882 Chinese Exclusion Act. This makes 4,000 Hawai'i Chinese eligible for U.S. citizenship. The Exclusion Act embarrasses the U.S., because China is our WW II ally. Roosevelt says the 1882 law is an "historic mistake."

December 28, 1943: HSPA scientists announce they are manufacturing penicillin, considered a "wonder drug" and a "potent germ killer" of deadly diseases. The mold is easy to grow here in 11-13 days.

January 11, 1944: Honolulu Teamsters Local 996 is chartered.

January 21, 1944: U.S. War Department announces a regular Selective Service draft for AJAs in detention camps because of the "excellent showing" and "outstanding record" of the 100th and 442nd.

4 million feet of barbed wire fences are posted on Oʻahu beaches. The Royal Hawaiian Hotel is in the background.

January 27, 1944: United Public Workers union is established.

February 2, 1944: Oʻahu prisoners produce 4,700 lbs. of rubber from Nāhiku Plantation, which had been abandoned for 30 years. 34 Oʻahu prison inmates started working at the plantation on January 21, 1943.

February, 1944: Camp Maui opens at Haʻikū with 19,000 4th Division Marines. The camp closes on November 3, 1945.

March 1, 1944: Kahoʻolawe Ranch subleases the entire island to the military for $238 a year until June 30, 1954. On November 1, 1945, the Army gives its lease to the Navy. In 1946, Angus McPhee sues the federal government to regain his lease, but he dies in 1948. The Navy cancels the Kahoʻolawe Ranch lease on September 30, 1952 before it is due to end.

March 14, 1944: The 442nd AJA soldiers adopt "Go for Broke" as their motto at Camp Shelby, Mississippi.

April 13, 1944: Federal Judge Delbert Metzger rules that martial law is illegal and ended on March 10, 1943. He also rules the Military Governor's Office was created illegally and has no control over civilian affairs. He releases Lloyd Duncan from jail because Duncan was tried in a military court after Metzger says martial law had ended.

April 30, 1944: Hawaiʻi Democratic Party Platform states martial law is "illegal" and "Hawaiʻi is not a conquered nation."

May 4, 1944: Military Governor Robert Richardson ends the 29-month blackout, but the 10 p.m. curfew remains. The ban on car and street lights ends on July 1, after 950 nights.

May 5, 1944: An Army Air Corps bomber crashes into an ʻAiea mountain after take-off from Hickam Air Force Base, killing all 10 people aboard.

May 21, 1944: A Pearl Harbor ammunition explosion kills 163 and injures 396 people. The "2nd Pearl Harbor disaster" is kept secret until 1962.

June 8, 1944: Two Army airplanes collide in the morning 1,000 feet above Kalihi, killing 10 civilians and 4 soldiers, and injuring 15 civilians.

June 17, 1944: U.S. Army designates the 100th Battalion and 442nd Infantry as one unit. A total 18,143 individual decorations for valor make it America's most decorated unit for its size and length of service.

July 3, 1944: ILWU publishes its first newspaper, THE DISPATCHER, HAWAIIAN EDITION with Jack Hall as editor, followed by the ILWU REPORTER, and VOICE OF THE ILWU, which continues today.

July 26, 1944: President Franklin Roosevelt begins a secret, war-related, 3-day Hawaiʻi visit to discuss war plans with General Douglas MacArthur and Admiral Chester Nimitz. It is his first visit since 1934, and his last. There are no parades or public announcements, yet most people in Hawai'i know the president is here. Due to military censorship, this visit is not reported in the local newspapers until August 10, about two weeks after the president had left.

July 27, 1944: U.S. Army General Mark Clark, Commander of the 5th Army awards the 100th Battalion with a Presidential Unit Citation, and says, "You are always thinking of your country before yourselves. You have never complained through your long periods in the line. You have written a brilliant chapter in the history of the fighting men in America...The whole United States is proud of you."

August 8, 1944: A citizens committee reports that Honolulu is the only large American city to openly tolerate prostitution, a $10-$15 million a year business. 250 women are registered with police. Prostitutes charge $3-$5 for a 3-minute visit.

September 20, 1944: Governor Ingram Stainback orders all Hawai'i prostitution houses closed. Prostitution had been "tolerated" by police and military during WW II because Hawai'i had 45,000 more men than women. The next day, Honolulu Police shut 15 regulated prostitution houses near Nu'uanu and Vineyard. The last time prostitution houses were closed was 1932.

October 24, 1944: President Franklin Roosevelt signs Executive Order 9489 to formally end martial law, restore the writ of habeas corpus, and end military authority in civilian zones. Hawai'i is now designated as a "military area," similar to other mainland areas.

October 30, 1944: Hawaii's 442nd Regimental Combat Team rescues the "Lost Battalion" of 211 Texas soldiers. In this and in other battles, 161 AJAs are killed and 2,000 wounded.

November 7, 1944: President Franklin Roosevelt is elected to a 4th term. He is the only president to be elected more than twice. He dies on April 12, 1945.

November 12, 1944: U.S. Army General John Dahlquist gathers the 442nd soldiers to honor them. He tells an aide, "I ordered all the men be assembled." The aide replies, "Yes sir. All the men are what you see."

December 18, 1944: Based on "military necessity," the U.S. Supreme Court rules that the 1942 removal of AJAs to internment camps was constitutional. However the court also rules that a loyal, law-abiding citizen can't be held against his will.

1944: A 3-year, $23 million excavation is completed at an unknown date near the pineapple fields of Schofield Barracks and Wheeler Field. It is known as "the hole." 250,000 square feet occupying 3 stories are built underground for airplane construction, and a cafeteria that can make 6,000 meals daily. The "hole" is now the Kunia Tunnel.

January 12, 1945: In a victory for union workers, the National Labor Relations Board rules that non-field workers, comprising most of Hawaii's sugar workers are protected by federal law, and considered part of labor bargaining units. The union wins 32 of 35 plantation elections. By November, 1945, labor unions win 132 elections in sugar, pineapple, railroads, stevedoring, etc., covering nearly 11,000 workers. Unions lose only 6 elections, covering less than 200 workers.

April 7, 1945: Japanese Central Institute closes, and donates $120,000 in real estate and assets to aid U.S. veterans. It was Hawaii's oldest Japanese language school. Rev. Takie Okumura opened the school on April 6, 1896.

April 9, 1945: Governor Ingram Stainback signs a law to repeal the 1923 anti-picketing law.

April 29, 1945: Hawai'i soldiers are among the first to liberate Holocaust victims of Nazi concentration camps and its 206,000 starving, skeleton-like prisoners. It is said the prisoners looked more dead than alive.

May 21, 1945: Governor Ingram Stainback signs the Hawai'i Employment Relations Act, known as the "Little Wagner Act." This law gives collective bargaining rights to agricultural workers, which the 1935 federal Wagner Act, gave to factory workers. This gives the ILWU the right to organize plantation workers and bargain collectively.

July 7, 1945: Military Governor Robert Richardson lifts all war-time blackouts and curfews, and rescinds the Hawai'i Defense Act. It is the first time since December 7, 1941 that civilians can walk the streets anytime, day or night.

July 19, 1945: USS INDIANAPOLIS refuels in Hawai'i then continues to Tinian with its secret cargo of the atomic bomb that will destroy Hiroshima, kill 70,000 people, and injure 100,000 more on August 6. The bomb will be delivered to the B-29 Bomber ENOLA GAY, which will drop the atomic bomb. After delivering the bomb, the INDIANAPOLIS is sunk by a Japanese ship on July 30. Only 316 of the 1,199 sailors survive, and many are killed by sharks. The survivors are rescued 4 days later. Captain Charles McVay III is court martialed in 1946 for "hazarding his vessel" by not following a zig zag pattern in dangerous waters.

August 3, 1945: Sugar growers and ILWU announce Hawaii's first negotiated labor contract for sugar. 20,000 workers gain 7¢ an hour raise. Ed Beechert and Ah Quon McElrath say the contract was signed on top of a garbage can, in a dark Waikīkī alley, lit only by a flashlight.

August 15, 1945: Gas rationing, labor controls and censorship end because Japan surrendered on August 14.

September 1, 1945: 135,000 people gather in downtown Honolulu to watch a V-J Day victory parade.

September 2, 1945: Japan formally surrenders aboard the USS MISSOURI in Tokyo Harbor. The USS MISSOURI is "homeported" in Hawai'i as a museum in 1998.

September 26, 1945: HONOLULU STAR-BULLETIN reports Hawai'i prisoner of war (POW) camps have 10,619 POWs – 4,841 Italians, 2,757 Okinawans, and 2,607 Koreans. Two were built in 1942 at Honouliuli Gulch and Wahiawā for temporary shipping of Japanese POWs to the mainland. In 1944, 4 camps were built for 5,000 "politically dangerous" Italians and one for 2,600 Koreans. Many Koreans were forced into the Japanese army. The 4 Italian camps were at Sand Island, Schofield Barracks, Fort Hase, and Kalihi Valley. Italian POWs were used as skilled laborers throughout the island. In July 1944 they built a Catholic chapel near Schofield Barracks to honor Mother Cabrini, who was being considered as an American saint by the Vatican. The chapel was finished in February, 1945, and was so attractive, many civilian Catholics celebrated mass on Sundays with the POWs. After the POWs returned to Italy, the chapel became overgrown with shrubbery, and was destroyed for the H-2 freeway. POWs also built a fountain with winged lions at Ft. Shafter's Richardson Hall.

October 23, 1945: Hawai'i Tourist Bureau reopens as the Hawai'i Visitors Bureau, and promotes Hawai'i through mainland magazine and newspaper ads, store displays, travel agencies, etc.

November 3, 1945: An Army Air Transport airplane crashes into the ocean 3 hours after leaving Honolulu for California, killing 18 people. The aircraft ran out of gas because someone forgot to fill the gas tanks.

November 12, 1945: The "Battle of Damon Tract" makes national headlines when 500 sailors riot and fight civilians near the airport and Fort Shafter. Police arrest 9. Reports say the riots are caused by sailors who were beaten by civilians.

November 14, 1945: The first large group of 450 Hawai'i AJAs return from mainland internment camps. Smaller groups began returning on July 11.

November 16, 1945: Pan American World Airways is the first to resume Hawai'i commercial flights after WW II. Before WW II, only 1% of Hawaii's visitors arrived by air.

November 19, 1945: The Outrigger Club apologizes to champion swimmer Keo Nakama when the club manager refused his admission. He was invited by member Bill Smith. The Outrigger Canoe Club had a policy of not allowing Asian guests to eat lunch at the club.

November 20, 1945: Governor Ingram Stainback urges Bishop Estate to sell some of its land to homeowners. In a letter, he says this would "remedy some of the evils of the large landholdings in the Territory and possibly prevent or delay legislation directed against such."

December 21, 1945: The 100th Infantry's Club Puka Puka becomes Club 100.

December 22, 1945: U.S. Secretary of Interior Harold Ickes officially recommends statehood for Hawai'i. Hawai'i is administered by the Department of Interior.

January 7, 1946: A U.S. House Committee on Territories holds statehood hearings in Hawai'i until January 17. The committee recommends legislation to admit Hawai'i as a state. During the next decade, the House generally supports statehood, but the Senate opposes it.

January 21, 1946: In his State of the Union speech to Congress, President Harry Truman is the first president to endorse Hawai'i statehood.

January 25, 1946: 31 Hawaii's sugar companies agree to pay $1.5 million to thousands of plantation workers in an out-of-court settlement for wages owed from 1939-1945. Workers will get $20-$400 each.

February 9, 1946: United Nations Charter says nations with territories are obligated to help their territories achieve self-government or independence. The United Nations drops Hawai'i from this list in 1959 after statehood. Many Hawaiians believe the 1959 vote for statehood was illegal because the voter ballot did not include an option for independence.

February 25, 1946: U.S. Supreme Court declares martial law in Hawai'i was unconstitutional. The court condemns using military courts for civilian cases.

April 1, 1946: Hawaii's worst tsunami disaster occurs on "April Fool's" day. An ocean earthquake near Alaska creates 500-mile an hour waves that travel 2,200 miles in 4 hours. The waves rise 55 feet at Hawai'i Island, 37 feet at O'ahu, and 45 feet at Kaua'i. In all, 173 people die,

Hilo residents run for their lives, just ahead of the destructive "April fools day" tsunami

163 are injured, 1,400 homes are destroyed, and there is $26 million damage. 5 teachers and 16 children at Laupāhoehoe School are killed and the school is destroyed. Most of the damage is in Hilo, caused by the 3rd and 4th waves. The Hilo wharf clocks stop at 7:06 a.m.

April 26, 1946: Former Governor Joseph Poindexter tells the HONOLULU ADVERTISER that General Walter Short "insisted" on martial law after Pearl Harbor, and promised to end it in a "reasonably short time." The governor was "reluctant," but it was a "necessary war measure."

May 8, 1946: President Harry Truman signs a law to unfreeze $1.3 million assets of Japanese aliens. This amends the 1941 War Powers Act.

June 14, 1946: When ILWU stevedores strike Castle and Cooke Terminals from June 11-14, leaving food on the ship, Governor Ingram Stainback issues an order to seize the ship in 24 hours and unload cargo.

June 18, 1946: The last ship with 800 Filipinos leaves the Philippines, bound for Hawai'i by July 4, when the Philippines gain independence, and mass plantation immigration ends. Their contract includes free return to the Philippines when the workers complete 3 years. From 1909-1946, 125,000 Filipinos arrived in Hawai'i.

July 1, 1946: Hotel Hāna opens. Hāna Ranch owner Paul Fagan also owns the Pacific Coast League baseball team, San Francisco Seals, which he brings to Hāna to train in March, 1947.

July 2, 1946: President Harry Truman signs a Nationality Act amendment to make Filipinos eligible for U.S. citizenship. As a result, thousands of Filipinos apply for their relatives to come to Hawai'i.

July 12, 1946: During contract negotiations, bus drivers cover the fare boxes and give "free rides" to passengers until July 15. On July 13, about 24 drivers are suspended for not collecting fares. On July 15, Teamster oil workers strike three oil companies in sympathy, and gas stations run out of gas for motorists. On August 1, a jury finds Teamster leader Art Rutledge and 5 others not guilty of telling bus drivers to refuse fares. A new Transit Workers Union of Hawai'i is established on July 22, 1946.

July 15, 1946: President Harry Truman awards the Presidential Distinguished Unit Citation to the 442nd Regiment at a White House ceremony. President Truman says, "You fought not only the enemy, but you fought prejudice – and you won. Keep up that fight, and we will continue to win..." AJAs and Japanese were 33% Hawaii's population and 65% of its soldiers. The current medal total for 442nd and 100th soldiers is 21 Congressional Medals of Honor, 7 Presidential Unit Citations, 32 Distinguished Service Crosses, 9,486 Purple Hearts, and 18,143 individual medals for bravery.

July 16, 1946: A Joint Congressional Committee submits a 492-page report after investigating the Pearl Harbor attack. The report criticizes General Walter Short and Admiral Husband Kimmel for "poor judgment," failure to inform radar workers that "war was at hand," and failure to share information with each other. They are also criticized for being overconcerned about sabotage, and for parking airplanes so closely together, the aircraft couldn't be quickly used during the attack.

July 25, 1946: PTA President Elizabeth St. John criticizes the Department of Public Instruction for "neglect of the public schools" and urges closing the English standard schools.

July 24, 1946: The first weekly Transocean Airlines charter flight arrives in Honolulu from San Francisco.

July 26, 1946: Trans-Pacific Airlines, founded by Richard and Rudy Tongg, begins interisland charter service. The airline becomes Aloha Airlines in 1958.

July 26, 1946: Organized labor calls off a pending strike threat against 4 public utility companies – gas, electric, phone and transit.

August 6, 1946: Two B-17 bombers fly 2,174 miles without a pilot, guided by radio controls, from Hickam Air Force Base to Edwards Air Force Base, California.

August 9, 1946: 4,000 people welcome the first large group of 241 soldiers of the 442nd Regiment returning to Hawai'i. The soldiers ride in a 60-car motorcade to 'Iolani Palace. Governor Ingram Stainback says, "By your heroic deeds you have done more to bring statehood for Hawai'i within the realm of near possibility than all the words of all the politicians during the last 40 years." Smaller groups of AJA soldiers had been returning since 1944.

August 12, 1946: The 442nd Veterans Club is established.

August 15, 1946: When Military Police kill an escaping Japanese POW, 2,000 Japanese POWs at Wheeler Field refuse to work.

September 1, 1946: 25,000 ILWU workers on 33 plantations begin a 79-day strike until November 18 – the first territory-wide, industry-wide strike. Workers want to end paternalism by converting "perks" such as free housing, etc. to cash, which workers say is worth about $25 million for last 6 years. Union workers gain a 20¢ an hour wage increase and an end to paternalism When the union wins the strike, national ILWU leader Harry Bridges says Hawai'i "is no longer a feudal colony."

September 20, 1946: U.S. Navy announces the last 5,000 Japanese and Okinawan POWs in Hawai'i will be sent home by January 1, 1947. Italian and Korean POWs have already been sent home.

October 21, 1946: Stanley White of the U.S. Labor Department, tries to mediate the 1946 sugar strike. He criticizes management – "I would have to conclude that no matter how costly it might be, the goal upon which you (the employers) had fixed (was) the extermination of unionism in the islands." Employers have "a public be damned" attitude.

November 5, 1946: ILWU-endorsed candidates win 14 of 15 seats in the Territorial House. The ILWU has influence there for the first time.

November 19, 1946: The 79-day territory-wide sugar strike ends. However Pioneer Mill's 1,067 workers strike another 45 days until January 2, 1947 because 11 sugar workers are fired for assaulting three luna.

December 26, 1946: One of the world's largest radio transmitters is built at Lualualei Valley. The U.S. State Department operates this 100,000 watt radio station, KRHO, to broadcast information and cultural affairs to the Pacific.

January 1, 1947: U.S. Pacific Command is established at Camp Smith, making Hawai'i the command center for U.S. military operations that today cover half of the world.

January 1, 1947: The 14,585 acre Honolulu Plantation closes. Most of the land and equipment is sold to O'ahu Sugar. The planation was established in 1899 by Seessman and Wurmser, the San Francisco owners of S&W Canned Foods. A sugar refinery was built here in 1906. Much of the land was taken by the military for Pearl Harbor Naval Base in 1907 and Hickam Air Force Base in 1935, as well as for Honolulu International Airport, Aloha Stadium and most of 'Aiea.

January 15, 1947: The Honolulu Star-Bulletin reports that recently-translated Japanese documents reveal that Japan cabinet members may have wanted to kill President Franklin Roosevelt in Honolulu. Japan's prime minister proposed a meeting aboard a Japanese ship in Honolulu on August 4, 1941. Roosevelt rejected the suggestion.

February 6, 1947: After months of investigation and publicity, the 1946 Police Graft Scandal is finally exposed. Honolulu Police Vice Squad Sgt. William Clark opens his bank safety deposit box in front of news reporters, prosecutors, and many onlookers. He shows $134,170, mostly cash, which he collected as bribes to protect Chinatown gamblers the past three years. Gamblers had paid police over $500,000 a year for protection. Sgt. Clark receives immunity for a confession, and identifies 13 police who are indicted for taking bribes. The 13 police are suspended, then reinstated after being found innocent. It is believed the 13 police are acquitted because the prosecutor's witnesses are two known gamblers and Sgt. Clark, who received immunity. Only one policeman, Captain Clarence Caminos is found guilty. On May 26, Caminos receives a 10-year prison sentence, but is paroled after two years. Police Chief Gabrielson resigned on April 12, 1946, allegedly for not doing enough to support the investigation. The IRS and Territorial Tax Office collect $500,000 in back taxes, and on June 13, 1947 an IRS agent is convicted of taking a bribe.

March 24, 1947: A Territorial Senate Select Committee report criticizes the lack of rights and services for Niʻihau. The report says "isolated" Niʻihau residents aren't allowed to own radios, can't own property, get inadequate school and medical attention, and "live in complete subservience" to the "paternal" island owners.

March 28, 1947: ILWU begins a 42-day strike against Hawaiian Pineapple. The strike begins when 18 pineapple workers are suspended for refusing to cross an ILWU picket line at Hawaiian Tuna Packers, where ILWU workers had been on strike since on March 20.

Congressional Delegate Joseph Farrington and entertainer Pualani Avon seek an early statehood.

March 31, 1947: A dozen Schofield soldiers try to escape from prison. More than 100 inmates take 3 guards as hostages and beat them. One inmate is killed, and 3 guards are wounded. On June 12, 1 inmate is acquitted, 6 inmates get 10-30 years of hard labor, and 5 inmates are not tried.

April 22, 1947: Schofield Barracks Private Garlon Mickles, age 19, is Hawaii's last capital punishment victim. He is hanged for raping and beating a War Department worker on Guam. In August 1945, two soldiers, Private Jesse Boston, age 36, and Private Cornelius Thomas, age 23, were executed at Schofield for murdering people on Maui.

April 25, 1947: United Airlines, which had served Hawaiʻi with military contracts since 1942, arrives with its first commercial flight from the mainland. Aboard the flight is United Airlines president William Patterson, the son of an Oʻahu Sugar Co. overseer. He visits his former Waipahu home for the first time in 32 years. He became airline president in 1931.

April 28, 1947: Governor Ingram Stainback signs a law to repeal the M-Day law and its civilian martial law powers.

May 2, 1947: Governor Ingram Stainback signs a law to rename the John Rodgers Airport as the Honolulu Airport.

May 15, 1947: Governor Ingram Stainback signs a law to establish a Hawai'i Statehood Commission to promote statehood from an office in Washington, D.C. By 1959, this organization spends $845,000 of public money and receives several million dollars in private donations to support statehood.

May 29, 1947: Honolulu Chamber of Commerce president John Walker says "destructive union policies and tactics" are responsible for 35 strikes in 18 months, which threaten Hawaii's economy.

June 30, 1947: U.S. House of Representatives passes a Hawai'i statehood bill for the first time, 196-133. The bill, introduced by Hawai'i Delegate Joseph Farrington, dies in the Senate.

July 11, 1947: A 5-day, territory-wide strike by 18,000 ILWU pineapple workers begins. More than 40 strikers are arrested.

August 16, 1947: U.S. Ambassador to Japan, George Atcheson and 9 others die when their Army B-17 airplane runs out of gas due to pilot error, and crashes in the ocean, 60 miles from O'ahu. Only 3 of the 13 aboard the airplane survive.

October 26, 1947: The first annual Aloha Week is held to promote tourism during a slow month. It is sponsored by a Junior Chamber of Commerce organization called Jaycee Oldtimers.

November 11, 1947: Governor Ingram Stainback says Communism preaches "fanatical violence" that seeks to destroy democratic governments by infiltrating schools and government. He promises to fire government workers that are Communists.

November 15, 1947: Ichiro Izuka publishes a critical 31-page brochure, THE TRUTH ABOUT COMMUNISM. He admits he was a Communist for 9 years, identifies local Communists by name, urges union workers to "wake up," and says Communists are loyal to Russia, not the U.S.

November 25, 1947: The Department of Public Instruction suspends two teachers, John and Aiko Reinecke. They are accused of being Communists, and for lacking the "ideals of democracy."

December 31, 1947: The Dillingham family and 250 friends take the last train ride of O'ahu Railway, which was founded in 1888. A small sight-seeing train now travels 6 miles from Kapolei to Wai'anae.

January 3, 1948: Army experts explode a 450 lb. Japanese mine from WW II that drifts to Kapapa, Kaua'i.

January 3, 1948: ILWU leader Ichiro Izuka tells an ILWU conference that he was a Communist from 1938-1946. He accuses the Communist Party of plotting union strikes – the first step to a Communist overthrow of the United States.

January 5, 1948: U.S. Senate Committee on Public Lands holds the first-ever Senate statehood hearings in Hawai'i until January 20.

March 21, 1948: Acclaimed singer Paul Robeson finishes 14 concerts in 11 days for the ILWU. He gets angry when asked if he's a Communist.

March 31, 1948: Maui's HC&S becomes America's largest sugar plantation when it merges with Maui Agriculture Company.

April 21, 1948: The Matson luxury ship, LURLINE with 722 passengers, returns to Honolulu after WW II. 100,000 people along the coast and 50,000 people at the dock welcome the ship, which is draped with a giant lei on its bow. During WW II, the military transported 736,000 soldiers on Matson ships.

May 14, 1948: Governor Ingram Stainback writes a letter to U.S. Undersecretary of the Interior Oscar Chapman – "As feared, the Communists have taken over the so-called Democratic Party organization in Hawai'i – lock, stock and barrel...Hawai'i is the most fertile field for Communism in the whole nation." Stainback says the most susceptible people are Japanese, Democrats and union workers.

May 20, 1948: U.S. Senate votes 20-51 to prevent a House resolution for statehood from reaching the Senate floor.

July 2, 1948: President Harry Truman signs the Japanese American Evacuation Claims Act to give partial compensation to AJAs for property losses from internment. There are 26,000 claims for $148 million, but the U.S. government pays just $38 million.

August 5, 1948: Koji Ariyoshi establishes the HONOLULU RECORD newspaper, originally named the PACIFIC RECORD. This progressive, alternative newspaper specializes in investigative reporting, and attains 5,000

National News

July 17, 1948: After walking out of the Democratic National Convention in opposition to civil rights, the Southern Dixiecrats select South Carolina Gov. Strom Thurmond as their presidential candidate.

circulation. The last issue is July 3, 1958. Ariyoshi is arrested in 1951 as an alleged Communist and "Hawai'i 7" member. An Appeals court reverses his conviction in 1958.

August 12, 1948: Castle and Cooke announces it is spending $1 million to plant macadamia nuts at its Royal Hawaiian Macadamia Nut Corporation, at Kea'au, and builds the first nut cracking and processing plant. It is Hawaii's largest macadamia nut orchard.

August 13, 1948: Former Communist Ichiro Izuka tells the Hawai'i School Commission that school teachers John and Aiko Reinecke are Communists, and he names 8 other Communists.

August 24, 1948: A B-29 crashes after take-off at Hickam Air Force Base, killing 16 of 20 crew.

September 3, 1948: HRT bus workers strike for 36 days until October 8.

September 10, 1948: A new $40 million, 14-story, Tripler Army Hospital opens with 1,500 beds as the main military hospital in the Pacific. It is named for General Charles Tripler, Medical Director of the Civil War Union Army. There is no official reason for the pink color, but maybe the wrong color was ordered or it was supposed to "hide" the red dirt that blows onto the hospital. The original Tripler Hospital was located in Honolulu in 1898 to treat Spanish-American war soldiers, then moved to Fort Shafter on July 1, 1907. It is re-named Tripler Army Medical Center on May 1, 1969.

October 11, 1948: 1,350 workers at 'Ola'a Plantation strike for 68 days until December 16, when sugar prices increase.

October 15, 1948: UH research chemist Charles Fujimoto resigns to work full-time as Hawaii's Communist Party chairman. It is the first time the Hawai'i Communist Party comes out in the open.

October 29, 1948: After 33 days of hearings, the Territorial School Commission fires Dr. John and Aiko Reinecke. Despite 37 combined years of teaching in Hawai'i, they are considered "untrustworthy" as teachers and disloyal because they are alleged Communist Party members.

November 1, 1948: U.S. Senator Hugh Butler, chairman of the U.S. Senate Interior Committee which reviews all statehood bills, has secret interviews in Honolulu with 77 people about Communism until November 12. He is a "one man committee" without public hearings. He wants to defer Hawai'i statehood "until the Communist menace is brought under control."

November 2, 1948: Eddie Tam is elected as Chairman of Maui County Board of Supervisors, a position he holds for 18 years until he dies on December 13, 1966. A son of immigrants, he had a ninth grade education. His famous office sign read – "You can't sell peanuts at the end of a parade."

December 7, 1948: Two Air Force bombers, B-36 and B-50, fly undetected over Oʻahu, and drop "dummy bombs" near Pearl Harbor. Both airplanes fly non-stop, roundtrip from Fort Worth, Texas. These undetected flights anger people in Hawaiʻi. Military officials admit Hawaiʻi is not high on the list of Russian targets.

December 27, 1948: A Federal Appeals Court rules that Hawaii's Unlawful Assembly and Riot law is unconstitutional. The plantations had used this 1929 law to break strikes and arrest strikers during the 1946 sugar and 1947 pineapple strikes. The U.S. Supreme Court overturns the Federal Appeals Court on October 22, 1951, which makes the law constitutional.

January 6, 1949: Mauna Loa erupts for 145 days. An airplane with 3 men disappears after flying near the volcano. The eruption is visible in Wailuku.

February 2, 1949: National Memorial Cemetery of the Pacific, commonly known as Punchbowl, begins burial services with an unknown soldier killed during the 1941 Pearl Harbor attack. The cemetery opens on July 19 with 10,000 graves, and it is officially dedicated on September 2. The first public burial is Ernie Pyle, the famous news reporter who died on April 18, 1945 during a war-time assignment. He was beloved by soldiers for writing about "GI Joe."

February 3, 1949: Territorial Budget Director Paul Thurston says the Welfare Department is broke, due to a record high 13,000 people on welfare caused by recent labor strikes. Thurston says the department needs $1.1 million.

April 4, 1949: A petition signed by 30,000 people is submitted to the Territorial Senate. The petition asks for the repeal of a Hawaiʻi law that prohibits teaching a foreign language to students.

April 23, 1949: Territorial Senator Herbert Lee's near 7-hour filibuster is Hawaii's longest. He protests legislation that would reduce Oahu's excise tax revenue from 55% to 52%, giving a larger share to the Neighbor Islands. Lee succeeds and Oʻahu keeps its share. As a result, all future Senate speeches are limited to 15 minutes.

April 26, 1949: Governor Ingram Stainback signs a Joint Resolution to establish a Commission on Communism and Other Subversive Activities. The Commission will investigate people or organizations that are believed to threaten or destroy the U.S. or our freedom. On October 26, 1949, Governor Ingram Stainback signs a law to create the Committee on Subversive Activities to investigate UnAmerican Activities. The Commission is abolished on June 24, 1969.

April 27, 1949: A bill to repeal prohibitions against certain business, work or conduct on Sunday becomes law without the signature of Governor Ingram Stainback.

May 1, 1949: The "Great Hawaiian Dock Strike" begins. It is Hawaii's longest maritime strike. 2,000 ILWU dock workers, led by Jack Hall, strike for 176 days until October 25, to obtain the same wages as west coast workers who load and unload the same ships. The 6-month strike creates an economic crisis and makes people do without basic amenities.

May 4, 1949: Governor Ingram Stainback signs a law to stop labor strikes against any public utility that affects the public interest, such as a dock worker strike. It is the first time Hawai'i government requires collective bargaining to settle an employer-worker dispute.

May 4, 1949: The first of 50 "Dear Joe" letters appear prominently on the front-page of the HONOLULU ADVERTISER. The letters are allegedly written by publisher Lorrin Thurston to call attention to the Communist influence of Hawaii's labor unions, and to accuse the ILWU of serving Russian dictator Joe Stalin. Hawaii's newspapers take a leading role in fueling the 1950s "Red Scare." The front-page letters are written as if an ILWU leader is writing to Stalin. The letters may have backfired when national publicity and politicians believe that Hawai'i is influenced or run by Communists. As a result, anti-Communism delays statehood.

May 14, 1949: 5,000 people send 3,500 cables to President Harry Truman, urging him to intervene to end the ILWU dock strike.

May 17, 1949: 10,000 people meet at Kapi'olani Park to protest the ILWU dock strike.

May 20, 1949: In a new approach to obtain statehood, Governor Ingram

Stainback signs a law to hold a territorial convention with 63 elected delegates to draft a state constitution. This approach had been used by 15 territories that obtained statehood.

May 31, 1949: 300 women, nearly all Caucasian, establish a "broom brigade" to protest the ILWU strike. Their brooms symbolize a desire to "clean out" the alleged Communist control of unions. They picket ILWU headquarters until August 7. Many picketers are the wives of Big 5 managers, and some arrive in chauffeured cars.

June 14, 1949: The Hawai'i Resident's Association, commonly known as IMUA, holds its first meeting with 300 women, many of whom are Broom Brigade members. The organization opposes Communism. As a result of publicity about IMUA and the Broom Brigade, many Congressmen become more concerned about Communism in Hawai'i than the reasons for the dock strike.

June 25, 1949: U.S. Senator Hugh Butler releases his "Butler Report" that opposes statehood because "Communism has a firm grip on the economic, political and social life in the Territory." Butler's concerns about Communism help to block Hawai'i statehood.

June 30, 1949: Labor leader and attorney Pablo Manlapit arrives in Hawai'i to visit his family. He'd been living in the Philippines since 1934. Unfortunately, he arrives during the dock strike, and U.S. Immigration officials makes him promise not to speak to the news media or attend public meetings. Governor Stainback is considering a pardon for Manlapit, but the dock strike makes it politically impossible. This is his last visit to Hawai'i, and he leaves on July 13.

July 1, 1949: Honolulu Mayor Johnny Wilson vetoes a resolution that would have allowed hotel construction on Kūhiō beach.

July 9, 1949: 250 picketing ILWU strikers are arrested from July 9-20 for blocking Hawai'i Stevedores from using strikebreakers to unload ships.

July 10, 1949: The $300,000 Kailua-Kona Airport opens.

July 26, 1949: Governor Ingram Stainback calls the Legislature into special session to end the dock worker strike. He wants to put the Territory into the stevedore business so shipping operations will continue.

July 26, 1949: Territorial Senate censures Senator William Nobriga for inserting amendments to a bill without telling anyone.

July 27, 1949: A 23-ounce meteor, 5 inches in diameter, falls through a Pālolo home. No one is hurt.

August 6, 1949: Governor Ingram Stainback signs a temporary 6-month law, the Dock Seizure Act to end the 3-month dock strike. This law requires workers to take a non-Communist oath, allows the governor to seize and operate stevedore companies, and hire workers to load and unload goods. On August 10, the governor seizes two companies, Castle and Cooke Terminals and McCabe Hamilton and Renny Stevedores. 1,000 unemployed workers sign up for jobs. On August 18, Governor Stainback signs a law to make picketing illegal at government operations. On November 1, Governor Ingram Stainback signs another Dock Seizure Act. A court says the law is constitutional.

August 29, 1949: Governor Ingram Stainback signs a law to make it illegal to picket a person's residence. The law is prompted when the homes of non-strikers are picketed.

September 13, 1949: Jackson College opens as a Baptist-owned, liberal arts college. The one-acre college is sold at an October 14, 1965 auction for $129,000 to the Hawai'i Mission of Seventh Day Adventists.

October 25, 1949: Hawaii's 6-month dock worker strike ends. Workers get a 21¢ an hour pay raise, but still earn less than west coast dock workers. The strike caused $100 million economic loss to Hawai'i in unemployment, lost wages, retail sales, and small businesses that go out of business. Hawaii's economy depends on shipping, so 34,000 Hawai'i workers lost jobs, and hotel occupancy fell to 36%.

October 25, 1949: 15,000 U.S. soldiers "invade" Wai'anae as part of Operation Miki war games.

October 26, 1949: Governor Ingram Stainback signs a law to prohibit government workers from striking.

October 26, 1949: U.S. Navy announces that submarines will launch a missile near Moloka'i on November 7.

November 1, 1949: Governor Ingram Stainback signs a law to create the Hawai'i Civilian Conservation Corps. This $3 million agency provides jobs and vocational training to single males, age 17-23.

November 11, 1949: Hawai'i is declared "E" for unemployment emergency for having more than 12% unemployment territory-wide – due to the 6-month dock worker strike. Hawaii's unemployment rate is about 15% – our highest-ever.

1949: Young Navy officer Jimmy Carter is the only U.S. president to have lived in Hawai'i. He and wife Rosalynn lived in Navy Housing near Pearl Harbor until 1950. His son Chip was born at Tripler on April 12, 1950.

1950-1959

March 7, 1950: U.S. House of Representatives passes a statehood bill, 262-110. It is the second time a statehood bill has passed the House.

March 8, 1950: U.S. Army opens Diamond Head crater to the public for the first time in 46 years.

March 28, 1950: The first family moves into A&B's fee simple residential homes in Kahului, known as "Dream City." About 3,160 homes are built for plantation workers in the next 30 years

April 1, 1950: Federal census begins. Hawai'i has 499,794 population – an 18% increase since 1940 – 17% Hawaiian, 25% Caucasian, 6% Chinese, 37% Japanese, 12% Filipino.

April 4, 1950:   A 63-member Hawai'i Constitutional Convention (Con Con) opens at 'Iolani Palace to draft a state constitution that will influence Congress to grant statehood.

April 5, 1950: A "snorkel-type" submarine, PICKERAL, arrives in Pearl Harbor after traveling 5,200 miles in 21 days underwater from Hong Kong. It is the longest known underwater trip. The sub features a unique breathing tube to the surface.

April 10, 1950: U.S. House UnAmerican Activities Committee (HUAC) begins 9 days of hearings in 'Iolani Palace to review alleged Communist influence in Hawaii's labor organizations. Con Con Delegate Richard Kageyama tells HUAC he was a Communist Party member in 1947, but he quit when he became "disillusioned." He names other Communists. On April 11, he resigns as a Con Con delegate, but doesn't resign from the Honolulu Board of Supervisors.

April 11, 1950: Former ILWU president Ichiro Izuka tells HUAC there were 130 Communists in Hawai'i in 1946, and 90% are ILWU leaders.

April 19, 1950: Marguerite Ashford, a Moloka'i Con Con delegate, authors a resolution asking Congress to repeal the 1920 Hawaiian Homes Commission law and to give current lessees the fee simple land title. She says the Commission "tends to create racial tension. It discriminates between citizens of race and even percentage of blood."

April 20, 1950: The last day of HUAC hearings. Throughout the hearings, many ILWU members "took the 5th" when asked if they are Communists. For refusing to testify, they are known as the "Reluctant 39," and charged with contempt of Congress. They are acquitted in January 1951. The issue of Communist influence becomes a major obstacle to statehood.

April 20, 1950: U.S. Senator Hugh Butler says Communism in Hawai'i "seems to be almost the rule" rather than the exception.

April 20, 1950: Constitutional Convention expels delegate Frank Silva when he is cited for contempt of Congress by refusing to answer questions from HUAC. On April 11, Izuka told HUAC that Silva is a Communist. Silva and Kageyama are the two Con Con delegates who depart for their Communist Party membership.

April 23, 1950: A front-page HONOLULU ADVERTISER story reports that the just-completed Congressional HUAC hearings "prove conclusively" that Communists control Hawaii's Democratic party and ILWU, and are trying to control education, government and labor.

April 30, 1950: Democratic Party Convention splits over concerns about Communist influence. More than 100 of 485 delegates walk out, and each group calls itself the Democratic Party.

June 1, 1950: Mauna Loa erupts for 23 days, sending three lava flows to the ocean. It is one of the largest Mauna Loa eruptions in recorded history, and is visible from Diamond Head, 200 miles away. Lava covers 112 square miles of land.

June 14, 1950: Hawaiian Air is the first U.S. airline to receive the National Safety Council's 20-year award for having no fatalities.

July 22, 1950: After 110 days, the Hawai'i Constitutional Convention approves a state constitution to take effect when Congress okays statehood. One delegate refuses to sign the constitution – Marguerite Ashford is home on Moloka'i "on principle" to oppose it.

August 1, 1950: Salvador "Dado" Marino is the first Hawai'i resident to win a boxing crown. He defeats Terry Allen of London for the world flyweight boxing championship. 10,000 fans attend the fight at Honolulu Stadium.

August 14, 1950: IMUA seeks to ban pro-Communism books and magazines from public libraries.

August 14, 1950: The first hurricane given a name, Hiki, has 80 mph winds, killing one person, and causing $200,000 damage on Kaua'i.

September 11, 1950: Mauna'olu College, a former seminary, opens on Maui as a junior college with 65 students.

September 23, 1950: The McCarran Internal Security Act becomes law when Congress overrides President Harry Truman's veto. The new law allows the federal government to intern any person during a national emergency. The law also requires Communist organizations to register with the U.S. government. Hawai'i Congressman Spark Matsunaga sponsors legislation to repeal this law, which President Richard Nixon signs on September 25, 1971.

October 13, 1950: President Harry Truman comes to Hawai'i for 16 hours. He visits military bases, then flies to Wake Island to meet General Douglas MacArthur. On his return trip, he stays one day.

November 7, 1950: Hawai'i voters ratify a proposed state constitution by an overwhelming 3-1 margin. The constitution has a strong anti-Communism clause.

December 22, 1950: A 35-day bus strike begins until January 26, 1951. On January 24, 1951, it is estimated that private jitneys carried 50,000 people a day during the strike.

January 19, 1951: Federal Judge Delbert Metzger acquits all of the "Reluctant 39" of contempt of Congress charges. They are defended by attorney Harriet Bouslog.

January 27, 1951: A HUAC report says the HONOLULU RECORD newspaper is a front for the Communist Party because it promotes Chinese Communists and a Hawai'i Civil Liberties committee.

February 10, 1951: ILWU organizer Jack Kawano tells the Territorial Subversive Activities Committee he's a former Communist, and urges workers to kick out "all Communists" from union membership. In the 1930s some labor leaders were attracted to Communism as a way to help unions fight the powerful plantations. Kawano says Communism is "destructive" to unions, and borders on "treason" to America, especially during the Korean War. On July 6, Kawano tells a Congressional HUAC hearing that he was a Communist from 1937-1949, and submits a list of ILWU members who are Communists.

February 27, 1951: A 7-month, 201-day strike by 750 Lāna'i workers against Hawai'i Pineapple Company begins. It is Hawaii's longest pineapple strike. The ILWU strike ends September 14, 1951. Workers win better wages and living conditions.

March 14, 1951: UH Regents cancel dedication ceremonies for a new Chemistry building and withdraw their invitation to Dr. Linus Pauling, a distinguished scientist and peace activist. Regents fear Pauling may have Communist sympathies because he objects to loyalty oaths. Pauling wins two Nobel Prizes – for Chemistry in 1954 and for Peace in 1962.

April 16, 1951: General Douglas MacArthur is welcomed by 100,000 people in Hawai'i, en route to Washington, D.C., where he will tell Congress on April 19, "Old soldiers never die, they just fade away." On April 11, President Harry Truman fired MacArthur as U.S. Commander of the Korean War effort.

May 4, 1951: Waikīkī Theatre hosts the world premiere of the MGM movie, GO FOR BROKE. Star Van Johnson attends. The movie is about the heroic 442nd soldiers that rescued the Texas "Lost Battalion." Several Hawai'i Nisei veterans play themselves in the movie.

Governor Oren Long

May 8, 1951: Oren Long becomes Hawaii's 10th territorial governor until February 28, 1953. He is appointed by President Harry Truman. He serves less than two years – the shortest term of any Hawai'i governor. He had been a Hawai'i school teacher and Superintendent of Public Instruction. In 1959 he will be elected to the U.S. Senate.

May 18, 1951: Governor Oren Long signs a law to allow women to serve on a Territorial jury.

May 21, 1951: Governor Oren Long signs 4 loyalty oath laws during the next 10 days. These laws require all government workers to take a loyalty oath, establish a Territorial Loyalty Board with powers to conduct secret investigations, and require government employees to testify if called before a judge or government agency.

June 6, 1951: Governor Oren Long signs a law to require physically fit, general assistance welfare recipients to work at government parks and public works jobs.

August 16, 1951: Chinese newspaper, CHUNG-HUA HSIN PAO, also known as NEW UNITED CHINESE PRESS, begins publication, and continues until April 29, 1998. It attains 4,000 circulation. The newspaper began in 1928 as CHUNG-HUA KUNG PAO, also known as UNITED CHINESE NEWS.

August 21, 1951: An earthquake near Kona measures 6.9 magnitude, and creates $600,000 damage.

August 28, 1951: FBI arrests 7 people known as the "Hawai'i 7," while another 48 are suspected of being Communist agents or advocating the overthrow of the U.S. government. ILWU leader Jack Hall, John Reinecke, Koji Ariyoshi, and 4 others are arrested for violating the federal Smith Act. Federal Judge Delbert Metzger is criticized for reducing the bail from $75,000 to $5,000. The trial begins November 10, 1952, and they are convicted on June 19, 1953. On July 3, most are sentenced by Federal Judge Jon Wiig to 5 years in jail. The guilty verdicts are reversed by a federal Appeals Court in 1958.

October 10, 1951: Hawaii's first tunnel on a public road opens. Lahaina tunnel is 315 feet long.

October 11, 1951: President Harry Truman responds to controversy about removing religious crosses from 13,000 graves at Hawaiian National Cemetery. He approves the Army's decision to provide flat headstones upon request for Hawaiian residents, while other military get crosses or Stars of David.

October 15, 1951: Journalist Bob Krauss begins work at the HONOLULU ADVERTISER. In the next 50 years, he writes nearly 8,300 columns and 14 books, and is honored as "a living treasure of Hawai'i."

December 24, 1951: Art Rutledge founds the Hawai'i Federation of Labor Memorial Association, which becomes Unity House in 1955, an organization of Teamsters, Hotel Workers and Transit Workers unions.

January 9, 1952: Governor Oren Long appoints Sakae Takahashi as Territorial Treasurer. He is the first AJA in a governor's cabinet.

January 15, 1952: Kāne'ohe Marine Air Station is commissioned. The former Kāne'ohe Naval Air Station was de-commissioned in May 1949, then assigned to the Marines Corps in 1951.

February 14, 1952: 800 workers strike three Matson-owned hotels for 15 days, following a 2-day strike on January 18. The hotels are Royal Hawaiian, Moana, and Surfrider.

March 26, 1952: U.S. Post Office issues an 80¢ air mail stamp with a picture of Diamond Head.

April 18, 1952: Hiram Fong and others establish Finance Factors to provide affordable home loans for people having difficulty with other banks.

May 24, 1952: Bishop Estate sells the historic and scenic Hale'iwa Hotel, which will be demolished.

June 20, 1952: Hawai'i Governor Oren Long signs a full pardon for labor leader Pablo Manlapit for his September 27, 1924 "criminal conspiracy" conviction for the Hanapēpē riot. As a pardon condition, Manlapit agrees never to live or work in Hawai'i, but he can visit his family.

June 27, 1952: Kīlauea erupts for 5 months until November 10. It is the first eruption since 1934, adding 300 feet to the crater floor.

June 27, 1952: U.S. Senate overrides President Harry Truman's veto of the Omnibus Immigration Law, known as McCarran-Walter Immigration and Nationality Act. The law establishes a quota of 105 immigrants annually from every Asian nation, and makes about 30,000 alien Japanese, Chinese, Koreans and Samoans eligible for U.S. citizenship.

September 1, 1952: ILWU Local 142 is established to consolidate longshore, sugar, pineapple, general trades, and tourism workers.

September 18, 1952: In secret session, the School Board adopts a policy to allow public school students to have an hour of weekly religious lessons not at a public school. It counts as public school attendance.

November 4, 1952: An Alaska earthquake sends a 13-foot wave to Mokule'ia and creates up to $1 million property damage in Hawai'i.

December 1, 1952: KGMB-TV broadcasts Hawaii's first live television program, seen by 10,000 viewers, followed by a Gene Autry movie. The program is hosted by Carl Hebenstreit (also known as Kini Pōpō). KGMB is initially affiliated with CBS, then NBC and ABC. On November 17, KONA-TV, half-owned by the HONOLULU ADVERTISER, tested the first telecast on two receivers.

December 11, 1952: President-elect Dwight Eisenhower arrives in Honolulu for 3 days, returning from a visit to Korea. He is welcomed by about 100,000 people. This is the first presidential visit to be televised.

January 21, 1953: For the first time, Hawai'i women serve on a federal court jury. Eight female jurors are selected for a narcotics trial.

January 25, 1953: Lyle Guslander opens Coco Palms Resort on Kaua'i. The site has a huge coconut grove, planted in 1896, and several lagoons. Queen Deborah Kūpule, Kauai's last queen,lived here. In 1954, the hotel held the first "Call to Feast" torch lighting ceremony at sundown, since copied by many hotels, and featured in the 1961 Elvis Presley movie, BLUE HAWAI'I. The ceremony is a nightly event until Hurricane 'Iniki in 1992, which closes the hotel.

February 2, 1953: President Dwight Eisenhower is the second president to support Hawai'i statehood. In his State of the Union speech, he says statehood "should be granted promptly."

February 20, 1953: President Dwight Eisenhower signs Executive Order 10436 giving the U.S. Navy full control of Kaho'olawe. The Order requires the Navy to restore the soil and make the island "reasonably safe for human habitation, without cost to the Territory."

Governor Samuel King

February 28, 1953: Samuel King becomes Hawaii's 11th Territorial Governor, and Hawaii's first part-Hawaiian governor until July 31, 1957. He is appointed by President Dwight Eisenhower. He gives much of his inauguration speech in Hawaiian, which is reprinted in the HONOLULU STAR-BULLETIN. He was Hawaii's Congressional Delegate from 1934-1944. After his governorship, he is elected to the Territorial Legislature. From 1917-1921, Secretary of Hawai'i Curtis I'aukea, a native Hawaiian, was acting governor whenever the governor left Hawai'i.

March 2, 1953: Hawai'i Territory Commission on Subversive Activities releases a report that says, "...Continuing Communist control of the ILWU in...Hawai'i will endanger the national security of the United States in the event of war" with Russia.

March 10, 1953: U.S. House passes a statehood bill, 274-138. It is the 3rd time the House has passed a statehood bill.

March 29, 1953: Former U.S. President Harry Truman arrives in Hawai'i for a one-month vacation on Coconut Island. The island is owned by Edwin Pauley, a wealthy Democratic Party fundraiser and oilman.

April 19, 1953: The Columbia Pictures movie, FROM HERE TO ETERNITY, based on James Jones' book, is filmed in Hawai'i for 3 weeks, starring Burt Lancaster, Deborah Kerr, and Frank Sinatra. The movie wins the Academy Award for Best Picture of the Year, and Sinatra wins for Best Supporting Actor. The famous beach scene is filmed near Hālona Blowhole. Jones was stationed at Schofield Barracks during WW II.

May 8, 1953: 1,000 people attend a House Finance Committee hearing. It is the largest crowd to date at a legislative hearing. People testify that school teachers are the "forgotten man" and deserve a pay hike.

May 9, 1953: HRT bus drivers take the first of 5 consecutive "weekend strikes" through June.

June 23, 1953: Territorial Supreme Court upholds the constitutionality of an 1894 gambling law to allow the prosecution of anyone watching or serving refreshments during any professional and social gambling.

June 25, 1953: The U.S. Navy is creating 220 civil service jobs to load and unload Navy ships because ILWU workers "walked out" the past weekend.

July 3, 1953: The "Hawai'i 7" are convicted of violating the federal anti-Communist, Smith Act. Six are sentenced to 5 years in prison and $5,000 fine. On June 19, ILWU protests the convictions with a 4-day strike of sugar, pineapple and dock workers. The convictions are over-turned by a federal appeals court in 1958.

July 11, 1953: All 58 people aboard a Transoceanic Airline flight die in an ocean crash en route to Hawai'i from Wake Island.

October 7, 1953: Vice President Richard Nixon arrives in Hawai'i for three days. He speaks to 3,000 students from Roosevelt and Stevenson schools. He came to Hawai'i earlier as a Congressman with HUAC, and returns on July 2, 1956, for a 10-hour stop en route to the Philippines and a round-the-world trip.

October 21, 1953: Carl "Bobo" Olson of Hawai'i wins the world middle-weight boxing crown. He defeats Randy Turpin in New York's Madison Square Garden.

October 29, 1953: The first airplane crash of a Hawai'i-to-mainland commercial flight kills all 19 people. The British Commonwealth and Pacific Airlines flight crashes near San Francisco Airport.

November 9, 1953: Hawaii's first freeway opens, with 3 west-bound lanes covering one mile between Old Wai'alae Road and Alexander Street. It is the first section of a 7-mile, $350 million Lunalilo Freeway, now called H-1. The east bound lanes open on January 5, 1954.

December 17, 1953: Federal Judge Calvin McGregor orders all property owned by Makiki Japanese Language School that was confiscated during WW II to be returned. The school had lost 42,000 square feet of land. School officials were interned during the war.

February 10, 1954: In a one-day effort, 116,000 people stand outside the Alexander Young Hotel to sign a one mile-long petition known as the "Statehood Honor Roll" urging Congress to grant statehood. "Midget" honor rolls are signed on Neighbor Islands. On February 26, the petitions are delivered to Vice President Richard Nixon in Washington, D.C. They are now filed in the National Archives.

February 15, 1954: Central Pacific Bank opens to better serve Hawaii's Japanese population. For most of the bank's existence, it is managed by former executives of California's Sumitomo Bank.

116,000 people sign the "Statehood Honor Roll" petition

April 1, 1954: By a 57-28 vote, the U.S. Senate passes a statehood bill that combines Alaska and Hawai'i into one bill, but the House refuses to consider it. This is the first time the Senate passes a Hawai'i statehood bill. From 1947-1954, the House passed 3 statehood bills. Prior to the favorable Senate vote, the Senate defeated an amendment 60-24, to give Hawai'i Commonwealth status, like Puerto Rico.

April 1, 1954: KHON radio disk jockey Hal "Aku" Lewis plays a successful April fool's joke. He tells listeners the U.S. Senate has approved statehood and will give Hawai'i residents an "immediate" refund of their 1953 federal income taxes. People jam the phone lines to the IRS for several hours.

April 22, 1954: More than 300 ILWU workers at Hutchinson Sugar Company at Nā'alehu, Hawai'i Island begin a 129-day sugar strike to support a fired worker. The strike ends on August 30, 1954.

May 3, 1954: The Territorial Health Department declares polio an epidemic on several islands, with 100 cases. By December 31, 1955, more than 65,000 people have received polio shots, and Hawai'i is among the nation's leaders for giving people the Salk vaccine.

May 31, 1954: Kīlauea erupts for 3 days with 500 foot fountains. It is the first eruption on the main crater floor since 1921.

July 15, 1954: Former Governor Ingram Stainback, now a Hawai'i Supreme Court Justice, rejects Hawai'i statehood and now prefers a commission government like Puerto Rico has. He writes 4 editorial articles in the HONOLULU ADVERTISER from July 15-18.

August 14, 1954: Wilson Tunnel caves in during construction, killing 5 people. The City and contractor E.E. Black agree on a $1 million out-of-court settlement on January 21, 1956. There are three more cave-ins in 1954, but no one dies.

October 22, 1954: When their boat sinks, August Duvachelle, age 40 and his 17-year old son August Jr., swim 10 hours through the 8-mile Moloka'i Channel.

November 2, 1954: Democrats win control of the Hawai'i Legislature for the first time. Since 1959, Democrats have usually won 2/3 or more of the Legislature.

November 2, 1954: Peter Aduja (R) of East Hawai'i is the first person of Filipino ancestry elected to the Hawai'i Legislature.

November 20, 1954: The first giant Galapagos tortoise born in a zoo, is born in Honolulu Zoo. It grows from 2 ounces to 112 lbs. in 10 years.

January 4, 1955: A new and rebuilt $400,000 Waikīkī Aquarium opens.

February 28, 1955: Kīlauea erupts for 88 days, requiring an evacuation of Puna. The lava buries 12 homes, and causes $3 million damage on 5,000 agriculture acres.

March 22, 1955: Hawaii's worst airplane crash. 800 miles after leaving Hickam for California, a Navy DC 6 radio doesn't work, so the airplane turns back and crashes into a Lualualei Valley mountain, killing all 66 people.

May 10, 1955: U.S. House of Representatives votes 218-170 to reject a bill to grant statehood to both Hawai'i and Alaska.

May 12, 1955: Kaua'i Board of Supervisors chairman Anthony Baptiste is found guilty by a jury for not filing a federal income tax return in 1952. He serves 10 months of a one year sentence, and returns to Kaua'i and continues serving as board chairman until 1961.

May 27, 1955: The Legislature adjourns and Hawaii's only 670-hour day ends. The 'Iolani Palace clock was stopped for 28 days. The Legislature finishes its work in special session.

May 28, 1955: Governor Sam King vetoes a joint resolution for water fluoridation.

June 10, 1955: Roy Kelley's $4 million, 350 room, Reef Hotel opens. It is Hawaii's largest beachfront hotel since 1927. The family-owned Outrigger Hotels will eventually open 21 hotels, becoming Hawaii's largest hotel company, with 7,500 rooms.

June 11, 1955: Matson opens its 3rd Waikīkī hotel, Ka'iulani Hotel with 300 rooms. Matson has one-third of Waikiki's 3,600 hotel rooms.

June 21, 1955: Ben Tashiro of Kaua'i is the first AJA to become a Hawai'i judge. He is nominated by President Dwight Eisenhower.

July 1, 1955: Joe and Ethel Murphy begin HAWAI'I ENGINEER magazine, which is renamed HAWAI'I BUSINESS AND INDUSTRY in 1964 and HAWAI'I BUSINESS in 1969. It is America's oldest regional business magazine.

July 11, 1955: A HONOLULU STAR-BULLETIN story reports a Stanford Research Institute study that says mainland companies are not likely to move here because Hawai'i is perceived as "too small and closely controlled" by government and the Big 5.

July 26, 1955: Stuart and Lee Fern establish the WAIKĪKĪ BEACH PRESS newspaper to promote tourism and inform tourists. By 1974, the newspaper advertises itself as the world's largest tourism newspaper, with 59,000 English and 35,000 Japanese circulation, and Neighbor Island editions. The newspaper ends publication on April 5, 1993.

July 26, 1955: City of Refuge National Historical Park is established on 164 acres. It was built about 1425 A.D. as a place where kapu breakers and defeated warriors could be safe.

September 12, 1955: St. Louis Junior College opens with 35 students. In 1957, it is renamed Chaminade College, and then Chaminade University on August 15, 1977.

September 18, 1955: Henry Kaiser opens his first Hawai'i hotel, the 100-room Kaiser-Burns Hawaiian Village. Rooms cost $6-$18 a night. Kaiser plans to expand to 3,200 rooms. He advertises the hotel on a popular national TV program, MAVERICK. The hotel becomes the Hilton Hawaiian Village in 1961.

September 28, 1955: Church College of Hawai'i opens as a two-year college with 150 students in Lā'ie. In 1974, the school is re-named Brigham Young University-Hawai'i.

January 1, 1956: 60 people injured from New Year's eve fireworks are treated at hospitals. On December 18, 1956, Mayor Neal Blaisdell signs a law to restrict fireworks, but he complains it is too weak.

January 5, 1956: President Dwight Eisenhower "urgently" requests statehood for Hawai'i in his State of Union message. He says, "Statehood would be a shining example of the American way to the entire earth." Hawai'i is "a unique example of a community that is a successful laboratory in human brotherhood."

January 31, 1956: U.S. Marine Corps Camp Smith is dedicated on 220 acres at a site formerly used as a WW II Navy hospital. It is named for General Holland "Howlin Mad" Smith, a former commanding general of the Marine's Pacific force.

March 24, 1956: The scenic Onomea Arch on the Hilo coast collapses in the center from erosion. Two large, unconnected walls are left, but the arch is missing.

April 6, 1956: Hawai'i Supreme Court suspends attorney Harriet Bouslog for "gross misconduct." In 1952, she said the "Hawai'i 7" aren't getting a fair trial in federal court. On June 29, 1959, the U.S. Supreme Court overturns her suspension. Bouslog often upset the establishment by winning many controversial civil rights and labor cases.

April 10, 1956: Governor Samuel King announces plans to build a 75-acre, $3.5 million island near Ala Moana Park, plus $1.5 million for site improvements for hotels and apartments.

August 1, 1956: Masaji Marumoto, a Honolulu attorney, becomes Hawaii's first AJA and non-Caucasian on the Hawai'i Territorial Supreme Court. He is nominated by President Dwight Eisenhower.

September 8, 1956: The $351,000 Waikīkī Shell opens with weekend concerts by jazz and military bands. On September 29, the Honolulu Symphony performs.

October 16, 1956: The U.S. Coast Guard rescues all 31 crew and passengers aboard a Pan American World Airways airplane, about halfway between San Francisco and Hawai'i.

November 10, 1956: ILWU chief Harry Bridges tells his 23,000 union members that U.S. Senator James Eastland wants to destroy the ILWU and deny statehood for Hawai'i. Bridges asks workers to protest the upcoming Senate hearings by walking off their jobs and attending the hearings. About 6,200 ILWU workers or one-third of Oahu's members walk off their jobs.

November 13, 1956: Hawai'i Attorney General Edward Sylva resigns at Governor Samuel King's request, for joining 700 people at a November 10 testimonial dinner honoring ILWU regional director Jack Hall.

Hall was convicted in 1953 of violating the federal Smith Act for Communist-related activities. His conviction is overturned in 1958.

November 15, 1956: Hawaii's Consumer Price Index for cost-of-living is 145, the highest ever, announced the Territory Department of Labor.

November 30, 1956: U.S. Senator James Eastland (D-Mississippi) brings his Senate Internal Security Subcommittee to Hawai'i to investigate Communism. The week-long hearings end on December 6. Eastland declares that "conspiratorial forces" influence Hawai'i and its labor unions. Four former Communists testify in Executive Session, and 20 of the 34 people called to testify take the 5th Amendment. Former Hawai'i Attorney General Edward Sylva tells the committee that the ILWU is not controlled by Communists.

January 3, 1957: John Burns becomes Hawaii's first Democratic delegate to Congress since 1932, and only the 3rd Democrat since annexation. He defeated Elizabeth Farrington on November 6, 1956.

January 15, 1957: A geodesic dome is built in 20 hours at Henry Kaiser's Hawaiian Village for the world movie premiere of AROUND THE WORLD IN 80 DAYS, attended by producer Michael Todd and his wife, actress Elizabeth Taylor. The $80,000, 49-foot high dome is designed by Buckminster Fuller, and made of Kaiser aluminum. The 2,000-seat dome is Waikiki's biggest nightclub. It is the home of the Don Ho show, which opens on December 26, 1981, and continues for 10 years.

February 9, 1957: Amfac announces plans for a major Neighbor Island tourist resort center at Kā'anapali.

March 9, 1957: An Alaska earthquake sends a 32-foot tsunami to Hā'ena, Kaua'i that destroys 30 homes. Two people die and $5 million damage is done territory-wide.

May 9, 1957: HVB reports that 70% of Hawai'i visitors go to a neighbor island, but O'ahu gets 91% of the tourist money. The 54-page report is the first HVB attempt to analyze neighbor island tourism.

May 11, 1957: Nu'uanu Pali Highway's $3 million tunnels open to traffic. The new highway is 8.3 miles.

May 13, 1957: Governor Samuel King signs a law to allow agricultural workers to collect unemployment benefits.

June 4, 1957: Governor Samuel King signs a law making Hawaii the 7th state to repeal the death penalty, and substitute life without parole. In all, 46 people were legally hanged in Hawai'i.

June 7, 1957: Governor Samuel King vetoes a bill to raise the excise tax from 2.5¢ to 3.5¢, but the Legislature overrides the veto during a special session

August 13, 1957: 20th Century Fox finishes filming the movie SOUTH PACIFIC at Kauai's Lumaha'i Beach, which is made famous by the movie. The $5 million cost is the biggest Hollywood budget to date. The movie, released in 1958, adapts the Rodgers and Hammerstein Broadway play, based on James Michener's Pulitzer Prize winning book, TALES OF THE SOUTH PACIFIC.

September 2, 1957: William Quinn becomes Hawaii's 12th and last territorial governor, and the first elected state governor until December 3, 1962. He is appointed by President Dwight Eisenhower. Quinn moved to Hawai'i in 1947 to practice law.

September 8, 1957: American Telephone and Telegraph Company (ATT) and Hawaiian Telephone complete two undersea $37 million telephone cables going east to California and west to Asia. They are the world's longest cables. The cables make phone conversation easy to hear.

September 9, 1957: An education report, prepared by William Odell of Stanford University, concludes – "Compared to public school systems in the United States, Hawai'i is spending only about 80-85% as much as the average and far less than the best." The report says that twice as many Hawai'i students are receiving less than a 5th grade education than on the mainland – 24% in Hawai'i and 11% on the mainland.

National News

September 24, 1957: President Dwight Eisenhower sends 1,000 Army troops to enforce racial integration in a Little Rock high school. On September 30, 1958, Arkansas Gov. Orval Faubus closes 4 high schools rather than integrate.

October 8, 1957: For the first time, a telephone connects the Atlantic, Pacific and Alaska via undersea and mainland cables. At a special ceremony in 'Iolani Palace, people in London, Alaska, New York and Honolulu speak on a telephone.

November 8, 1957: A Pan American airplane crashes into the ocean, midway from San Francisco to Honolulu, killing all 44 people aboard. The biggest search ever in the Pacific involves 135 airplanes and 35 ships.

November 30, 1957: Hurricane Niña passes 60 miles from Kaua'i, killing one person, and causing $200,000 damage.

January 15, 1958: Dr. Kenneth Emory a Bishop Museum anthropologist says Tahitians came to Hawai'i beginning 750 A.D., and South Point was settled by 957 A.D. In 1950, he took the first radiocarbon date, which proved the occupation of Kuli'ou'ou in the 10th or 11th century.

January 20, 1958: A federal Appeals Court reverses the June 19, 1953 convictions of the "Hawai'i 7" for violating the Smith Act. The court ruling is based on a 1957 U.S. Supreme Court decision that membership in the Communist Party does not violate the Smith Act. After this ruling, the anti-Communist hysteria in Hawai'i quickly fades.

February 1, 1958: A 128-day strike by 13,000 ILWU sugar workers against 26 plantations begins. It is known as "The Aloha Strike" because the union allows some members to continue working so everyone won't lose their jobs. The strike results in major union gains – big wage hikes and a 40-hour work week. Governor William Quinn helps to negotiate a final settlement.

February 20, 1958: Trans Pacific Airlines becomes Aloha Airlines when Dr. Hung Wo Ching is named president and CEO of the airline, and Rudy Tongg is named chairman of the board. On November 13, Dr. Ching tries to buy Hawaiian Air Lines. In January 1959, he is the first Asian-American elected to the Bank of Hawai'i board of directors.

February 21, 1958: USS GUDGEON, the first U.S. submarine to travel around the world – it took 150 days – visits Pearl Harbor.

March 1, 1958: Author James Michener finishes writing his 12th book, HAWAI'I, which becomes a national best-seller and is made into a movie. The book is severely criticized here, allegedly for not presenting the truth. The novel is about immigrants who become a "Golden People," influenced by Eastern and Western ideas, and how they eventually learn "to live together in harmony."

March 5, 1958: Hawai'i gets 17 inches of rain in 24 hours.

National
News

April 16, 1958: Nuclear scientist Dr. Edward Teller warns the U.S. Senate that stopping nuclear bomb tests would endanger the lives of millions of Americans if there is an atomic war.

April 19, 1958: A small 30-foot boat, GOLDEN RULE, owned by Captain Albert Bigelow, a former Navy Lt. Commander, arrives in Honolulu with a crew of 4 pacifists. He is en route to the Eniwetok nuclear test area to protest U.S. nuclear testing. On May 7, federal Judge John Wiig finds Bigelow guilty of contempt, and sentences him to one-week in jail. Bigelow and his crew defy an Atomic Energy Commission order not to sail to Eniwetok, and they are arrested by the Coast Guard on June 4 after sailing 5 miles. He spends 60 days in jail for ignoring a court order to avoid the test area. He gets one-year probation. On June 28, 1958, Bigelow sells the ship.

May 29, 1958: During war exercises, the destroyer USS SILVERSTEIN collides into the $10 million submarine STICKLEBACK. All 82 crew are rescued before the sub sinks, 19 miles from Pearl Harbor.

June 27, 1958: Kūhiō Theatre hosts the world premiere of the movie SOUTH PACIFIC. All ticket sales are donated to the USS ARIZONA memorial. Author James Michener speaks at the premiere.

June 28, 1958: Nuclear submarine NAUTILUS stops in Honolulu for several weeks to teach its nuclear program to the Navy. The sub traveled 6,000 miles underwater to get here. The first atomic-powered submarine based in Hawai'i is the USS SARGO, which arrives in October.

July 7, 1958: President Dwight Eisenhower signs a law to make Alaska the nation's 49th state. Granting statehood to Alaska first is a compromise strategy negotiated by Hawai'i Congressional Delegate John Burns, because it will improve Hawaii's chances for statehood.

August 1, 1958: Night becomes day at 1 a.m. when the U.S. explodes a nuclear bomb above Johnston Island, 700 miles away. The explosion creates a white flash followed by flashes of several bright colors. The bomb is a surprise because the military didn't give any advance notice to Hawai'i. Governor William Quinn asks the military for advance notice about future nuclear explosions. Two more nuclear bombs are dropped above Johnston Island, on July 8 and November 1, 1962. Each explosion is one million tons of TNT or 50 times more powerful than Hiroshima.

August 20, 1958: Honolulu City pays $2 million to buy the 23-acre Ward Estate, known as "Old Plantation," built in 1880. The Southern mansion home and grounds are surrounded by a tall fence and covered in mystery. On September 20, 1959, 4,000 people tour the estate, which is open to public view for the first time. The Blaisdell Center is located here, with the original lagoon and many of the coconut trees.

September 20, 1958: A 12-ton raft, LEHI IV, with 4 sails and a 4-man crew arrive in Kahului after deliberately drifting 2,800 miles from San Pedro, California in 69 days. The 20 x 18 foot raft is built for $30,000. Skipper Devere Baker said his trip proves that Hawai'i could have been settled by North Americans, as the BOOK OF MORMON says, and the settlement of the world's population could have been influenced by ocean currents. He is greeted by 2,000 people in Kahului. Baker's first words are, "Where's the nearest hamburger stand?" The arrival receives national news coverage.

September 21, 1958: Former Honolulu news reporter, Roy Essoyan of Associated Press, is expelled from Russia for allegedly violating Soviet censorship laws. He leaves September 26. He is the 4th reporter expelled this year.

September 21, 1958: St. Andrew's Church is dedicated 90 years after King Kamehameha V laid the cornerstone on March 5, 1867.

October 10, 1958: Aloha Airlines rejects Hawaiian Airline's $700,000 purchase offer. On November 13, Aloha offers to buy Hawaiian under similar terms that Hawaiian had offered Aloha.

January 3, 1959: Alaska becomes the 49th state, and Hawai'i gains 2 more Senate votes to ensure statehood.

January 22, 1959: Hung Wo Ching, president of Aloha Air, is the first non-Caucasian elected to the Bank of Hawai'i board of directors.

February 15, 1959: On a "dare," first-time writer and Hawai'i military housewife Heloise Cruise writes her first newspaper column about housekeeping tips, although she had never cleaned a toilet until her marriage 6 months earlier. The HONOLULU ADVERTISER gives her column, "Readers Exchange," a 30-day trial, and it eventually becomes nationally syndicated as "Hints from Heloise." On June 21, 1961, editor George Chaplin says, "It's the most fantastic rapport between columnist and readers I've ever known." Chaplin credits her for a huge circulation increase.

March 11, 1959: U.S. Senate passes a Hawai'i statehood bill, 76-15.

March 12, 1959: The U.S. House of Representatives passes a statehood bill, 323-89.

March 18, 1959: President Dwight Eisenhower signs the Hawai'i state-hood Admissions Act to make Hawai'i the 50th State on August 21. The U.S. transfers former Hawaiian Government and Crown lands to the State of Hawai'i, and puts the land in a public trust for native Ha-waiians and for specific public purposes. It took 61 years for Hawai'i to become a state. Only New Mexico waited longer for statehood. From 1935-1959, Congress held 22 statehood hearings, 15 in Wash-ington, D.C., and 7 in Hawai'i. Since 1919, 63 Hawai'i statehood bills were introduced in Congress.

April 9, 1959: America's "original 7" Mercury astronauts are introduced, and two have ties to Hawai'i. They are Wally Schirra, whose parents live in Foster Village, and Gordon Cooper, who attended the Univer-sity of Hawai'i as an Engineering student from 1946-1949.

April 19, 1959: HONOLULU STAR-BULLETIN reports that representa-tives of several airlines – Pan Am, United, Japan Air, Cana-dian Pacific – say Hawai'i is losing $30 million a year be-cause there aren't enough hotel rooms here, so they aren't fly-ing tour groups to Hawai'i.

May 11, 1959: The last Territorial Legislature adjourns.

May 12, 1959: Hawaii's two wealthiest men insult each other in public. Henry Kaiser, age 77, and Walter Dillingham, age 84, argue at a Wai'anae public meeting about Kaiser's proposed Mā'ili cement plant project. Kaiser accuses Dillingham of "underhanded" tactics to pre-vent competition and Walter Dillingham, who owns Hawaiian Cement, calls Kaiser "a visitor here." Dillingham says, "I don't think it is a very nice thing for a visitor to Hawai'i, no matter how many millions he's spent here, to attack a son of mine, and of Hawai'i."

June 1, 1959: Matson sells its 4 Waikīkī hotels to Sheraton for $18 mil-lion. The hotels are Royal Hawaiian, Moana, Surfrider and Princess Ka'iulani.

June 10, 1959: During the general election campaign, Governor William Quinn promises a "second Mahele." He would divide thousands of acres of state lands into one-acre homesites, and sell the land to native Hawaiians for as low as $50 an acre. This campaign promise may have helped Governor Quinn defeat John Burns by 4,000 votes. Quinn submits a proposal to the Legislature on September 1, 1959, but it doesn't pass.

June 20, 1959: The United Filipino Council of Hawai'i is established.

June 23, 1959: The HONOLULU ADVERTISER publishes a 300-page statehood issue that weighs 4 lbs. It is Hawaii's largest newspaper.

June 27, 1959: Hawai'i voters approve a statehood referendum by a 17-1 margin. Voter turnout is 90%. Ni'ihau is the only island to reject statehood. This public vote is required by the U.S. statehood law, but it wasn't offered in 1897-1898 when the U.S. annexation of Hawai'i was debated and finally approved.

June 30, 1959: The first commercial jet lands in Hawai'i. Quantas Airways Boeing 707 connects Sydney and San Francisco via Honolulu.

July 3, 1959: The first "Starlight Concert" is held at Waikīkī Shell, featuring the star folk singers, Kingston Trio and the Honolulu Symphony. Two of the original Trio are from Honolulu – boyhood friends Bob Shane and Dave Guard. The group won two Grammy awards and had several #1 national hit songs and albums. The song TOM DOOLEY sold 3 million copies. Guard leaves the group in 1961.

July 7, 1959: America's top rocket scientist Wehner von Braun tells 1,500 people – the largest UH audience for a lecture – how we will get to the moon.

July 28, 1959: Hawaii's first statehood general election has a 93% turnout of registered voters. President Dwight Eisenhower says that this puts U.S. democracy at work. Incumbent Territorial Governor William Quinn (R), a Caucasian, is Hawaii's first elected state governor and James Kealoha (R), a native Hawaiian is elected Lt. Governor. Hiram Fong (R), a Chinese, and Oren Long (D) a Caucasian, are elected to the U.S. Senate. Daniel Inouye (D), an AJA is elected to the U.S. House. Fong is the first Senator of Asian and Chinese ancestry. Inouye is the first Congressman of Asian and Japanese ancestry.

August 6, 1959: Hurricane Dot hits Kaua'i with 100+ mph winds, causing $20 million damage.

August 10, 1959: Governor Bill Quinn appears on the cover on TIME MAGAZINE, and 13 pages are devoted to Hawai'i.

August 13, 1959: The $28 million, 50-acre Ala Moana Shopping Center opens with 87 stores. It is Hawaii's first major shopping center. From

1953-1959, Hawaiian Dredging and Construction filled the former swamp land with coral from the new yacht harbor at Ala Moana Park. Walter Dillingham bought the property in 1912 for $25,000 from the descendants of Princess Bernice Pauahi Bishop.

August 21, 1959: President Dwight Eisenhower proclaims Hawai'i as the 50th U.S. state. Governor William Quinn takes office.

August 21, 1959: U.S. Post Office issues a 7¢ stamp to celebrate Hawai'i statehood.

August 31, 1959: Hawaii's first State Legislature meets in a lengthy special session until October 22, then another special session from November 9-14. The first regular session opens on February 17, 1960.

September 16, 1959: Rev. Martin Luther King Jr. tells 1,200 people at McKinley High School that America must remedy "its racial problems at home." On February 18, 1964, he urges people at Central Union Church to support civil rights legislation in Congress.

October 1, 1959: Honolulu has Los Angeles-type smog "pollution" called "inversion" from car exhaust, industry and burning waste. People complain they can't see.

October 6, 1959: Wilfred Tsukiyama becomes Hawaii's first AJA Supreme Court Chief Justice on the court's first meeting as a state Supreme Court.

October 7, 1959: The ABC-TV program, HAWAIIAN EYE, starring Robert Conrad is broadcast for 4 years until April 2, 1963. It is the first of several television crime series set in Hawai'i. The TV promotion says, "If you haven't visited the newest state yet, 'Hawaiian Eye' television series is the next best thing." Very little filming is done here.

October 13, 1959: EXPLORER VII satellite is the first satellite to be tracked from Pacific Missile Range at Barking Sands, Kaua'i.

October 15, 1959: Amfac announces the $40 million Kā'anapali Beach Resort as a "second Waikīkī" with 10 hotels on 500 acres during the next 10-15 years on two miles of beachfront. It is Hawaii's first planned resort destination. Amfac Vice President J. Curtis Ednie says, "I envision Maui as a destination area for jets. They will come directly from the mainland instead of stopping in Honolulu." The first hotel opens in 1962.

November 14, 1959: Kīlauea-Iki erupts for 36 days, with Hawaii's highest recorded fountains, 1,900 feet high. It is the 3rd recorded eruption at that site since 1832 and 1868.

1960-1969

January 12, 1960: Puna records 1,000 earthquakes, indicating there will be an eruption soon.

January 13, 1960: Kīlauea erupts for 36 days. The eruption destroys Kapoho village and $1.5 million in crops. On February 3, lava stops when it reaches the Cape Kumukahi Lighthouse and goes around it.

January 30, 1960: Singer Alfred Apaka, age 40, dies. He is one of Hawaii's most popular singers. Comedian Bob Hope gave him his "break" on a national radio show.

February 5, 1960: Transocean Airlines, a California company, officially ends its popular Hawai'i route after 13 years. The airline had provided low-cost charter group flights since July 24, 1946.

February 7, 1960: Halema'uma'u floor collapses 364 feet.

February 17, 1960: Hawai'i State Legislature opens its first regular session, which ends with a special session on July 1.

March 29, 1960: Kahala Community Club votes 407-3 to protest the proposed Kahala Hotel and seek public hearings. Critics charge it is "not sound planning" to turn a residential neighborhood into a "hotel zone." On May 5, City Planning Commission rejects the hotel. However the City Council changes the city Master Plan on July 5, and rezones the land on August 16. The City Council overrides Mayor Neal Blasidell's veto.

April 1, 1960: Federal census begins. Hawai'i has 632,772 population, a 27% increase since 1950 – 16% Hawaiian, 32% Caucasian, 6% Chinese, 32% Japanese, 11% Filipino, 2% Korean.

May 14, 1960: President Dwight Eisenhower signs a law to create the Center for Cultural and Technical Interchange between East and West – to be known as the East-West Center – located at the University of Hawai'i campus. The bill originated when UH faculty desired more cultural interchange, and U.S. Senator Lyndon Johnson wanted to bring Asians to Hawai'i to learn American science and technology. On September 26, 1960, the Center welcomes its first student, Abdul Qavi

Zia, of Pakistan, to pursue a Ph.D. On January 1, 1962, Dr. Alexander Spoehr is the first Chancellor of the East-West Center.

May 19, 1960: In an education survey, Hawai'i public school teachers admit they lack skills to teach speaking, creative writing, and Hawaiiana.

May 23, 1960: A 9.6 Chile earthquake on May 22 creates a 440-mile an hour tsunami that rises 35 feet and kills 61 people in Hilo, injures 282 people, destroys 537 buildings, and causes $23 million damage. The tsunami moves 22-ton rocks and destroys Hilo harbor.

June 5, 1960: Roosevelt High School's graduating class is the last for an English standard school. On May 22, DPI Superintendent Walton Gordon said eliminating standard schools is "...a step forward against any possible taint of segregation in the schools." In 1949, Governor Ingram Stainback signed a law to begin a 12-year phase out.

June 20, 1960: President Dwight Eisenhower visits Hawai'i for 6 days on his return from Korea. Governor William Quinn declares a half-day holiday, and 200,000 people welcome the president. President Eisenhower tells the airport crowd, "Here we have a true example of men living together in human dignity, men of every race and creed, that can possibly exist on this earth. They have lived together to their mutual benefit, their mutual profit, and mutual satisfaction, and possibly even deeper than that, to their mutual self-respect." On June 24, UH gives President Eisenhower an honorary degree.

Visitors learn Hawaiian culture at Ulu Mau Village in He'eia

June 20, 1960: Malia and Herman Solomon open Ulu Mau Village in Ala Moana Park. The village has demonstrations of poi pounding, weaving, fishnets, crafts, etc. and workshops. On May 5, 1966, an arsonist burns two buildings, and a new village opens in He'eia on June 6, 1969.

June 22, 1960: Hawaii County Police Chief Anthony Paul is found guilty of assault and battery against another police officer, and disorderly conduct. His sentence is suspended.

July 4, 1960: A 50th star is officially added to the U.S. flag, commemorated with a new 4¢ flag stamp issued by the U.S. Post Office. Federal law requires adding a new star to Old Glory on the July 4th after admission. 10,000 people watch the flag raising at 'Iolani Palace.

Governor William Quinn

July 23, 1960: Only 2 of Hawaii's 27 public high schools are nationally accredited, but all schools meet state education standards. DPI says it isn't concerned with national accrediting agencies. Only McKinley and Baldwin meet the national standards. On October 16, 1962, the principals of Maui and Baldwin High Schools complain that public high school education in Hawai'i is substandard.

July 28, 1960: Hawaii's first prison riot in 40 years involves 49 inmates. On September 26, a mainland consultant releases a critical report that says "Inmates have the upper hand" at O'ahu Prison. There is a bitter 6-month "war of words" between prison Warden Joe Harper and his boss, Social Services Department Director Mary Noonan. On October 3, Harper tells the HONOLULU ADVERTISER that Noonan used brainwashing techniques to try and make him quit.

August 3, 1960: Just one-week after the Republican National Convention, Vice President Richard Nixon begins his presidential campaign in Hawai'i with a two-day visit of 4 major islands.

October 2, 1960: Frank Sinatra sings at a John Kennedy fundraising event at Waikīkī Shell. Sinatra is paid the standard union minimum of $38 for singing 50 minutes.

November 3, 1960: An 8-foot Arcas Rocket is the first rocket launched from Pacific Missile Range at Barking Sands, Kaua'i. The rocket will improve weather forecasting. It flies 31 miles high at 3,600 feet-per-second. Missile tracking is also done at 'Ohana Point O'ahu and South Point Hawai'i.

November 8, 1960: Hawai'i makes presidential history. In a Hawai'i recount, John Kennedy defeats Richard Nixon by 115 votes out of 184,705. Hawai'i sends representatives of both Democrat and Republican parties to the Electoral College until the close vote is official.

November 22, 1960: After 7 years of construction and several cave-ins, the Wilson Tunnel opens full-time. The $25 million Pali Highway and Wilson Tunnel are dedicated on December 21, 1962. On December 15, 1953, county Supervisors named the tunnel for former Mayor John Wilson, the engineer who built the first Pali Road, and urged it to be widened. The Old Pali Road closes on January 3, 1961.

January 19, 1961: Conrad Hilton buys the Hawaiian Village from Henry Kaiser for $21 million, and renames it the Hilton Hawaiian Village.

February 1, 1961: Mayor Neal Blaisdell appoints Duke Kahanamoku as "official city greeter."

February 16, 1961: Governor William Quinn's State of the State speech urges lawmakers to resist both "land misers" who would do nothing with public land and "land spendthrifts" who would sell all public land.

March 17, 1961: Elvis Presley begins filming the movie, BLUE HAWAI'I. It is his biggest movie success, earning nearly $5 million at the box office. Two million albums of the movie soundtrack and song, BLUE HAWAI'I, are sold worldwide. Elvis' 1961 recording is the 3rd for this song, written in 1930s by Leo Robin and Ralph Rainger, who also wrote the Bob Hope theme song, THANKS FOR THE MEMORIES.

March 25, 1961: Elvis Presley sings at a Bloch Arena concert that raises $52,000 of the $500,000 needed for the USS ARIZONA Memorial Fund, and he adds $5,000 of his own.

April 2, 1961: Author James Michener tells the NEW YORK POST newspaper that he left Hawai'i because discrimination bothered his Nisei wife, Mari, who rarely complains. On July 28 he tells HONOLULU STAR-BULL-

ETIN reporter Clarice Taylor that three country clubs don't admit Orientals as members, and he couldn't buy a home in Kahala because "discrimination prevents any Japanese from moving in." He explains that discrimination affects mostly the wealthy.

April 4, 1961: U.S. Census Bureau announces that Hawai'i has the nation's largest non-Caucasian population, about 67%.

April 20, 1961: The minor league Hawai'i Islanders, a Pacific Coast League baseball team, plays its first game before 6,000 fans at Honolulu Stadium, defeating the Vancouver Mounties 4-3. The Hawai'i Islanders play their last game in 1987, and move to Colorado Springs.

April 27, 1961: Henry Kaiser and Bishop Estate sign a development agreement for Hawai'i Kai, a $350 million planned community on 6,000 acres of Bishop Estate land. It will be Hawaii's second largest city with 14,000 homes and 50,000-70,000 population. To support slow sales in Hawai'i Kai's beginning years, he plans a resort at Queens Beach and a minor league baseball team to play at a 50,000 seat stadium in Hawai'i Kai.

May 9, 1961: Vice President Lyndon Johnson visits Hawai'i while en route to Asia. He speaks to the Legislature, and participates in the East-West Center groundbreaking. UH gives him an honorary degree.

May 23, 1961: Governor William Quinn signs a law to prohibit billboards on public highways.

Henry Kaiser and Hawai'i Kai

July 1, 1961: Governor William Quinn signs the nation's first law to create State Land Use Districts – Conservation, Agricultural and Urban – to guide planning. The law also creates a Land Use Commission to make the state responsible for zoning via land classifications. Land is assessed according to value, which encourages land development for highest and best purposes. On June 17, 1963, Governor John Burns signs a law to add a 4th Land Use District, Rural. This allows low density development, such as one house per half-acre.

July 1, 1961: Haleakalā National Park is dedicated as America's 30th national park. It is a dormant volcano, elevation 10,023 feet, known as the "House of the Sun," which last erupted in 1790. The crater is deep enough to hold all of Manhattan Island. The rare, 6 foot silversword plant, 'āhinahina, grows here and blossoms once every 20 years.

July 10, 1961: Kīlauea erupts for 7 days, with 700 foot fountains.

July 10, 1961: Governor William Quinn signs the nation's first condominium law, known as the Horizontal Property Regimes Act, to protect condo buyers from "hidden clauses" and other deceiptful practices.

September 21, 1961: Chinn Ho is appointed to the board of directors of Theo Davies. He is the first person of Asian descent to serve on a Big 5 board.

September 22, 1961: Kīlauea erupts for 3 days.

September 29, 1961: Governor William Quinn is the first governor since 1929 to visit Ni'ihau.

October 31, 1961: Libby McNeill and Libby closes the Pauwela Cannery on Maui, which it purchased on June 3, 1926.

November 15, 1961: Honolulu Police Department bans Henry Miller's book, TROPIC OF CANCER. Police arrest a book distributor for violating a state law that prohibits obscene literature.

November 18, 1961: Despite objections by Elizabeth Farrington, the Farrington Estate announces the sale of the HONOLULU STAR-BULLETIN to Chinn Ho, president of Capital Investment Product. The $11 million sale includes the STAR-BULLETIN, radio and TV stations, the HILO TRIBUNE-HERALD, and printing companies.

December 18, 1961: Bishop Museum Planetarium opens.

January 15, 1962: U.S. Secretary of Defense Robert McNamara tells military officials in Honolulu the U.S. has "no intention" of sending U.S. troops to South Vietnam.

January 15, 1962: Several Waikīkī lei sellers ignore a street sales ban that begins today. The City Council passed a resolution on October 3, 1961 to impose the ban.

February 19, 1962: A Honolulu City Council resolution requires Hawaiian names for all streets. The practice is formally adopted by the Planning Commission on June 27, 1968. All counties have adopted the practice.

March 17, 1962: Former Korean Premier Syngman Rhee, exiled to Hawai'i since 1960 and living in Kāne'ohe, apologizes to the Korean people for his past mistakes, but the Republic of Korea won't allow him to return. He dies in Hawai'i on July 19, 1965 at age 90, and is returned to Korea for burial.

May 25, 1962: Governor William Quinn signs a tax cut law to reduce the sugar and pineapple excise tax from 2 to 1/2% by 1964.

May 30, 1962: USS ARIZONA Memorial is dedicated. It is designed by architect Alfred Preis, who was imprisoned in a Hawai'i internment camp because he held a German passport when WW II began. 1,177 sailors are interred in the ship.

June 1, 1962: Hawai'i Newspaper Agency is established when the HONO-LULU STAR-BULLETIN and HONOLULU ADVERTISER agree to a 30-year joint operating agreement. The two newspapers will save money by sharing non-editorial functions such as printing, advertising, circulation, and a building. The profits are divided, with 60% to the STAR-BULLETIN, and 40% to the ADVERTISER. The agreement saves the weaker ADVERTISER, with 64,000 circulation, while the STAR-BULLETIN has 105,000 circulation. Newspapers in 20 other cities have similar agreements. On July 1, the two newspapers combine to produce different sections of a single Sunday newspaper.

June 16, 1962: Maui's twisting, 55-mile, "improved" Hāna Highway opens with wider lanes and graded curves.

July 19, 1962: Lahaina Restoration Foundation is established. It operates tours of Hale Pa'i Printing House, Hale Pa'ahao Prison, Old Lahaina Courthouse, Brig Carthaginian, and other historic buildings.

July 22, 1962: A Canadian Pacific Airlines flight crash lands at Honolulu International Airport, killing 27 of the 40 people on board. It is Hawaii's second worst civilian air disaster and the first commercial airline to crash. The airplane had engine problems soon after leaving Honolulu, and it crashes while landing.

July 27, 1962: Hawaii's first phone call is made via TELSTAR, a 36-inch American communication satellite, 3,000 miles in space.

July 31, 1962: Dr. Kenneth Emory and Dr. Yoshito Sinoto of Bishop Museum, discover evidence that Hawaii's first immigrants came from the Marquesas about 500 A.D. or earlier, followed by Tahitians about 1000 A.D.

August 21, 1962: Hawaii's first gangland killing. Two known gamblers, Joseph K. Hong and Joseph Y. Hong are shot in the face in the back seat of a car in Hawai'i Kai. The crime is unsolved.

October 3, 1962: Kōke'e Tracking Station is established on Kaua'i to follow the orbiting astronauts. After Walter Schirra's space capsule SIGMA 7 orbits the earth 6 times, 50 workers at Kōke'e help Schirra re-enter earth, and guide his capsule recovery from the ocean 1,300 miles northwest of Honolulu.

October 6, 1962: Astronaut Walter Schirra flies to Hickam Air Force Base for a day. He arrives with 3 of America's 7 original astronauts.

October 18, 1962: Waikiki's tallest building to date, the 25-story, Foster Tower, is dedicated. It was criticized during construction for blocking views of Diamond Head.

National News

October 22, 1962: The Cuban Missile Crisis begins. President John Kennedy gains national and international respect for his diplomacy. Russia removes nuclear missiles from Cuba, and war is avoided.

November 6, 1962: Helene Hale, a Hawai'i Island Democrat, is Hawaii's first elected female chair of a County Board of Supervisors.

November 6, 1962: For the first time, Democrats win the governorship, both houses of the Legislature, and all 3 seats in Congress. Democrat John Burns defeats William Quinn for Governor. Daniel Inouye is elected to the U.S. Senate, and Spark Matsunaga and Thomas Gill are elected to Congress. William Richardson, a Hawaiian, is elected Lt. Governor. Inouye is the first U.S. Senator of Japanese ancestry.

December 3, 1962: John Burns becomes Hawaii's 2nd state governor. He serves until December 2, 1974. Previously he was a police officer, businessman, Congressional Delegate, and Democratic Party leader.

December 6, 1962: A homemade bomb with 6 dynamite sticks is discovered in an abandoned briefcase at the former Honolulu Airport. FBI officials say the bomb was left in a 10¢ locker in October, 1961.

January 18, 1963: The $4.7 million Sheraton Maui Hotel is the first hotel to open at the 500-acre Kā'anapali Beach Resort. Kā'anapali is Hawaii's first master-planned resort, now on 1,200 acres, with a 3-mile beach.

February 18, 1963: U.S. Interior Secretary Stuart Udall suggests a 97,000 acre Kaua'i National Park to preserve Waimea Canyon and Nā Pali Coast. The federal government's formal proposal in 1965 creates controversy because most of the park is on state land. After several years, the national park idea is dropped because it lacks local support.

February 27, 1963: State Senator Kazuhisa Abe introduces legislation to establish a one-day "holiday for religious worship" in Hawai'i. This would eliminate Christmas and Good Friday, but it doesn't pass. Abe, a Buddhist, wants to test the constitutionality of religious holidays, but he is called the legislator who wants "to destroy Santa Claus." He also introduces a bill to establish Wesak Day to honor Buddha's birthday.

March 18, 1963: George Mason of Crossroads Press publishes the first issue of PACIFIC BUSINESS NEWS, an 8-page weekly that specializes in business news.

May 3, 1963: By one vote, the State Legislature defeats a land reform bill modeled after a Maryland law. Senator George Ariyoshi casts the deciding vote. Land reform is a cornerstone of the Democratic Party because it would take land from the large estates and allow homeowners to own their land. Bishop Estate and native Hawaiians oppose the bill because lease rents support Kamehameha Schools.

May 9, 1963: Olga Waterhouse becomes chairwoman of the Honolulu Police Commission – the nation's first chairwoman of a Police Commission.

May 15, 1963: Astronaut Gordon Cooper makes America's 6th manned space flight. He orbits earth 22 times in 34 hours aboard the FAITH 7, which travels at 17,546 mph. On May 18, about 150,000 people welcome him along Honolulu streets as the first kama'āina astronaut. On August 21-29, 1965, he is the first American astronaut to make a second trip into space, and he orbits earth 120 times in 190 hours.

June 3, 1963: Governor John Burns signs a law to establish April 8 every year as "Buddha Day" to promote religious understanding, but not as a state holiday. On March 1, the Hawai'i Buddhist Council gave the Legislature a petition with 40,000 signatures, asking for "Buddha Day."

President John Kennedy, Governor John Burns and U.S. Senator Daniel Inouye in 1963

June 8, 1963: President John Kennedy speaks about civil rights to the National Conference of Mayors in Hawai'i. 10,000 people welcome him at the airport, where he says, "Hawai'i represents all we are and all we hope to be...We are proud of this...state and what it stands for."

June 21, 1963: Hawaii's first newspaper strike begins. The 47-day strike by 7 unions comprising 850 employees of the HONOLULU ADVERTISER and HONOLULU STAR-BULLETIN ends on August 6.

July 19, 1963: Japanese multi-millionaire Kenji Osano pays $9 million to buy the Princess Ka'iulani hotel from Sheraton. From 1963-1974 he also buys the Moana, Surfrider, Sheraton Kaua'i, Sheraton Waikīkī (Hawaii's largest hotel), Royal Hawaiian, and Sheraton Maui. He becomes Hawaii's largest individual hotel owner, with 20% of the hotel rooms. In 1981, he is convicted of making illegal payoffs to Lockheed, an American company, and in 1986, he is convicted of lying to Japan's Diet (Congress). He is sentenced to 10 months in prison, but he dies in 1986 before going to jail. His hotels are owned by Kyo-ya Company, a subsidiary of Kokusai-Kogyo, in Japan.

August 20, 1963: The Caledonian Society is established to educate people about Scottish heritage.

September 25, 1963: Governor John Burns praises the ILWU for preventing racial problems in Hawai'i "no less violent than that in Alabama." He criticizes the "oligarchy" for discrimination, and says he is satisfied that "Orientals and other non-Caucasians have earned high positions...both in government and in the business world."

October 12, 1963: Polynesian Cultural Center in Lā'ie opens with a Maori hymn and 2,500 guests. The 15-acre, $500,000 park is operated by the Mormon Church. It is one of Hawaii's most popular tourist destinations, and provides jobs for many students.

December 4, 1963: The $2 million Kennedy Center opens at the East-West Center, just two weeks after the president was assassinated.

December 12, 1963: Board of Education passes a rule to require all students to work one-day a month in their school cafeteria.

December 14, 1963: Several days of newspaper stories report complaints from realtors that Bishop Estate is responsible for unwritten "gentlemen's agreements" that prevent non-Caucasians from buying homes in Kahala. Bishop Estate denies the charge. Realtors say there is a special desk in Bishop Estate's office where realtors must bring home buyers, allegedly for an ethnic check. If a spouse is absent, the buyer must bring a photo of the spouse or a wedding photo. In 1963, author James Michener said he left Hawai'i because he couldn't buy a home in Kahala, and his AJA wife experienced discrimination here.

December 31, 1963: Honolulu Police arrest 93 people and warn 288 others for illegal fireworks. 77 fires are started during New Years eve and day. As a result, Honolulu Police Chief Dan Liu, Fire Chief William Blaisdell, and insurance underwriters urge a total ban of fireworks. Only Maui County bans fireworks.

January 17, 1964: HONOLULU STAR-BULLETIN sells the HILO TRIBUNE-HERALD to Donrey Media Group of Las Vegas. On March 2, the newspaper's name is changed to HAWAI'I TRIBUNE-HERALD.

January 20, 1964: U.S. Justice Department files an anti-trust civil suit, charging 4 of the Big 5 – A&B, Castle and Cooke, C. Brewer, and Amfac – with illegal restraint of trade as Matson's owners. On July 13, A&B receives approval from the U.S. Justice Department to buy a 74% controlling interest in Matson Navigation for $22 million from Amfac, C. Brewer, and Castle and Cooke.

January 22, 1964: Conrad Hilton opens the $11 million, "secluded" Kahala Hilton luxury resort, on 6,485 acres, with 10 stories, 300 rooms, and 1,800 feet of beach. On December 31, two porpoises are added to a one-acre lagoon. The hotel suffers from low occupancy in its first two years, so management turns on mauka room lights at night to create the impression the hotel has good business.

January 24, 1964: UH dedicates the Mees Solar Laboratory. It is the first solar observatory atop Haleakalā. Haleakalā now has 5 major telescopes for UH, military and civilian programs.

February 29, 1964: 'Ilikai Hotel opens with more than 1,000 hotel and condo rooms, making it the world's largest condominium. The $22 million, 27-story building is Waikiki's tallest. Financier Chinn Ho builds the hotel near his parents former home.

May 3, 1964: Sea Life Park in Waimānalo opens. It features dolphins, penguins, sea lions, and wholphins – a combination of false killer whale and dolphin.

May 10, 1964: Frank Sinatra nearly drowns near Wailua Bay on Kaua'i. He tries to save the wife of his executive producer, Mrs. Howard Koch from drowning, but an undertow traps him for 15 minutes. He is rescued by residents with surfboards and the Fire Department.

May 31, 1964: The Sunday ADVERTISER and STAR-BULLETIN reports it is the nation's #1 paid circulation newspaper, for highest percentage distribution. Standard Rate and Data Service reports the Sunday newspaper goes to 91% of O'ahu households or 145,305 average paid circulation.

June 18, 1964: A 6,300-mile, $84 million undersea cable connecting Hawai'i to Tokyo is completed. President Lyndon Johnson and Japan Prime Minister Hyato Ikeda talk directly, then Governor John Burns talks to Tokyo Governor Ryutaro Azumka. The phone call is broadcast in the 'Iolani Palace throne room. The new cable allows 128 phone calls at the same time at $9 a minute during weekdays.

August 10, 1964: Congressman Tom Gill complains the U.S. Navy dropped bombs at Miloli'i on June 29 and July 2, just 40 feet from a canoe and

National News

August 17, 1964: Congress passes the Gulf of Tonkin resolution to allow President Lyndon Johnson to escalate the Vietnam war.

150 feet from a fisherman. The Navy gave no prior announcement about the bombing.

September 12, 1964: After a March 7 opening, the $14 million Honolulu International Center is dedicated, featuring Art Linkletter's Party of Hollywood Stars. On September 13, the Honolulu Symphony performs the first concert there. Controversy erupts because no Hawaiian musicians are invited for the 9-day opening, so union leaders threaten to picket the non-union Polynesian Cultural Center performers. The Polynesian Cultural Center withdraws, and is replaced by many notable Hawaiian entertainers. It is renamed the Neal Blaisdell Center on January 14, 1976 to honor Mayor Neal Blaisdell, who died on November 5, 1975. He was mayor from 1955-1968.

November 3, 1964: Voters approve a constitutional amendment to change the School Board from appointed to elected positions.

November 3, 1964: Neighbor Island voters approve charter amendments to replace the chairman of the Board of Supervisors with a mayor.

November 3, 1964: Spark Matsunaga and Patsy Mink are elected to Congress. Mink is the first Asian-American woman to serve in Congress. Voter turnout is 89%.

December 9, 1964: Maui's Kamehameha's Brick Palace is excavated. It is probably Hawaii's first Western-style building, built by two former British prisoners from Australia's Botany Bay Penal Colony.

January 19, 1965: 15 NASA astronauts train 5 days at Volcano National Park lava fields for walking and driving on the moon. Between 1965-1972, about 3 dozen astronauts train here.

January 27, 1965: Honolulu Advertiser reports about an Oʻahu Transportation Study for a Waikīkī-Pearl Harbor waterway along the Ala Wai Canal, with land right-of-way for monorail, buses and cars.

January 27, 1965: Plans are announced for a $7 million, 23-story, 800-room Bali Haʻi Hotel in Waikīkī. This hotel is intended for budget-minded visitors, featuring $9.75 room rates.

January 27, 1965: The National Science Foundation announces plans to drill 3 miles into the earth, under the ocean near Kāʻanapali. Project Mohole is intended to study what's under the earth's top layer. It would have begun in 1968 and brought $70 million a year into Hawaii's economy, but it was cancelled in 1966 because it cost too much.

February 4, 1965: Hawaiian Wax Museum opens. It presents the history of Hawai'i with 59 statues and 18 scenes.

February 6, 1965: 500 lbs. of TNT are blasted on Kaho'olawe to test the effects of a nuclear blast on coastal ships. A 3rd test on June 24 damages a Navy ship.

March 21, 1965: Kamehameha Schools says it will admit non-Hawaiian students for the first time, during summer school, on a "space available basis." On July 28, 1972, Hawai'i Supreme Court Justice Kazuhisa Abe suggests that Kamehameha Schools admit all races and hire non-Protestant teachers.

June 19, 1965: A new $2 million Chain of Craters Road opens in Volcano National Park. It loops near the craters for 19 miles.

July 24, 1965: Mauna Kea Beach Hotel is dedicated. The $15 million, 154-room luxury hotel is built on 2,000 acres of former Parker Ranch land in Kawaihae by Laurance Rockefeller. Governors Quinn and Burns had asked Rockefeller to build a hotel.

August 3, 1965: An unidentified rocket with a red glow hits the ocean, 10 miles from Po'ipū Beach. No one says if it is American or Russian.

August 31, 1965: During a morning Hawaiian Airlines flight from Honolulu to Kamuela, a drunken teenage passenger threatens a stewardess and some of the 20 other passengers at knife-point. When the airplane returns to Honolulu the youth continues to hold a stewardess at knife point until he is subdued.

September 17, 1965: Hawai'i Pacific College opens with 56 students. On September 19, 1966, Hawai'i Christian College and Hawai'i Pacific College merge to become Hawai'i Pacific College, a 4-year college.

October 3, 1965: Standing next to the Statue of Liberty, President Lyndon Johnson signs the Immigration and Nationality Act to repeal the discriminatory provisions of earlier immigration laws. The new law puts Asian immigrants on equal standing with Europeans for the first time. Each Asian nation gets a new quota of 20,000 immigrants.

October 5, 1965: No one is hurt when the U.S. Navy mistakenly drops 8 bombs on a Ni'ihau beach, thinking it is Ka'ula Rock, 22 miles away. U.S. Senator Hiram Fong calls this "gross carelessness." The Navy had been bombing Ka'ula, a mile-long islet, since 1952. On March 2, 1961, the Kaua'i Board of Supervisors passed a resolution asking the Navy to stop the bombing. In February 1979, the Navy agrees to drop unexploded dummy bombs that won't disturb the whales. In January, 1980, a U.S. Fish and Wildlife Office rules the bombing violates the Migratory Bird Species Act because the islet is visited by up to 100,000 sea birds.

October 13, 1965: Two nuclear submarines, the BARB and SARGO, collide underwater, 15 miles west of Barber's Point. No one is hurt, no radiation is leaked, and there is minimal damage to the subs.

October 21, 1965: Judge Ronald Jamieson rules that Kamehameha Schools must hire non-Protestant teachers. His decision is unanimously overruled by the Hawai'i Supreme Court on September 21, 1967.

November 7, 1965: The 1st Hawaiian Open golf tournament is held at the Wai'alae Country Club. Gay Brewer Jr. wins first prize, $9,000. It is Hawaii's first national Professional Golf Association event.

January 9, 1966: Hawai'i State Federation of Labor, AFL-CIO is established by 44 unions and 30,000 workers to replace the Central Labor Council of Honolulu. Hawai'i is the last state to create such an organization. On July 17, 1980, the name changes to Hawai'i State AFL-CIO.

January 18, 1966: The $20 million Downtown Cultural Plaza project is announced. Plans include 1,000 apartments and a 150-room hotel with commercial space and cultural facilities to promote tourism and business. It is completed on January 1, 1975.

February 5, 1966: President Lyndon Johnson arrives in Hawai'i for a 3-day meeting at Camp Smith with cabinet members, military advisors, and South Vietnam leaders. 5,000 people and a few protesters greet the president. President Johnson makes headlines by stopping the motorcade at Kūhiō Beach Dairy Queen for ice milk. Attending the meeting are Vice President Hubert Humphrey, Secretary of State Dean Rusk, Secretary of Defense Robert McNamara, South Vietnam President Nguyen Van Thieu, and Premier and General Nguyen Cao Ky.

February 18, 1966: Hotel workers strike the 'Ilikai Hotel for two weeks until April 15.

National News

March 22, 1966: General Motors President James Roche apologizes to consumer advocate Ralph Nader for spying on his personal activities. Nader's book, UNSAFE AT ANY SPEED accuses GM of putting sales before safety.

March 21, 1966: 400 UH students almost riot when East-West Center student Noel Kent and former UH student Peter Lombardi are arrested for allegedly desecrating the U.S. flag. They made a paper flag with daggers and dollar signs instead of stripes and stars. On December 9, Circuit Court Judge Masato Doi reverses Kent's May 25 guilty verdict. Lombardi returns to the mainland and is not prosecuted further.

March 25, 1966: Lt. Governor William Richardson becomes Hawai'i Supreme Court Chief Justice, replacing Wilfred Tsukiyama, 68, who died. He is Hawaii's first part-Hawaiian chief justice since the monarchy.

April 25, 1966: U.S. Supreme Court changes the Hawai'i State Senate reapportionment plan. The court plan, based on population instead of voter registration, transfers Senate control to O'ahu from the less-populated Neighbor Islands.

June 5, 1966: Former First Lady Jackie Kennedy and her two children arrive in Hawai'i, welcomed by 5,000 people at the Honolulu Airport. She stays several weeks, and attends the Kamehameha Day Parade.

July 15, 1966: Bishop Estate's annual appraisal report is submitted to the Attorney General. The report urges Bishop Estate to sell some of its land because it is earning just 1% return on its investments, which is considered too little. Bishop Estate owns about 9% of Hawai'i land.

August 3, 1966: The first American soldiers on rest and recreation from the Vietnam War arrive in Hawai'i. From 1966-1974, about 49,000 soldiers visit Hawai'i each week, and most are met by family. They occupy 1,600 Waikīkī hotel rooms. The HVB reports that returning soldiers bring $46 million annually to Hawaii's economy.

October 3, 1966: Lyle Guslander's Island Holidays buys the Royal Lahaina Hotel for $3.5 million, becoming the first company to own a hotel on every major island.

October 4, 1966: KCCN, the first all-Hawaiian music radio station, begins broadcasting "all Hawaiian...all the time."

October 18, 1966: President Lyndon Johnson makes his second visit to Hawai'i this year, and gives a television speech from the new East-West Center. 200,000 people welcome the president along the motorcade route. To ensure a big turnout, Governor Burns proclaims "Aloha Johnson Day" with a school holiday.

October 25, 1966: Honolulu housewives establish the Consumer Action Council. Similar groups are established statewide and nationwide to protest high food prices. On November 27, the Consumer Action Council has nearly 5,800 petition signatures against supermarket prices. On November 2, boycotts begin against Foodland, Times and IGA, and the stores respond with media ads. On November 29, Foodland owner Maurice Sullivan says supermarkets make only 1% profit. Safeway is added to the boycott in January, 1967.

December 3, 1966: Entertainer Kui Lee, age 34, dies of cancer. He wrote 200 songs including I'LL REMEMBER YOU, LAHAINALUNA, and ONE PADDLE, TWO PADDLE.

December 13, 1966: 3,000 people attend a Honolulu city hearing on fluoridation. It is the largest crowd to attend a city hearing.

Academic Freedom: Oliver Lee

May 4, 1967: Waikīkī Lions Club members urge that UH Political Science Professor Oliver Lee be denied tenure because of his anti-war activities. The Lions repeat their request on May 18. On May 29, Lee receives a "letter of intent" to grant tenure in one year. On May 31, a student organization that Lee advises, distributes a statement urging U.S. troops to commit sabotage. On June 5, UH President Thomas Hamilton withdraws the promise to grant tenure, and on June 28, the UH Regents agree.

December 23, 1967: UH President Thomas Hamilton says he supports "academic responsibility" and resigns after 5 years as president because he loses faculty confidence. A day earlier, a UH faculty committee reported that President Hamilton violated Professor Oliver Lee's academic freedom and due process by withdrawing his tenure approval.

May 20, 1968: 75 UH students occupy the UH Administration Building, Bachman Hall, to protest Professor Oliver Lee's denial of tenure. The next day, 300 students continue the sit-in, and Lee is arrested with 151 students and several professors. The loitering charges are dismissed in September.

May 22, 1968: UH Regents refuse to renew Prof. Lee's contract, but they pay him a year's salary as "severance pay."

April 14, 1969: Board of Regents yield to pressure from the American Association of University Professors, and reinstate Professor Lee with a promise of tenure in one year. Professor Lee teaches another 33 years at UH, then retires.

January 13, 1967: Don Ho's song, TINY BUBBLES is a national hit. On May 27, 1969 NBC-TV televises the HAWAI'I-HO! special, featuring Don Ho and 500 students of the Kamehameha School choir. The TV special is filmed in many Hawai'i locations. In 1976, Ho stars in a brief TV variety series, THE DON HO SHOW.

January 16, 1967: The Governor's Committee on Food Prices holds its first hearing, with Lt. Governor Tom Gill as chair. Hawai'i supermarkets charge 16% more than San Francisco, but most of that difference is due to shipping costs. On March 15, the Governor's Committee report says food prices can be lowered by eliminating trading stamps and games. The HONOLULU ADVERTISER and STAR-BULLETIN will publish a weekly survey of prices of 54 food items at 18 supermarkets. The prices are tracked by a University of Hawai'i computer. The purpose of the weekly survey is to inform consumers about food prices and increase grocer competition.

March 1, 1967: Hawaii's longest bus strike begins. Teamsters strike 67 days until May 8. Honolulu Rapid Transit (HRT) chairman Harry Weinberg forces a strike by seeking higher fares. As a result, Governor John Burns signs a law on June 16, 1967 to allow county government to condemn, buy and operate a mass transit system. MTL (Mass Transit Lines) will replace HRT.

April 13, 1967: Meadow Gold dumps 4,000 gallons of contaminated milk.

May 21, 1967: HAWAI'I TRIBUNE-HERALD employees strike 56 days until July 24.

June 12, 1967: Governor John Burns signs a law to promote public art. Hawai'i is the first state to set aside 1% of construction costs to buy art for state buildings.

June 23, 1967: Bishop Museum scientists discover the "most amazing...unique" petroglyphs behind Kona Village Hotel. They find the first-ever petroglyph of a kite, and petroglyphs of human sacrifice, and a man surfing or dancing. The date 1820 is carved in rock, which is the earliest date found at a petroglyph site.

June 24, 1967: The Hawai'i Land Reform Act becomes law without the signature of Governor John Burns. The law encourages fee simple land ownership by allowing lessees to force landowners to sell the fee interest, and allows the state to condemn land. About 3/4 of Hawaii's privately-owned land is held by a few large estates and landowners. The law had been debated for 18 years. Hawai'i is the only state with a leasehold reform law.

June 24, 1967: The nation's first Ombudsman's Office is created to investigate public complaints about government agencies. Governor John Burns allows the bill to become law without his signature. The Ombudsman job is vacant for two years.

June 30, 1967: The first international telephone call via by the orbiting LANI BIRD satellite, 22,300 miles in space, is from Hawai'i to Japan. The 190 lb. satellite is launched on October 26, 1966, and travels 6,900 miles per hour.

August 7, 1967: 14,000 visitors attend a 4-day American Bar Association convention in Waikīkī, the largest convention held in Hawai'i. U.S. Vice President Hubert Humphrey gives the keynote speech.

August 24, 1967: Henry Kaiser, age 85, dies. One of America's most successful industrialists, he came to Hawai'i in 1954 to retire at age 72. He builds and opens $80 million in new Hawai'i businesses – the 6,000-acre Hawai'i Kai community, KHVH radio and TV, Kaiser Health Plan, Kaiser Cement, Waikiki's largest hotel, the Hawaiian Village, and a record company to promote singer Alfred Apaka.

September 7, 1967: Christian College of the Pacific opens with 51 students. The college is later renamed Hawai'i Loa College.

September 18, 1967: UH Medical School opens with 27 students.

October 1, 1967: United and Pan American begin direct jet flights from the mainland to Hilo.

October 29, 1967: To improve traffic flow, a 105-year old banyan tree at King and Ke'eaumoku is cut down despite 20 years of protests by the Outdoor Circle and general public. In December 1947, the Board of Supervisors ordered the tree to be removed, but it was saved by a petition with 3,000 signatures.

November 5, 1967: Kīlauea erupts for 8 months until July 8, 1968. It is the second longest eruption of the 20th century.

December 28, 1967: Hawai'i achieves a tourism milestone, as 1 million visitors arrive for the first time in a single year.

January 22, 1968: Duke Kahanamoku, age 77, dies of a heart attack. He traced his ancestry through Bernice Pauahi to Kamehameha. He won 5 medals in 4 Olympics from 1912-1932, popularized swimming and surfing, and promoted Hawai'i tourism as an ambassador to the world. He appeared in 30 movies as a Hollywood silent screen actor during the 1920s, was elected O'ahu Sheriff from 1934-1961, and was appointed Official City Greeter in 1961.

February 8, 1968: 5,600 ILWU pineapple workers strike for 61 days.

February 27, 1968: To reduce traffic to Waikīkī, Honolulu City Council approves a two-level highway on Kapiʻolani from McCully to Kalākaua. In May, 1950, the Board of Supervisors proposed a similar 4-lane, $350,000 overpass.

National News

March 16, 1968: U.S. soldiers kill 450 South Vietnamese civilians, including women and babies. The My Lai massacre is revealed on November 16, 1969.

March 20, 1968: Kauaʻi Supervisors complain that "hippies and beach-bums" create problems with nudity, drugs and park use such as camping. They fear thousands of hippies will come to Kauaʻi. On April 9, 1969, 13 hippies are sentenced to 90 days in the county jail for vagrancy – camping without a permit in a public park. On May 8, 1969, the County Council taxes campers "to control hippies and freeloaders who mess up our parks," but the fee backfires when it discourages other campers.

April 9, 1968: Congressman Spark Matsunaga casts the deciding vote, 8-7, in the House Rules Committee to support civil rights legislation to prohibit housing discrimination. A month earlier, Hawaiʻi's two U.S. Senators Hiram Fong and Daniel Inouye cast the deciding votes to stop a filibuster of that bill. These votes confirm previous Southern opposition to Hawaiʻi statehood for fear that Hawaiʻi would support civil rights legislation. President Lyndon Johnson signs the Fair Housing Act on April 11.

April 11, 1968: 4,100 soldiers with the Hawaiʻi National Guard are activated for the Vietnam War. Many soldiers complain that Hawaii's National Guard is over-represented in the war, compared with National Guards of other states.

April 11, 1968: 12 UH students burn their draft cards at Hemenway Hall to protest the Vietnam War.

April 15, 1968: President Lyndon Johnson meets South Korea President Park Chung Hee in Hawaiʻi for 3 days. They discuss the Vietnam War and North Korea.

April 16, 1968: The Pacific Club ends its 117-year racial restrictions and admits its first Chinese-American member, Philip Ching, and its first AJA member, Asa Akinaka. Some members quit in protest. On January 3, 1963, Governor John Burns was the first governor to reject honorary membership, to protest Pacific Club rejection of Supreme Court Justice Masaji Marumoto. The Club had rejected an attempt to admit Asians in 1954 and 1957, and had rejected a rule change to admit Asians as 5% of its membership. However the first Asian members, Dr. Wah Kai Chang and Ernest Kai, were "inherited" in a merger with the University Club in its first post-merger meeting on October 10, 1930. Other Oʻahu clubs also have an unwritten racial policy.

May 18, 1968: When 3,000 Hawaiʻi National Guard and reservists are called to active duty, an anti-war protest erupts. UH Religion Professor James Douglass and 12 students protest by sitting on Kalia Road, in front of trucks taking soldiers to Schofield Army Barracks. The 13 are arrested for loitering. On July 10, Douglas is sentenced to 15 days in jail. Ten students pay a $25 fine, and 2 students spend 5 days in jail for refusing to pay.

June 3, 1968: The new Central Oʻahu community known as Mililani Town, opens as one of Oahu's few projects selling fee simple homes. It is built by Oceanic Properties Inc., on 3,500 acres, with plans for 60,000 population. In 1986, the National Civic League names Mililani as Hawaii's only All-America City.

July 2, 1968: Maui County Chairman Elmer Cravalho says 100 hippies are violating community standards and causing the most unrest since WW II. On April 14, 1970, Mayor Cravalho asks police to enforce a March 13 eviction notice against Mākena campers on private property. Maui County publishes a brochure for hippies about laws such as drugs, bathing, nudity, camping, hitchhiking, littering, etc.

July 15, 1968: Hawaii's second Constitutional Convention opens with 82 delegates at McKinley High School. The 72-day convention ends on September 24.

July 18, 1968: President Lyndon Johnson visits Hawaiʻi for 3 days to meet with South Vietnam President Nguyen Van Thieu and discuss the Vietnam War. This is President Johnson's second visit here in 1968.

July 30, 1968: Developer Bert Williams sells La Pietra, the former home

of Walter Dillingham, in order to
save the mansion from being
demolished. The home is sold to
Hawai'i School for Girls for $1 mil-
lion, and another 5 acres is sold for
$10 million for a future condo-
minium site.

July 31, 1968: The West HAWAI'I TODAY
newspaper begins publication.

August 7, 1968: The chairman of
Hawaii's Republican Party, Edward
Johnston, nominates U.S. Senator
Hiram Fong as a "Favorite Son" can-
didate for president at the Republi-
can National Convention.

August 26, 1968: U.S. Senator Daniel
Inouye gives the keynote speech at
the Democratic National Convention. Inouye says it is his "proudest

U.S. Senator Hiram Fong

hour." He says war, poverty, discrimination and race riots must end.
Two days later, he is considered a vice presidential nominee.

September 7, 1968: Former Judge Calvin McGregor, a Kamehameha
Schools graduate, complains that the Bishop Estate trustees lack a Kamehameha alumnus.

September 13, 1968: Congressman Spark Matsunaga introduces a bill to
establish a cabinet-level U.S. Department of Peace. This idea was first
suggested in 1779 by Dr. Benjamin Rush, who signed the Declaration
of Independence.

September 30, 1968: Bishop Estate trustee Atherton Richards resigns as
president of Bishop Estate's Kamehameha Development Corporation.
He says he isn't going to be a "puppet or rubber stamp" for the August
sale to Texas millionaire Troy Post for a half-interest in its Keauhou-
Kona resort project. Post pays about half of what the land is worth. On
March 6, 1973, the Hawai'i Supreme Court voids the agreement. The
development company was established in 1966 to allow Bishop Estate
to develop its Kona properties. Bishop Estate proceeds to build hotels
at Keauhou-Kona.

September 30, 1968: The CBS-TV program, HAWAI'I FIVE-O, starring Jack
Lord, is broadcast for 12 years until April 5, 1980. It is the first TV
show filmed entirely in Hawai'i. The program is about a fictional state
police force that some people believed existed. It has been said the TV

series attracted $100 million in tourism here. Jack Lord also did a lot to promote Hawai'i as a center for movies and TV production.

November 5, 1968: Frank Fasi is elected Honolulu mayor for the first of six times. He will be Honolulu's longest serving mayor, almost 22 years, from 1969-1980, and 1985-1994. Each neighbor island county elects a mayor for the first time, and County Councils replace the Boards of Supervisors. The Neighbor Islands elect their County chairmen as mayors – Elmer Cravalho of Maui, Antone Vidinha of Kaua'i, and Shunichi Kimura of Hawai'i Island. Cravalho had been Speaker of the House from 1959-1967, and resigned to run for chairman.

November 13, 1968: President Lyndon Johnson's daughter, Luci Johnson Nugent and her 16-month old baby visit Hawai'i to be with her soldier-husband, who is on leave from the Vietnam war.

November 22, 1968: Two Schofield soldiers Henry Peters and attorney David Schutter write a petition urging that Hawaii's National Guard be deactivated. They obtain 1,400 signatures from Schofield soldiers. A smaller percentage are sent to Vietnam than originally planned.

December 21, 1968: HONOLULU ADVERTISER reports a Carnegie Foundation survey of 22,000 teachers nationwide reveals Hawai'i high school teachers are more concerned about student behavior, lack of parental support, vandalism, theft, violence, racial problems, and larger classes than teachers in other states.

December 28, 1968: The first humans to orbit the moon are welcomed by 20,000 people at Hickam Air Force Base. The 3 Apollo 8 astronauts – Frank Borman, James Lovell Jr. and William Anders – circled the moon 10 times at 24,000 mph on December 23. They were retrieved from their space craft on December 27 about 1,000 miles from Hawai'i.

January 4, 1969: An unannounced bombing of Kaho'olawe almost destroys a Hawaiian Air Tour airplane, with 19 people aboard, that is legally flying over the island.

January 13, 1969: Admiral Fred Bakutis supports military use of Kaho'olawe. He says it is "convenient...like a final practice before a big game. You get a good idea how good" your "personnel, planes and weapons" are without having to find out "under enemy fire." On October 30, Admiral John Hyland says "It's the only place around that is suitable. I think the island is of very little use for anything else."

January 14, 1969: 26 sailors are killed and 85 hurt in an explosion on the nuclear aircraft carrier USS ENTERPRISE, 70 miles from Honolulu.

February 16, 1969: The $2 million Paradise Park opens on 15 Mānoa acres, with 600 rare and exotic birds.

February 20, 1969: Governor John Burns, in his State of the State speech, urges lawmakers to "keep Hawai'i Hawaiian..." He also says our population of immigrant descendants suffers from "a subtle inferiority of spirit..." which is totally unwarranted, but it becomes a "social and psychological handicap in life." Burns says people who grew up in pre-WW II Hawai'i "know full-well what I mean."

February 20, 1969: Hawai'i had the nation's highest combined state and local tax burden in 1967, says the Advisory Commission on Intergovernmental Relations.

February 22, 1969: Kīlauea erupts for 6 days.

March 13, 1969: A&B announces it will build an $850 million resort on 1,500 Wailea acres with Northwestern Mutual Life Insurance Co. Matson agreed to buy the land from 'Ulupalakua Ranch on May 10, 1957. Wailea will have 3,000 hotel rooms and 8,000 condominiums. The resort opens in 1976.

March 15, 1969: A new $28 million State Capitol building opens. 'Iolani Palace had been the seat of government for the Provisional Government, Republic of Hawai'i, Territory and State from 1893-1969.

May 23, 1969: State Legislature approves a resolution for high rise buildings on the 35-acre Magic Island, but repeals it on May 12, 1970. Magic Island is really a peninsula. It opens as a $430,000 park in April 1971. Other proposals for Magic Island have included building hotels (1947, 1954 and 1961), a theme park (1966), and an airport (1968).

May 24, 1969: A huge Kīlauea eruption lasts almost 2 1/2 years. It creates the Mauna Ulu shield and covers 50 square miles.

June 4, 1969: Mayor Frank Fasi says he won't give any future information to HONOLULU STAR-BULLETIN reporter Toni Withington because she deliberately "discredit(s) my administration." The mayor refuses to let HONOLULU STAR-BULLETIN reporters attend city news conferences or to speak with city department directors. On October 16 he extends the ban to Associated Press. The 11-month ban ends in May 7, 1970.

June 7, 1969: President Richard Nixon visits Hawai'i for a day, enroute to Midway Island for Vietnam war talks.

June 12, 1969: 29 Honolulu Police officers are suspended for one day for a beer party at Hanauma Bay – for failing to report a violation, and causing embarrassment to the department.

July 2, 1969: Hawai'i Island Mayor Shunichi Kimura vetoes rezoning to prevent Boise Cascade from building the 25,000 acre Waikōloa Resort. The County Council overrides the veto on December 4.

July 9, 1969: During a national strike of Associated Press workers, 750 employees of the HONOLULU ADVERTISER and STAR-BULLETIN refuse to cross the picket line of a striking AP employee for nearly 3 days.

July 20, 1969: University of Michigan scientists fire 400 laser light beams from Haleakalā to the astronauts' moon landing site. It is the first time light is bounced off the moon. The purpose is to measure the exact distance of the earth to moon.

July 22, 1969: The U.S. Civil Aeronautics Board awards commercial routes to 4 airlines – American, Braniff International, Continental, and United. These airlines fly to Hawai'i from 35 mainland cities.

July 26, 1969: The first humans to land on the moon – astronauts Neil Armstrong, Michael Collins, and Edwin Aldrin Jr. – are retrieved from the Pacific Ocean in their Apollo 11 space craft, COLUMBIA 3 by the USS HORNET, and taken to Pearl Harbor and Hickam Air Force Base. Aldrin and Armstrong walked on the moon on July 20. 25,000 people welcome them to Pearl Harbor. Their space capsule remains here several days. En route to Hawai'i, Armstrong entertains the other astronauts by playing the 'ukulele. On July 24, a 60 lb. bag of moon rocks arrived in Hawai'i, and was shipped immediately to Houston.

July 31, 1969: A&B and the Cameron family agree to buy and trade A&B stock for the 30,000-acre Maui Pineapple Co., which is renamed Maui Land and Pineapple Co. on September 10, 1969. Colin Cameron is a great-great-grandson of missionary Dr. Dwight Baldwin.

August 6, 1969: A military soldier takes sanctuary in the Church of the Crossroads, to protest the Vietnam War. After a Waikīkī peace march of 400 supporters, another 7 take sanctuary. By September 12, 34 military have taken sanctuary, mostly in the Church of the Crossroads, but a few are inside Unitarian Church at Pali and one at the Quaker Society of Friends in Mānoa. On September 12, 40 military police raid the churches at dawn. They kick in the door at Church of the Crossroads, refuse to say if they have a search warrant, and arrest 8 servicemen. Others are eventually arrested, surrendered, or escape to Canada.

August 10, 1969: 16 people are hurt in a race riot of 250 Marines at Kāne'ohe Marine Corps Air Station. Black Marines had complained of racism and discrimination. Caucasian Marines objected when 50 Blacks gave a "Black Power" salute when the U.S. flag was raised.

September 20, 1969: 500 teenagers riot for three hours, throw rocks and storm the gates at a Honolulu International Center rock concert. Two police are injured and 5 teens are arrested.

September 20, 1969: HONOLULU STAR-BULLETIN reports a First Hawaiian Bank prediction that in 1971, Waikīkī will have 31,000 hotel rooms – the nation's 2nd highest total – surpassed only by New York. Waikīkī is getting 5 new hotels with 1,000 rooms each.

September 22, 1969: U.S. Army Secretary Stanley Resor admits the Army secretly tested non-toxic chemical and biological nerve gas on Oʻahu and Hawaiʻi Island from 1965-1968 without notifying state officials. On March 8, 1977, the U.S. Army again admits past testing of non-toxic nerve gas. The Army also admits testing germ warfare in Hawaiʻi, and other national locations from 1949-1969. On April 4, 1979, the U.S. Navy admits in a HONOLULU STAR-BULLETIN editorial page story, that submarines dumped nearly 5 million gallons of low-level radioactive water into Pearl Harbor from 1964-1973.

September 27, 1969: The U.S. Navy can't explain how an unexploded 500 lb. bomb is dropped on Māʻalaea pasture land, just 200 yards from the Honoapiʻilani Highway. The land is owned by Maui Mayor Elmer Cravalho. On January 5, 1970, the Navy admits the bomb accidentally fell from an airplane in 1966. Soon after this discovery, U.S. Senator Hiram Fong and Congressmen Spark Matsunaga and Patsy Mink urge Defense and Navy officials to stop bombing Kahoʻolawe.

September 29, 1969: Seven people among 50 protesters are arrested for creating $10,000 damage to exhibits at a convention of the American Bankers Association at Honolulu International Center. Two are found guilty and sentenced to 6 months in jail. They are protesting banks that ignore the needs of third world nations.

November 15, 1969: Molokai's 104-acre Kualapuʻu reservoir is dedicated. It is the world's largest butyl-rubber lined lake, holding 1.4 billion gallons of water. The reservoir is part of a $10 million irrigation project that brings water to dry West Molokaʻi.

December 1, 1969: A 50-foot wave hits Oahu's North Shore. It kills two people, creates $1 million damage, destroys 35 homes, and leaves 300 people homeless.

December 22, 1969: U.S. Senator Daniel Inouye accuses Navy Admiral Donald Davis of lacking candor when Davis says the Navy can clear 70% of the 10,000 tons of unexploded bombs on Kahoʻolawe.

1970-1979

January 6, 1970: Governor John Burns joins business leaders and the general public at the Travel Industry Congress to plan a tourist-based economy. The goal of more tourism is to improve the state economy, create jobs and improve the quality of life. The next day, delegates urge Neighbor Island development and controls on Waikīkī growth.

February 10, 1970: Governor John Burns submits a proposal to the Legislature to buy Niʻihau and prevent commercial development in case the island is sold. Niʻihau has an assessed value of $300,000. On March 3, the Robinson family, which owns Niʻihau, says the island isn't for sale at any price, and the bill fails to pass.

March 5, 1970: For the first time, biologists find the pesticide DDT and the chemical PCB in the unhatched egg of a Hawaiian ʻIo (hawk). The egg is sent to the Museum of Natural History in Washington, D.C.

March 11, 1970: The first jumbo jet arrives in Honolulu. A Pan American Airlines 747 brings 281 passengers from Los Angeles.

March 11, 1970: Hawaiʻi is the first state to legalize abortion. Governor John Burns, a Catholic, lets the bill become law without his signature.

April 1, 1970: U.S. Navy stops bombing Kaunā Point in South Kona. The Navy had been using this area for target practice since 1959.

April 1, 1970: Federal census begins. Hawaiʻi has 769,913 population, a 21% increase since 1960 – 9% Hawaiian, 39% Caucasian, 7% Chinese, 28% Japanese, 12% Filipino.

April 18, 1970: President Richard Nixon welcomes three astronauts of the near-disastrous Apollo 13 flight, at the Honolulu Airport. The 3 astronauts are James Lovell, Fred Haise Jr., and John Swigert. President Nixon says their success is "a triumph of the human spirit." Nixon also attends services at Kawaiahaʻo Church.

April 23, 1970: 200 UH students occupy the Air Force ROTC building for 6 days. They want to abolish ROTC because it is "pro-death" and incompatible with higher education. On October 29, the Board of Regents refuse to renew the teaching contract of Rev. Larry Jones, a Reli-

President Richard Nixon comes to Hickam Air Force Base to welcome home Apollo 13 astronauts (l-r) John Swigert, Fred Haise Jr., and James Lovell. The astronauts receive the nation's highest civilian award, Presidential Medal of Freedom.

gion lecturer who participated in the sit-in. However Jones is rehired as a lecturer on December 17.

April 23, 1970: Civil Aeronautics Board gives Aloha Airlines a $630,000 temporary subsidy to reduce its financial difficulties. Both local airlines got federal subsidies until January 1, 1967.

April 25, 1970: Frank Correa pickets outside Washington Place, holding an American flag. He is protesting the student occupation of the UH ROTC building, and lack of action by judges. In the coming months, 300 people join him to support "law and order" concerns.

May 6, 1970: UPW members ignore a law prohibiting government worker strikes and begin a 3-day strike of state and county governments for higher pay. 1,500 workers protest at the State Capitol.

May 7, 1970: Many UH students begin a one-week strike to protest the secret U.S. bombing of Cambodia, as college students do nationwide.

May 12, 1970: Campbell Estate announces a 20-year plan for a Second City and West Beach resort , with 80,000-120,000 population. On February 2, 1977, Mayor Frank Fasi signs the Honolulu General Plan, which identifies 'Ewa-Makakilo (renamed Kapolei) as the "second area urban center." On June 4, 1987, Campbell Estate unveils plans for Kapolei, a city for 150,000 people and mid-range, affordable housing.

National News

May 15, 1970: Police kill 2 Jackson State College students protesting the Vietnam War. On May 4, National Guard soldiers killed 4 Kent State University student war protestors.

May 27, 1970: Matson ends its mainland-to-Hawai'i passenger cruise service. Matson sells its luxury cruise ship LURLINE, followed by the MARIPOSA and MONTEREY. This was Matson's 3rd LURLINE.

May 28, 1970: Bishop Museum displays a 1.5 ounce, walnut-size moon rock collected by astronaut Neil Armstrong last July. The rock is estimated at $81 million value, and is viewed by 34,000 people at several Hawai'i museums for 11 days.

June 22, 1970: Governor John Burns signs a law to allow the counties to establish shoreline setbacks of at least 20-40 feet from construction.

June 23, 1970: Governor John Burns signs a law to allow the governor to waive the requirement for government employees to take a loyalty oath.

June 23, 1970: Castle and Cooke buys Libby's lease to a 12,000 acre Moloka'i Plantation, and a processing plant in Kalihi. The plant closes in 1972, and the plantation closes in 1975.

June 26, 1970: A new $5 million, 88 inch telescope is dedicated at the Mauna Kea observatory. It is the world's highest observatory, at 13,796 feet elevation. Mauna Kea now has 13 telescopes – more than any other mountain in the world.

June 30, 1970: Governor John Burns signs a law giving government workers the right to bargain collectively with a limited right to strike.

July 3, 1970: 100 hippies living at a 7-acre "banana patch" on Maui are quarantined under 24-hour guard by Maui Police because they have contagious hepatitis. The hippies have the owner's permission to reside there, but they are cited for having too many unrelated people on the property. It is Maui's first quarantine in several decades.

August 3, 1970: The Ala Moana Hotel opens 540 of its 1,300 rooms. The 38-story, $36 million hotel is owned by American Airlines and Dillingham Corp. It is Hawaii's tallest building to date.

August 12, 1970: U.S. government orders Hawai'i to establish and enforce clean air standards.

September 8, 1970: UH Hilo expands to a 4-year college with B.A. Degree programs. Hawai'i Community College opens with 600 students.

September 23, 1970: Hawai'i is one of four cities to hold a world premiere of the 20th Century Fox movie, Tora! Tora! Tora!, which gives Japan's version of the Pearl Harbor attack.

September 25, 1970: An audit of Bishop Estate says the charity "is doing virtually nothing" to help Hawaiian youth get a good education and prevent Hawaiian students from failing in public schools. The report says the charity is not earning enough from its $300 million assets to operate Kamehameha Schools, and must "do something for Hawaiians" because Kamehameha educates only 5% of Hawaiian children.

September 29, 1970: U.S. Senator Hiram Fong attempts to stop the Kaho'olawe bombing with an unsuccessful amendment to a bill. It is the first attempt in Congress to stop the bombing.

October 9, 1970: 2,000 ILWU hotel workers strike 10 Neighbor Island hotels for 75 days until December 18.

October 23, 1970: State Senator Larry Kuriyama is murdered at home during a week of violent organized crime. A suspect is acquitted at trial, and the crime is unsolved.

October 28, 1970: At the State Capitol, 500 Hawaiians protest Bishop Estate's attempts to evict Kalama Valley pig farmers for a housing subdivision.

October 28, 1970: UH students vote to discontinue future athletic events with BYU. Students say the Mormon church is biased against African-Americans. Students also vote to allow military recruiters on campus.

December 8, 1970: Stockholders approve a merger of Aloha and Hawaiian Airlines, but the deal doesn't happen. Both airlines accuse the other of unfair, monopolistic practices. On February 14, 1975, a federal jury awards Aloha Airlines a $4.5 million victory, but the two airlines agree to an out-of-court settlement of $1.8 million on August 23, 1976. Budget Rent-a-Car agrees to pay $400,000 to Aloha.

December 9, 1970: Hawaii State Teachers Association is established.

December 18, 1970: Land Use Commission adopts a 40-foot shoreline setback. Also, 600 people jam the State Capitol auditorium to protest

Honolulu Mayor Frank Fasi waves his Cowboy hat as he drives one of 20 new buses that arrives from Dallas

the Commission's previous urban rezoning of Olomana, which resulted in developer Joseph Pao illegally stripping the hillside. The same day, Pao's Island Construction Company pleads no contest to grading the hillside without a permit for a 692-unit townhouse project.

January 1, 1971: When HRT cuts wages, bus drivers strike for 60 days until March 1. A HONOLULU STAR-BULLETIN editorial says the worker strike is justified.

February 25, 1971: MTL bus company signs an agreement with Honolulu city government to take over Honolulu Rapid Transit. Mayor Frank Fasi drives a new bus that arrives from Dallas. On September 25, 1970, Honolulu City Council passed an ordinance to authorize the city to buy HRT from Harry Weinberg at a price to be set by the PUC.

February 26, 1971: University of Hawai'i ROTC building is destroyed by fire, with $65,000 damage. A week later, on March 5, a fire burns the temporary School of Travel Industry Management building, just 400 yards from ROTC. In 1973, former UH student Rev. Robert Warner turns himself in for setting the ROTC fire, and serves 6 months in jail.

March 4, 1971: The Waikīkī Improvement Association says it will provide free air and hotel room to crime victims willing to testify in court.

April 13, 1971: HONOLULU STAR-BULLETIN reports that President Harry Truman had pardoned 282 Nisei draft resisters, including some from Hawai'i, in January 1948. President Truman gave them full citizenship rights, but they were never told.

April 14, 1971: The first Merrie Monarch Hula Festival is held in Hilo for 5 days, featuring 350 dancers, performing 100 hula. The festival began in 1964 without hula competition, which was added in 1968.

April 26, 1971: U.S. Senator Daniel Inouye introduces a bill to stop the bombing of Kaho'olawe, return the island to Hawai'i control by year's end, and to require the federal government to remove 10,000 tons of unexploded bombs. After 31 years of bombing, Inouye says, our "patience has worn thin."

May 1, 1971: The $10 million Keāhole Airport opens in Kailua-Kona.

May 11, 1971: 50 police arrest 32 non-violent protesters for trespassing, as Kalama Valley homes are bulldozed. 80-150 low income residents and pig farmers had been living for many years on month-to-month leases from Bishop Estate. This protest represents the first modern native Hawaiian fight for land rights. In an August trial, all are found guilty with sentences suspended. On December 13, the city drops its appeal challenge, which acquits all.

June 1, 1971: Herbert Choy becomes Hawaii's first federal judge of Korean ancestry. He is appointed by President Richard Nixon.

June 4, 1971: The $62 million, 1,900 room Sheraton Waikīkī Hotel opens as Hawaii's largest hotel.

June 15, 1971: Governor John Burns appoints Lt. Governor George Ariyoshi to head a Kohala Task Force to help 400 Kohala Sugar workers when Castle and Cooke closes the 108-year old company by 1975. On May 15, 1973, Governor John Burns signs a law to provide $4 million for the Task Force, matched by $1.6 million in county loans to create agricultural businesses and job opportunities.

June 18, 1971: Hawai'i Supreme Court selects Matsuo Takabuki as a Bishop Estate trustee. A former City Councilman and political ally of Governor John Burns, Takabuki is condemned by mass protests of Hawaiians, who want more Hawaiians appointed as trustees. On June 21, Kawaiaha'o Church Rev. Abraham Akaka says, "We felt like strangers in our own homeland." When Takabuki takes his oath, Kawaiaha'o

Church bells ring 45 minutes in protest. On July 17, 1,000 people march through Waikīkī in protest. As a trustee, Takabuki guides investments to erase the Estate's $1 million deficit. Once considered "land rich, cash poor," Bishop Estate gets the highest possible credit rating from Moody's and Standard and Poor. Takabuki serves as a trustee for 21 years.

U.S. Congresswoman Patsy Mink

June 21, 1971: Governor John Burns signs a law to reduce sugar excise taxes from 4% to 1/2% for 5 years, despite cutting funding for non-profit agencies. Governor Burns also signs a law to exempt movie and TV production from all state taxes for 5 years.

July 29, 1971: Maui Mayor Elmer Cravalho and Life of the Land file a federal lawsuit to stop the bombing of Kahoʻolawe until the Navy submits an Environmental Impact Statement (EIS), as required by 1969 federal law. The Navy submits an EIS on April 28, 1972, and Judge Nils Tavares dismisses the lawsuit on May 16, 1972.

September 24, 1971: Kīlauea erupts for 5 days, with 250-foot fountains.

November 4, 1971: Board of Education adopts the Kamehameha Elementary Education Program (KEEP) to teach reading in public schools.

November 19, 1971: Kumu Kahua Theatre opens with its first play. It produces plays about Hawaii's history and ethnic traditions.

January 12, 1972: Congresswoman Patsy Mink announces that she is an anti-Vietnam war candidate for U.S. president. On May 23, she gets 2% of the Oregon Democratic primary vote and drops out the race.

February 3, 1972: Kīlauea erupts for 2 1/2 years.

February 17, 1972: President Richard Nixon spends two days in Hawaiʻi en route to his historic visit to mainland China, the first ever by a U.S. president.

February 28, 1972: 300 IBEW workers strike 48 days against Dynalectron Corporation, at Barking Sands Missile Range, on Kauaʻi until April 10. They seek the same pay as workers at Kōkeʻe Tracking Station.

March 22, 1972: Hawai'i Legislature is the nation's first to ratify the U.S. Equal Rights Amendment – just one hour after Congress votes for it.

March 27, 1972: Catholic Action of Hawai'i and mainland peace groups say the U.S. military is storing 3,000 nuclear weapons on O'ahu. The groups say many nuclear weapons are in Pearl Harbor, not far from the airport runway, which makes the weapons a greater hazard in an airplane crash. The groups give leaflets to Hawai'i-bound airline passengers at 11 mainland airports nationwide. The leaflets say O'ahu is the "most militarized island in the world" and criticize "Genocide in Indo-China." 20% of O'ahu urban land is used by the military, including the possible storage of nuclear weapons. In 1966 and 1967, the 3,156 nuclear weapons were stored in Honolulu and the military tested nerve gas near Hilo. 50,000 military are stationed in Hawai'i. Catholic Action is led by Jim Albertini, who is frequently arrested in the 1970s and 1980s for peace, anti-nuclear and civil disobedience activities.

May 30, 1972: U.S. Post Office issues an 11¢ air mail stamp to honor the City of Refuge (now called Pu'uhonua 'O Honaunau National Historic Park). The stamp is part of a National Parks Centennial series.

June 5, 1972: Governor George Ariyoshi signs a law to establish the Hawai'i Public Broadcasting Station, known as KHET-TV.

June 20, 1972: The Newspaper Preservation Law becomes law without the signature of Governor John Burns. This legalizes the Joint Operating Agreement of June 1, 1962, which established the Hawai'i Newspaper Agency.

June 23, 1972: President Richard Nixon signs a law, known as Title IX, to prohibit sex discrimination in education, especially admissions and athletics. Congresswoman Patsy Mink is responsible for the legislation.

July 20, 1972: The Stop H-3 Association and others file a lawsuit in federal court. They contend the proposed H-3 freeway violates federal laws. On March 3, 1972, the U.S. Environmental Protection Agency said the H-3 shouldn't be built because it will encourage overdevelopment of the windward area. The $250 million freeway, known as the "defense highway," connects three military bases – Kāne'ohe Marine Corps Base, Pearl Harbor and Hickam Air Force Base – and also helps civilian commuters. Opponents complain that the freeway is costly, unnecessary, insensitive to Hawai'i culture, and an environmental eyesore. Design and construction plans were completed before archaeological surveys. Historic preservation is not considered until federal, state, and OHA agencies sign an agreement in August, 1987. Five archeologists quit in protest during the construction.

August 17, 1972: Pu'u Koholā Heiau National Park is established on

Hawai'i Island to preserve the heiau built by Kamehameha I in 1792 for human sacrifices. The park also preserves John Young's property.

August 30, 1972: President Richard Nixon visits Hawai'i for two days of meetings with Japan Prime Minister Kakuei Tanaka. He also greets 650 VIP guests at a party hosted by Clare Booth Luce, a Hawai'i resident for several years. She is a former U.S. Ambassador, and widow of TIME MAGAZINE founder Henry Luce.

October 5, 1972: About one-half the public school teachers or 4,900 teachers, don't go to work. Teachers protest the Department of Education's delay on a new contract.

November 3, 1972: Judge Norito Kawakami overrules Lt. Governor George Ariyoshi, and allows Republican Party "get-out-the-vote" efforts to check the names of registered voters at polling places.

November 7, 1972: Voters approve a constitutional amendment to ratify the age 18 vote and national Equal Rights Amendment.

November, 1972: A commercial use for gene splicing results from a late night meal in a Waikīkī deli, and an agreement by two scientists to work together. Stanley Cohen of Stanford University and Herb Boyer of the University of California at San Francisco are attending a Honolulu conference about bacterial plasma. Boyer establishes Genentech in 1976 and appears on the cover of TIME MAGAZINE on March 9, 1981. They received $40 million in royalties for their patent.

December 16, 1972: Hawai'i receives 2 million tourists in a year, for the first time.

January 14, 1973: 1.5 billion people in 40 nations watch Elvis Presley's television special, ALOHA FROM HAWAI'I via satellite from Honolulu International Center. Elvis gives $75,000 to the Kui Lee Cancer fund. In all, Elvis made three movies in Hawai'i and gave 3 concerts here.

February 8, 1973: U.S. Senator Daniel Inouye is selected as one of 7 Senators to a Select Committee to investigate the Watergate scandal. Hearings begin on May 17. Inouye says the scandal is "unparalleled in our country's history." 40 presidential aides are indicted, and several resign or go to jail. On July 27, without realizing his microphone is "on," Inouye says "what a liar" of former presidential aide John Ehrlichman. On August 1, John Wilson, the lawyer for former presidential aide Bob Haldeman calls Senator Inouye "that little Jap." Wilson later says he didn't know it was an insult.

February 14, 1973: As part of "Operation Homecoming," the first group of 20 POWs from the Vietnam War arrive in Hawai'i. They stop at Hickam Air Force Base, en route to the mainland. On April 2, 600 more stop here for several days.

April 2, 1973: The nation's first state-wide teacher strike. 9,000 Hawai'i public school teachers strike 21 days until April 23, for higher pay and smaller classrooms. On March 22, Judge Norito Kawakami rules the strike is illegal. On April 11, Judge Masato Doi fines HSTA $100,000 plus $10,000 a day.

April 26, 1973: Hilo earthquake causes $15 million damage. It is the Hawaii's biggest earthquake since 1951, with a 6.2 magnitude.

May 22, 1973: Governor John Burns signs a law to establish public rights of way at Hawai'i beaches.

U.S. Senator Daniel Inouye

June 1, 1973: HONOLULU ADVERTISER reports that organized crime is taking hundreds of thousands of dollars in "protection" payments, and murder is involved. Several Honolulu Liquor Commissioners resign when they receive threats and their homes are burglarized.

June 6, 1973: Hawai'i Tax Foundation reports that $4 in every $10 in wages goes to government workers. Government workers are one-fourth of all workers in Hawai'i.

June 22, 1973: Hawai'i Supreme Court rules that all land created by new lava belongs to the state, not to property owners who try to claim it.

July 1, 1973: Seibu Corporation says it is buying 1,000 acres in 'Ulu-palakua and Mākena for $7 million, and will build the Prince Hotel.

July 27, 1973: Charlie Maxwell, president of Aboriginal Lands of Hawaiian Ancestry (ALOHA), seeks reparations from the U.S. government for land seized when the monarchy was overthrown. He demands the return of Kaho'olawe to Hawaiians, and not to the State. He says, "Our kupuna saw it first." ALOHA was Hawaii's first sovereignty organization, established by Louisa Rice in 1969.

December 16, 1973: Duncan MacDonald wins the first Honolulu Marathon. 151 of 167 runners finish the race.

December 21, 1973: Hawai'i Visitor's Bureau withdraws its financial support for HAWAI'I CALLS radio program to the mainland after 38 years. The HVB decides to spend $700,000 on magazine advertisements. HAWAI'I CALLS continues another two years until August 16, 1975, with funding from the Hawai'i Corporation.

December 31, 1973: C. Brewer buys Royal Hawaiian Macadamia Nut Co. from Castle and Cooke, and renames it Mauna Loa Macadamia Nut Corporation.

January 7, 1974: Federal Judge Sam King rules that Honolulu Mayor Frank Fasi can't ban HONOLULU STAR-BULLETIN reporter Richard Borreca from press conferences because it is "a form of censorship." Mayor Fasi responds the next day by excluding both the ADVERTISER and STAR-BULLETIN from his press conferences.

January 28, 1974: Hawai'i is the first state to restrict gasoline sales to odd or even-numbered days, based on license plate number. A nationwide oil shortage began when the Middle East stopped selling oil in 1973. Car lines at gas stations are long, and the cost of gasoline rises. The program ends on April 30, 1974.

March 9, 1974: 9,000 ILWU sugar workers strike 39 days until April 16. On April 7, about 6,000 ILWU pineapple workers strike until April 29. It is the first time in Hawai'i that both sugar and pineapple workers strike at the same time.

April 16, 1974: Ben Menor is the first Filipino to become a Hawai'i Supreme Court Justice.

May 7, 1974: 3,300 IBEW workers strike Hawaiian Telephone for 38 days until June 13.

May 14, 1974: 500 Registered Nurses strike four O'ahu hospitals for two weeks. It is Hawaii's first nurses strike.

May 17, 1974: Vice President Gerald Ford visits Hawai'i and tells a Republican State Convention, "If the Committee to Re-Elect the President (Nixon) is wrong, they will go to jail."

June 3, 1974: U.S. Supreme Court refuses to review how the Hawai'i Supreme Court justices select Bishop Estate trustees.

June 12, 1974: Acting Governor George Ariyoshi signs the Prepaid Health Care Act. Hawai'i is the first state to require employers to provide health insurance for workers.

July 13, 1974: Federal Judge Martin Pence stops the state from giving Unemployment Insurance to striking IBEW workers of Hawaiian Telephone because the company has not shut down. On October 14, 1975, Judge Pence rules that a state law that gives unemployment benefits to strikers when the business doesn't close is unconstitutional. This is the first time a judge rules against any state with a similar law. On January 22, 1986, the Hawai'i Supreme Court rules that striking workers can collect unemployment insurance if the employer continues "substantially" in business.

July 19, 1974: Kīlauea erupts for 3 days, with 150 fountains, and covers 3 square miles with lava.

National News

August 9, 1974: President Richard Nixon resigns to avoid being impeached. On September 8, President Gerald Ford pardons Nixon for any crime he may have committed.

August 16, 1974: The first annual Na Hōkū Hanohano awards are presented. Multiple winners include Cecilio and Kapono, Melveen Leed, The Brothers Cazimero, and Palani Vaughn.

August 26, 1974: Aviator Charles Lindbergh, age 72, is buried at Kīpahulu, Maui, which brings international attention to Maui. He was flown to Maui from New York so he could die in his Hāna home, where he lived part-time since 1971.

September 1, 1974: Church College of Hawai'i is renamed BYU-Hawai'i.

September 13, 1974: Honolulu city officials reject a proposed 186-foot condo at the base of Punchbowl. The condo would have been as tall as the rim of the crater.

September 24, 1974: Hawaii's longest strike begins. 50 Teamsters strike 14 months against Edward Sultan Manufacturing Company, a jewelry company. After 7 months, NLRB rules the strike is illegal because the union ignored the collective bargaining agreement.

September 25, 1974: A "moratorium" on Waikīkī construction begins when Mayor Frank Fasi does not sign an ordinance passed by the City Council. It lasts until September 30, 1975. Developers rush to submit $240 million of projects before the moratorium begins.

November 4, 1974: George Ariyoshi is elected as the nation's first governor of Japanese ancestry. He takes the oath of office on December 2. Previously he was a state legislator and Lt. Governor.

November 4, 1974: Eduardo Malapit is elected Kaua'i mayor, the first mayor of Filipino ancestry in the U.S.

November 4, 1974: Hawai'i Island voters reject water fluoridation by a 4-1 margin. This is the first county referendum held in Hawai'i. 10,000 voters signed referendum petitions after the County Council approved fluoridation on April 17.

January 4, 1975: President Gerald Ford signs the Native American Programs Act to recognize Hawaiians and Native Alaskans as Native Americans.

January 31, 1975: Lt. Governor Nelson Doi tells the state to "control the violence or close the schools." He accuses the DOE of "fumbling along" and says bathroom gangs must be controlled.

February 10, 1975: For the 3rd time in two years, the Hawai'i National Guard is sent to the State Prison. Warden Ray Belknap resigns and 45 officials are reassigned.

April 5, 1975: Former Governor John Burns, age 66, dies of cancer. He was a leading voice for statehood, and for the multi-racial, ethnic and Democratic Party takeover of Hawai'i.

April 6, 1975: Refugees from Vietnam and Hmong from Cambodia stop briefly in Hawai'i. "Operation Babylift" and "Operation Newlife" send 93,987 orphans and refugees to Hickam Air Force Base and Wake Island en route to the mainland from April 6-September 30.

May 1, 1975: After 23 years of trying, Honolulu Policewoman Lucille Abreu is Hawaii's first policewoman promoted to Detective. She scored highest on her last civil service test, but 30 men who scored lower were promoted ahead of her, so she filed a discrimination complaint in 1972.

May 8, 1975: "Nappy" Pulawa, the reputed leader of Hawai'i organized crime, is convicted in a federal court of tax evasion and sentenced to 24 years in prison. Prosecutors say he "imposed a reign of terror."

May 15, 1975: Russian scientist Vyacheslav Kovalev, age 27, defects to the U.S. while in Honolulu.

June 15, 1975: Sea Flite makes its first hydrofoil trip with interisland passengers at 57 mph on a 2 1/2 hour trip from O'ahu to Maui.

July 1, 1975: Lex Brodie establishes the Small Business Association of Hawai'i – renamed Small Business Hawai'i on May 1, 1983 – as a result of a dispute with the State Labor Department. First, Brodie

Governor George Ariyoshi

protested when two of his employees voluntarily quit and got unemployment payments. Later he objected when striking Hawaiian Telephone Company workers got unemployment payments.

July 1, 1975: Bishop Museum scientists, led by Patrick McCoy, discover a large stone tool "manufacturing plant" for Hawaiian adz, dated about 1100 A.D., atop Mauna Kea. This is the largest adz quarry in Polynesia, and perhaps the world. On January 4, 1939, the HONOLULU STAR-BULLETIN reported a large adz quarry was discovered inside Haleakalā.

July 25, 1975: One-day after returning to earth, 135 miles west of Ni'ihau, 3 Apollo-Souyez astronauts receive medical attention at Tripler Medical Center for lung irritation. Thomas Stafford, Vance Brand and Donald "Deke" Slayton and their families vacation for 10 days at Kāne'ohe Marine Corps Base. This was the last Apollo space flight, and first joint operation for the U.S. and Russia, which docked space ships while orbiting the earth.

July 28, 1975: Maui County signs an $11 million water agreement to bring 'Iao Valley water to Kīhei-Mākena. A&B, Wailea Development, and Seibu pay most of the water development costs so they can build hotels. This is the first time private companies agree to spend money to develop a public water project. Maui County's share is $4 million.

September 12, 1975: Dole Corp. closes its Maunaloa Plantation on Moloka'i, which had been growing pineapples since 1925.

September 12, 1975: The $33 million, 50,063 Aloha Stadium opens. 32,000 football fans attend the first sports event – UH loses to Texas A&I, 43-9. The movable stands are the first of its kind in the nation. They move by air cushions into different configurations for different events. Despite assurances by the contractor that the aluminum wouldn't rust, it did, resulting many years of legal battles.

October 15, 1975: State Transportation Director E. Alvey Wright tells Niu Valley residents about a $32 million light-rail transit system for Kalaniana'ole Highway. Other suggestions for study include a $334 million mountain-top highway and a $100 million reef highway.

October 16, 1975: Campbell Estate trustee Fred Trotter says "The time has gone for the leasehold system. The public doesn't care for (it)." He predicts Campbell Estate will sell its leasehold properties in 5 years.

October 16, 1975: Alu Like is established to provide educational, health, economic and job training services to Native Hawaiians. It is the first private sector agency to receive federal funds for native Hawaiians.

October 25, 1975: The Hale Koa Hotel opens with 420 rooms in Waikīkī. The $17 million, 15-story hotel serves the military, their families and retirees. Rooms are $20 for a double.

November 28, 1975: President Gerald Ford signs a military construction law that includes a provision added by Senator Daniel Inouye to restore Kaho'olawe and review returning the island to the state.

November 29, 1975: A "triple event" occurs today – an earthquake, tsunami and a brief Kīlauea eruption – for the first time since April 2, 1868. A 7.2 earthquake, Hawaii's biggest in 100 years, causes $4 million damage, and creates a tsunami that kills two people. The Boy Scout camp at Halapē, Hawai'i Island is now under water.

December 4, 1975: State Agriculture Director John Farias admits the Kohala Task Force has failed since 1971 to help former sugar workers find jobs after Castle and Cooke phased out its North Kohala Sugar Plantation. The Kohala Sugar Mill closes on December 31, 1975.

December 6, 1975: United Airline employees begin a nationwide strike. United brings a majority of Hawaii's tourists.

December 7, 1975: President Gerald Ford visits Hawai'i for one day after returning from China. He speaks at the East-West Center and visits Pearl Harbor. He has visited Hawai'i many times before and after his presidency.

December 23, 1975: Kukui Plaza, a controversial, city-private housing project is completed. The $50 million, 900-unit housing project provides 227 units for low and moderate income families on two city blocks. Mayor Frank Fasi is indicted, but not convicted of taking a bribe. The developer goes to prison.

December 24, 1975: U.S. Environmental Protection Agency allows pineapple companies to use some pesticides, such as heptachlor and chlordane, despite banning most other chemicals and pesticides that cause human cancer.

January 4, 1976: Nine Hawaiians and supporters make the first secret visit to Kaho'olawe to demand an end to the bombing. Kaho'olawe becomes a symbol of Hawaiian sovereignty.

January 14, 1976: Protect Kaho'olawe Association, soon renamed the Protect Kaho'olawe 'Ohana (PKO) is founded after the second secret visit to Kaho'olawe on January 12. On January 15, PKO persuades the U.S. Navy to protect historic sites, eliminate goats, control erosion, and allow monthly visits for religious, cultural, scientific and educational purposes. The group is led by Walter Ritte, Dr. Emmett Aluli, and George Helm. On February 13, the U.S. Navy approves 65 people to visit Kahoʻolawe for religious ceremonies.

January 15, 1976: Wailea's first hotel, the 600-room Maui Inter-Continental Wailea opens. On June 30, 1984, A&B buys Northwestern's interest for $30 million, and creates Wailea Development Company, which sells over 500 Wailea acres to Shinwa Golf Group for $197 million on February 10, 1989.

January 28, 1976: 800 Registered Nurses strike 6 Oʻahu hospitals and Kauai's Wilcox Hospital until February 16.

January 28, 1976: HONOLULU ADVERTISER says Honolulu Chamber of Commerce releases a 100-page report that says an inter-island ferry would cost too much, hurt the state economy, and require a state subsidy.

February 19, 1976: President Gerald Ford signs a proclamation to cancel Executive Order 9066. Ford says, "Not only was the evacuation wrong, but Japanese Americans were and are loyal Americans."

February 19, 1976: Former Punahou president John Fox says in an oral history, "I inherited an Oriental quota when I arrived (in 1944)...Eliminating it (in the late 1960s) was the biggest problem I ever faced." A 10% quota for Asian students was established in 1896 because Punahou alumni complained about too many Asian students at the school.

February 20, 1976: Marine Corps Pacific Commander General John McLaughlin says the Marines might leave Hawaiʻi if Kahoʻolawe is returned to Hawaiʻi jurisdiction. He says the Marines use Kahoʻolawe for target practice to improve their bombing skills.

February 26, 1976: U.S. Post Office issues a 13¢ stamp to honor the Hawaiʻi State flag, commissioned in 1816 by King Kamehameha I. The stamp is part of the American bicentennial series.

March 31, 1976: 60 UH students occupy Bachman Hall to protest fee hikes and education cuts. Two dozen students are arrested on April 1.

May 1, 1976: The double-hulled, 60-foot sailing canoe, Hōkūleʻa ("Star of Gladness") sails from Maui with a crew of 17, and arrives in Tahiti on June 4. It sails 2,400 miles without the aid of modern navigation instruments. As an expression of cultural pride, 17,000 Tahitians welcome the ship. The Hōkūleʻa returns to Hawaiʻi on July 26, welcomed by 15,000 people at Magic Island. The voyage, captained by Micro-

The Hōkūleʻa proves that Polynesians could travel long distances

nesian navigator Mau Piailug, proves that ancient Polynesians did sail long distances, guided by the sun, moon, stars, ocean currents, winds, etc. The voyage also symbolizes a cultural renaissance in Hawaiʻi. The Hōkūleʻa was first launched on March 8, 1975, sponsored by the Polynesian Voyaging Society.

May 20, 1976: U.S. Senator Daniel Inouye is named to the U.S. Senate Select Committee on Intelligence, to oversee the CIA and American spying. During Senator Inouye's two-year chairmanship, the Senate is told in advance about spying activities for the first time in U.S. history.

July 2, 1976: Hawaii's deepest geothermal well, at 6,450 feet, known as HGP-A, near Pahoa, discharges 676° steam and hot water. The well produces electricity for HELCO in 1982. The state closes HGP-A on December 13, 1989. Some people say geothermal is important because Hawaiʻi imports 90% of its oil, and we pay twice the national average for electricity. Hawaii's geothermal efforts are marked with years of protest by Hawaiians and environmentalists.

July 4, 1976: 100 members of Hui Alaloa, a Molokaʻi organization, protest the lack of public beach access. On March 12, they interrupted a press conference that announces the construction of the Sheraton Kaluakoi Hotel.

July 29, 1976: The $100 million luxury Hyatt Regency Hotel opens in Waikīkī with 1,260 rooms. The hotel is Hawaii's largest private construction project to date.

November 2, 1976: Daniel Akaka is the first Hawaiian elected to Congress. 3 Hawaiians – Robert Wilcox, Jonah Kūhiō and Sam King – were elected as non-voting Delegates during the territorial years.

November 15, 1976: A U.S. Navy ship accidentally catches a megamouth shark near Kāneʻohe that dies while entangled in a parachute line. It is the first ever seen in the world. It is 12 feet long, weighs a ton, and has a mouth one yard wide with small teeth. Waikīkī Aquarium Director Leighton Taylor nicknames the shark "megamouth."

December 3, 1976: 5,000 union construction workers march from Blaisdell Center to City Hall to protest a proposed construction moratorium of high rise buildings. They picket for 90 minutes, and create an enormous traffic jam by double and triple parking their trucks on Kapiʻolani, King and Beretania streets.

December 7, 1976: U.S. Army Museum of Hawaiʻi opens at Fort DeRussy to document and present Hawaii's military history.

December 20, 1976: A Virginia company, Marinco, says it isn't possible to remove all bombs and make Kahoʻolawe safe. It would cost up to $130 million to clear the island. The report is criticized as "a snow job" that exaggerates cost.

December 29, 1976: Maui County pays a $51,000 out-of-court settlement to the owners of the former New Newspaper. In exchange, the newspaper owners drop a $1.25 million lawsuit and exonerate Mayor Elmer Cravalho, Police Chief Abe Aiona, and County Attorney Arthur Ueoka. It all began when Ueoka sent a "confidential" May 10, 1972 letter to the wrong newspaper, the Lahaina Sun, threatening libel if a story about an April 7 Civil Service Commission hearing is made public. When the New Newspaper published the story on June 6-10, 1972, police visited Maui printers to find out who was printing the newspaper, and confiscated newspapers from news stands. A September 22, 1972 lawsuit alleged that county officials intimidated printers and newspaper sellers, and police confiscated newspapers illegally.

December 31, 1976: Bank of Hawaiʻi Economist Thomas Hitch says no single agricultural crop will replace sugar as a prosperous crop.

January 26, 1977: In his State of State speech, Governor George Ariyoshi proposes a "state plan" for controlled growth, which is adopted in 1978 as the nation's first. He says, "If we are not careful, overpopulation, overbuilding and overdevelopment will destroy the Hawaiʻi that we know." Ariyoshi prefers selective growth to no growth, and urges more development on the Neighbor Islands.

February 27, 1977: To preserve an agricultural lifestyle and prevent construction of a golf course and expensive homes at the Lester Marks Estate, Governor George Ariyoshi says the state will buy 600 acres of Waiāhole Valley for $6 million. Residents were to be evicted on March 1.

April 18, 1977: President Jimmy Carter says energy conservation is "the moral equivalent of war." The U.S. depends too much on foreign oil.

March 7, 1977: James Kimo Mitchell and George Helm die at sea while paddling a surfboard from Maui to Kahoʻolawe to get Walter Ritte and Richard Sawyer, who had been on Kahoʻolawe since January 30 to protest the bombing. Helm's surfboard is found near Lānaʻi. On February 11, George Helm had addressed the Hawaiʻi Legislature and urged the return of Kahoʻolawe.

March 21, 1977: Oʻahu Grand Jury indicts Mayor Frank Fasi for bribery in the Kukui Plaza scandal, and the mayor announces he will run for governor. All charges are dropped on December 27 when the prosecution's key witness, Kukui Plaza developer Hal Hansen, refuses to testify. The indictment says Mayor Fasi selected Hansen as the developer of the $50 million project in exchange for a $500,000 payoff, and Fasi supporter Harry Chung is the middleman. Fasi accuses Governor George Ariyoshi of a "political vendetta."

May 10, 1977: Federal Judge Samuel King declares several hotels to be guilty of fixing room rates and keeping rates at non-competitive levels from 1966-1974. When the hotels plead "no contest," Judge King fines them $150,000 – Sheraton Hotels and Hilton Hotels Corporation $50,000 each, Cinerama Hawaiʻi Hotels and Flagship International $20,000 each, and the Hawaiʻi Hotel Association $10,000.

June 2, 1977: Governor George Ariyoshi signs a law to allow former public school teachers John and Aiko Reinecke to sue the state for their dismissal on October 29, 1948. On October 7, 1976, the Board of Education restored John's teaching certificate. On March 9, 1978, Reinecke reaches an out-of-court settlement with the state for $250,000.

June 5, 1977: Governor George Ariyoshi orders the Hawai'i National Guard to "Operation Destroy." 13 tons of marijuana worth $53 million are uprooted on Maui, Moloka'i and Kaua'i. This is may be the beginning of "Operation Green Harvest." Maui Mayor Elmer Cravalho and Deputy Police Chief Joseph Cravalho are threatened with harm.

June 8, 1977: Governor George Ariyoshi signs the Coastal Zone Management Law to better protect and develop Hawaii's coastal areas.

June 21, 1977: A London art dealer pays $238,000 for a rare Hawaiian feather cloak at a London auction. It is displayed at Bishop Museum on September 28, 1977 – the first time in Hawai'i since 1825. The cloak is made of feathers from mamo, 'Ō'ō and 'I'iwi birds.

June 23, 1977: Five native Hawaiians of Protect Kaho'olawe 'Ohana are found guilty of trespassing on Kaho'olawe, a restricted military area, to try to stop the bombing. On August 26, a federal court sentences two frequent protestors, Walter Ritte and Richard Sawyer to the maximum 6 months in prison.

June 24, 1977: First Lady Rosalynn Carter dedicates the new $37 million Prince Jonah Kūhiō Federal Building.

June 24, 1977: With the support of native Hawaiians, Governor George Ariyoshi stops a lease auction of 33,000 acres of Hawaiian Homes pasturelands. Ariyoshi wants the land to go to Hawaiians on the waiting list. Since 1920, only 25,032 acres had gone to Hawaiians.

July 11, 1977: People Against Chinatown Evictions (PACE) begin a 10-day occupation at the Aloha Hotel rooming house to protest "redevelopment." They finally leave on July 21 when they are promised another place to live.

July 17, 1977: LOS ANGELES TIMES reports Punahou School is named one of the 10 best schools in the U.S., according to college admissions officers.

August 17, 1977: 860 Ironworkers begin a 4-month strike until December 12. The strike halts construction statewide, affecting 10,000 workers in all construction trades.

September 12, 1977: Samuel Kealoha Jr. is released from jail after 41 days and given 3-years probation for trespassing on Kaho'olawe. He says he'll return if the bombing continues. He was arrested on Kaho'olawe on February 22, 1977, found guilty on July 18, and chose jail because he refused bond.

September 13, 1977: Kīlauea erupts for 18 days.

October 15, 1977: Governor George Ariyoshi defends the $3.7 million Kohala Task Force. He declares, "What price is hope and dignity? Let the critics answer that." By 1980, 3 of the 5 business projects are still operating when the government loans end.

October 20, 1977: Prudential Insurance announces plans for 6 hotels with 4,200 rooms and a golf course on 875 acres of Oahu's North Shore. The $500 million-$1 billion, 22-year project would create 4,000 jobs, and have only 20% fewer rooms than Waikiki. The hotel is now known as the Turtle Bay Hilton. Two months later, on December 15, Prudential buys one-half of Hilton Hawaiian Village.

October 25, 1977: Judge Arthur Fong rules the city must stop searching people at Blaisdell Center rock concerts. On October 14, the city agreed to stop searching people at the Waikīkī Shell.

November 5, 1977: State Health Department reports that Hawai'i has the nation's highest rate of tuberculosis, mostly from foreign-born people. Hawaii's rate is 5 times the national average.

December 6, 1977; Hawai'i Council on Portuguese Heritage is established to preserve Portuguese heritage and culture in Hawai'i.

December 12, 1977: Kukui Plaza developer Hal Hansen is sent to Hālawa Correctional Center until he agrees to testily against Mayor Frank Fasi and Harry Chung in a bribery trial. Hansen pleads the 5th Amendment and refuses to testify. On August 14, 1978 Hansen is sentenced to 1 1/2 year in prison for federal tax and wire fraud violations.

December 13, 1977: The National Center for Health Statistics reports that people in Hawai'i live 4 years longer than the mainland average, and more than 2 years longer than people in any other state.

January 20, 1978: U.S. Post Office issues a 13¢ stamp to recognize the 200th anniversary of Captain Cook's arrival in Hawai'i.

March 17, 1978: At the beginning of a second Hōkūle'a voyage to Tahiti, the canoe overturns in a rough storm, and crew member Eddie Aikau volunteers to swim to Lāna'i for help. He disappears before reaching Lāna'i. The other 15 crew are rescued on March 17-18, and the voyage is canceled. The phrase, "Eddie would go," honors his heroism.

March 17, 1978: "Women Against Rape" submit 22,613 petition signatures to the Hawai'i Supreme Court. They ask for a hearing on the fitness of Judge Robert Richards,on who dismissed a rape charge against a defendant.

May 1, 1978: The Brothers Cazimero perform their first annual May Day concert at the Waikīkī Shell.

May 22, 1978: Governor George Ariyoshi signs the Hawai'i State Plan to guide future development through comprehensive planning that considers socio-economic, geographic and cultural concerns.

June 3, 1978: Governor George Ariyoshi signs a law that declares the Hawaiian language is the "native language of Hawai'i."

June 20, 1978: "Talk Story," the first-ever conference to recognize Hawaii's ethnic literature is held.

June 23, 1978: 4,600 petition signatures for an initiative are given to the Kaua'i Council. It is the state's first initiative to qualify for a ballot. The initiative would limit building height to 55 feet, but it was defeated by 34 votes on November 7, 1978, 6,680-6,646.

July 5, 1978: Hawaii's 3rd Constitutional Convention since 1950 begins, and lasts 90 days. The 102-delegate Convention is influenced by "Palaka Power," advanced by David Hagino in a pamphlet. The palaka shirts of plantation and dock workers have interlocking patterns that "represent a link to our past...to make one people and one culture." Hagino opposes religious conservatives who are anti-union and says liberals aren't progressive enough. The agenda seeks to control population and growth, tax tourism with funds for Hawaiian preservation, support Hawaiiana and union issues.

August 1, 1978: Hawai'i Crime Commission Report says organized crime has infiltrated political and social circles. Polls show crime is Hawaii's #1 concern. Hawaii's 9 organized crime gangs have killed an average of 6 people a year for a decade. The report is criticized for failing to "name names."

August 15, 1978: Hawai'i County Police Chief Gabe Paul estimates 250,000 lbs. of marijuana, worth $250-$750 million, is exported from his island each year. On January 7, 1985, law enforcement officials estimate marijuana statewide is worth $1 billion, which is more than sugar.

September 4, 1978: National Guard arrests 51 Hawaiians for trespassing near the runway at the Hilo Airport. Also 9 news reporters are arrested while covering the story. The airport is located on ceded lands. Judge

Ernest Kubota dismisses all charges on March 6, 1979. Protesters complain about the high percentage of Hawaiians in prison, the Kahoʻolawe bombing, and Bishop Estate mismanagement.

September 24, 1978: Hawaii's biggest campaign rally – 49,701 people rally at Aloha Stadium to support Democratic Governor George Ariyoshi.

October 24, 1978: President Jimmy Carter signs the Federal Airline Deregulation Law, which results in lower fares, more routes, and more visitors to Hawaiʻi.

November 7, 1978: Voters approve all 34 constitutional amendments submitted from a Constitutional Convention. Amendments create open primary elections, provide partial public financing of elections, transfer property taxes to counties, and create a spending limit for state government with a tax refund.

November 7, 1978: Voters approve 4 constitutional amendments affecting native Hawaiians. One amendment creates the Office of Hawaiian Affairs. OHA is a 9-member elected board to serve as the state's primary agency for native Hawaiians. A 2nd amendment requires the state to "promote the study of Hawaiian culture, history and language" in public schools. A 3rd amendment protects the customs of subsistence, cultural and religious rights of native Hawaiians regarding fishing, water use, and access, etc. A 4th amendment makes Hawaiian and English the two official languages of Hawaiʻi.

November 7, 1978: A "resign-to-run" constitutional amendment passes. It seeks to prevent Mayor Frank Fasi from running for governor.

November 10, 1978: President Jimmy Carter signs a law renaming the City of Refuge National Historical Park as Puʻu Hōnaunau National Historic Park.

November 10, 1978: Kaloko-Honokōhau National Historical Park is established on 750 acres to preserve Hawaiian culture and a fishpond.

December 22, 1978: Kauaʻi Police raid County Council offices during "friendly" gambling by county officials. The Council window is covered with cardboard to block anyone outside from seeing the gambling.

March 6, 1979: Hawaiian Airlines has the nation's first all-female crew. Captain Sharyn Emminger flies a 30-passenger airplane with a female co-pilot and stewardesses.

March 26, 1979: TIME MAGAZINE publishes a 6-page story about Maui as a desirable tourist destination.

April 23, 1979: DOWNTOWN PLANET is published by Diane Logsdon and Susie Thiemen.

May 14, 1979: Governor George Ariyoshi signs the Housing Loan and Mortgage Act, better known as Hula Mae, to provide low interest mortgage loans to help thousands of first time home buyers.

June 7, 1979: U.S. Post Office issues a 15¢ stamp with a picture of Hawaii's Wild Broadbean, which grows only on Hawai'i Island. The stamp is part of a series that honors endangered flora.

July 1, 1979: President Jimmy Carter arrives in Hawai'i for 90 minutes. He is returning from an Asia visit.

July 6, 1979: America's largest infrared telescope is dedicated on Mauna Kea. The 120-inch telescope costs $10 million. On November 22, 1880, King Kalākaua said he wanted to establish an observatory in Hawai'i.

July 24, 1979: Maui Mayor Elmer Cravalho officially resigns, one-year after winning re-election. He had been county chairman since 1967 and mayor since 1969.

September 12, 1979: Former President Richard Nixon visits Kaua'i for two days, en route to China.

October 1, 1979: U.S. Post Office issues a 10¢ stamp and postcard to honor 'Iolani Palace as part of an historic preservation series.

October 20, 1979: Hannibal Tavares receives a 51% vote total and defeats 17 candidates to win a special election as Maui mayor. He will serve 11 years as mayor.

October 22, 1979: 7,000 United Public Workers union members begin a 41-day strike against state and county governments until December 3. Most schools are closed for 13 days, and residential garbage is uncollected. This is the first government union to legally strike, based on a 1970 law to allow government employees a limited right to strike. A court orders 900 "essential workers" back to work because they are necessary to public health and safety, but they continue to strike.

December 8, 1979: UH Wahine volleyball team wins its first national championship – the first national collegiate championship ever won by a UH team. The team wins a second national title on December 19, 1982.

December 21, 1979: U.S. Navy submits an Environmental Impact Statement that supports using Kaho'olawe.

1980-1989

January 23, 1980: 18 Sand Island residents are arrested for refusing to leave their homes, and ignoring state eviction notices. The site is now a state park. In 1977, there were similar confrontations at Waiāhole and Waikāne Valleys.

January 27, 1980: 50,000 fans attend the National Football League's first Pro Bowl game in Hawai'i.

April 1, 1980: Federal census begins. Hawai'i has 964,691 population, a 25% increase since 1970 – 12% Hawaiian, 33% Caucasian, 6% Chinese, 25% Japanese, 14% Filipino, 2% Korean.

June 28, 1980: The American Hawai'i Cruises ship, INDEPENDENCE, is the first to begin regular 7-day interisland cruises.

July 31, 1980: President Jimmy Carter signs into law the Commission on Wartime Relocation and Internment of Civilians to study WW II internment, and to recommend a remedy. The bill was first introduced by U.S. Senator Daniel Inouye on August 7, 1979. The final report, PERSONAL JUSTICE DENIED, is issued on February 24 and June 16, 1983. The report says internment was based on "race prejudice, war hysteria and a failure of political leadership," not military necessity. A bill to provide $20,000 payment per survivor becomes law on August 10, 1988.

August 15, 1980: Iwilei oil tanks catch fire at the Honolulu waterfront, causing $3 million damage and killing two people. It is Hawaii's biggest fire since Chinatown 1900. On January 5, 1983, a jury awards Hawaii's largest compensation, $27.7 million to the families of the two men who died. The award is appealed, and on May 2, 1984, it is reduced to $15 million in an out-of-court settlement.

August 23, 1980: Hālawa Prison inmates riot. Six guards and 7 inmates are injured.

November 4, 1980: Eileen Anderson is elected as Honolulu mayor. She is Hawaii's first female mayor. Helene Hale was elected chairwoman of the Hawai'i Island Board of Supervisors in 1962.

November 4, 1980: By a 2-1 margin, Kaua'i voters approve a referendum to remove resort zoning for a Hilton resort at Nukoli'i Beach. The Kaua'i County Council had approved the zoning on February 1, 1979, but the referendum restores the 25-acre property to agriculture zoning. The project includes 150 luxury condominiums and a 350-room hotel, built by Graham Beach Partners.

December 1, 1980: Federal Judge William Schwarzer issues a Consent Decree to give PKO access to Kaho'olawe. The U.S. Navy and PKO agree to a joint use of Kaho'olawe. The Navy must clear 4,000 acres.

December 11, 1980: The CBS-TV program, MAGNUM P.I., starring Tom Selleck is broadcast for 8 years until May 8, 1988. The TV program spends $200 million on production here.

December 22, 1980: President Jimmy Carter signs a law to create the 11,000 acre Kalaupapa National Park. The same law also creates the 9-member Native Hawaiians Study Commission to study the culture, needs and concerns of native Hawaiians.

National News

January 20, 1981: 52 American hostages – held captive by Iran students and revolutionaries since November 4, 1979 – are set free.

January 31, 1981: A homemade pellet bomb explodes on Saturday night, outside the Kaua'i Mayor's Office window, perhaps to protest the Nukoli'i resort. No one is hurt.

February 9, 1981: Kaua'i Judge Kei Hirano rules that Nukoli'i construction can continue despite a voter referendum to stop it. He says the developer has vested rights that come with a legal building permit which the county gave to the developer a day before the election. He also says the condominium is 22% completed.

March 2, 1981: Two teens hijack a tour bus with 40 Japanese tourists. They steal $11,000 cash and jewelry. They are arrested on March 4.

March 15, 1981: Mid-Pacific Airlines begins interisland air service, at reduced rates, and sells thousands of discount coupons.

May 30, 1981: U.S. Navy agrees to clear 10,000 acres or 1/3 of Kahoʻolawe in an area with religious and cultural significance.

June 2, 1981: 250 inmates at the Oʻahu Correctional Center seize an overcrowded cellblock building for a few hours.

June 23, 1981: With a $241 million surplus, Governor George Ariyoshi signs a law to give each taxpayer a $100 income tax credit. The state constitution requires a tax credit when there is a surplus, and the General Fund balance exceeds 5% of general fund revenues two years in a row. For 14 straight years, the State gives a tax credit, usually just $1, but the rebate is $25 in 1982 and $125 in 1989. On May 21, 1983, the Legislature passes a law that says a tax credit might not be in the public's best interest, but the tax credit is a "Quixotic Act."

July 7, 1981: Alexander Young Hotel in downtown Honolulu is demolished after 77 years. Since 1970, the historic hotel housed only offices. The site is renamed as Bishop Square and Tamarind Park, where two office towers, 28 and 30-stories, are built in 1983-1984. The $45 million project is owned by Northwestern Mutual Life Insurance.

July 18, 1981: Hawaiian Electric Light Co. dedicates a 3 megawatt plant. Hawaiʻi is the second state to produce commercial geothermal power.

July 22, 1981: Hawaiian Electric creates its parent company, Hawaiian Electric Industries. Within 6 years, the parent company of this government-regulated utility owns Hawaiian Tug and Barge Corporation and Young Brothers Ltd., Hawaiian Insurance Group, American Savings Bank, and Malama Pacific Corporation – banking, insurance, transportation and real estate development companies.

November 1, 1981: The 1st Annual Hawaiʻi International Film Festival is held at the East-West Center. There are free movies, and appearances by actors and writers.

November 13, 1981: Public radio station KHPR begins broadcasting classical music, news, and fine arts programs.

November 23, 1981: The 130-year old Love's Bakery is sold to First Baking Company of Japan for $7 million.

December 18, 1981: The $65 million Maui Marriott Hotel opens in Kāʻanapali with 720 rooms. It is Marriott's first Hawaiʻi hotel, and the company's 100th hotel.

January 8, 1982: 125 people celebrate the Makahiki festival for the first recorded time on Kahoʻolawe.

January 25, 1982: Federal Judge Martin Pence stops legislative reapportionment. The court appoints a citizen panel to create districts based on census population not voter registration. On May 4, a new plan eliminates electing more than one legislator from a district. Some legislators represent more than one island, called "canoe districts."

April 8, 1982: U.S. Post Office issues a 20¢ stamp to honor Hawaii's nēnē and hibiscus as part of a series that recognizes state birds and flowers.

April 21, 1982: Meadow Gold Dairies dumps thousands of gallons of milk, worth $122,000, after traces of heptachlor, a toxic pineapple pesticide, are found in its milk products. O'ahu dairies are closed, and federal and state officials order Meadow Gold to stop selling milk. On August 11, State Senator Ben Cayetano says the State Health Department waited more than 3 months before testing milk products for contamination. Recent studies have shown no significant health effects from heptachlor exposure. A HONOLULU STAR-BULLETIN story on January 7, 1995 reports there was heptachlor contamination in 1970 at Del Monte pineapple, and there were other pesticides in O'ahu milk in 1975.

April 30, 1982: Honolulu's first woman mayor, Eileen Anderson receives a customary membership to the all-male Pacific Club, but it is not accepted. When the 1983 Legislature responds by considering two bills to deny a liquor license to any social club that discriminates, the Pacific Club changes its mind. On December 7, 1983 the club votes to approve women as members, and Andrea Simpson is accepted in 1984.

June 5, 1982: Up to 40 million tuna cans packed at Hawaiian Tuna Packers plant at Kewalo Basin, are recalled nationwide because two cans have holes. Castle and Cooke owns Bumble Bee Tuna, which owns Hawaiian Tuna.

July 31, 1982: C. Brewer begins a 10-year plan to convert 8,000 acres of sugar to macadamia nuts at Hāmākua and Ka'ū.

August 11, 1982: A Palestinian terrorist hides a small bomb on a Pan Am flight from Tokyo to Honolulu. A 16-year old boy dies when the bomb explodes under his seat, about 20 minutes before landing in Honolulu. The bomb makes a 1x3 foot hole in the floor. Sixteen people are injured.

October 14, 1982: The State Supreme Court rules that voters have the right to make land use decisions. This requires Kaua'i County to withdraw developers' permits and stop resort construction at Nukoli'i Beach.

November 2, 1982: By a 394-vote margin, voters revise the Hawai'i Island County Charter to give voters the right to decide financial issues with the referendum and initiative ballot. The issue is supported by people seeking lower property taxes.

November 23, 1982: Hurricane 'Iwa strikes Kaua'i with 117 mph winds, killing four, making 7,000 Kaua'i and O'ahu people homeless, and causing $250 million damage. Kauai's economy plunges.

December 23, 1982: In the nation's biggest college basketball upset, Chaminade University basketball team coached by Merv Lopes, defeats the nation's top-ranked University of Virginia team, 77-72 at Blaisdell Center. Virginia, led by All-American and future NBA All-Star Ralph Sampson, had been hospitalized a few days earlier in Japan.

December 25, 1982: First Aloha Bowl college football game is held. Ten million TV viewers watch Washington beat Maryland, 21-20.

December 31, 1982: Hawai'i receives 4 million tourists in a year, for the first time.

January 3, 1983: Kīlauea, the world's most active volcano, begins erupting at various times for 20 years. Lava covers 100 square miles, adds more than 500 acres of new land to Hawai'i Island, destroys nearly 200 Kalapana homes, causes more than $60 million damage, destroys Kaimū Beach, also known as "Black Sand Beach." A 6.2 earthquake near Kalapana causes $1 million damage.

January 20, 1983: Six native Hawaiians, claiming their aboriginal rights, are arrested for living at Mākua Beach without a permit. The state bulldozes their tents and buildings as the Hawaiians protest peacefully.

February 9, 1983: State officials close Mānoa Finance and Great Hawaiian Financial Cooperative. This freezes $55 million in savings of 13,000 people. On February 10, Mānoa Finance files bankruptcy after losing too much money from real estate investments. On June 3, 1985, Governor George Ariyoshi signs a $10.5 million "loan" of state tax money to repay depositors at three financial institutions. On October 29, 1986, Mānoa Finance owner Hirotoshi Yamamoto is sentenced to 4 months in prison for embezzling $118,000, and he is ordered to repay it.

February 10, 1983: Hawaii's biggest voter fraud cases begin. Senator Clifford Uwaine, aide Ross Segawa, Rep. Gene Albano, and 22 others are indicted for voter fraud for the 1982 primary election and for illegally registering dozens of voters. Segawa was defeated for the House in November 1982, while Albano and Uwaine were defeated for re-election in 1984. On May 6, 1983, Segawa is expelled from UH Law School, and 9 other indicted law students are reprimanded and suspended. On August 17, 1984, Segawa receives a one-year prison sentence. On February 11, 1987, he is released from jail after serving 2 months because he testified against Uwaine. On October 28, 1986, Uwaine receives a 3-month prison sentence. On May 9, 1985, Albano receives a 5-year prison sentence, but he flees to the Philippines. On

July 11, 1987, Albano is deported and returns to Hawai'i. After 18 months in prison, he is paroled on December 5, 1988.

March 3, 1983: A Kīlauea eruption destroys Kalapana homes for the first time since 1960. It is the most lava produced from Kīlauea in 500 years. Lava continues for 20 straight years.

April 1, 1983: Hal "Aku" Lewis of KSSK radio creates his last big practical joke – a non-existent parade with celebrities, attracting hundreds of people to the streets, looking for a parade. He dies on July 21, after a 30-year career on KGU, KSSK, and KPOA.

June 23, 1983: The federal Native Hawaiian Study Commission issues its final report, concluding that Hawaiians have no legal claim under federal law to financial reparations or lands lost in 1893. The two-volume report gives majority and dissenting viewpoints, plus a history of the overthrow and annexation, as well as the social, economic and government conditions affecting native Hawaiians. The dissenting report is written by the three Hawai'i commissioners – Rodger Betts, Kina'u Kamali'i, and Winona Beamer.

August 9, 1983: KSSK radio premieres the Perry and Price show, featuring Michael Perry and Larry Price.

August 15, 1983: A Federal-State Task Force report for the U.S. Department of the Interior repeats the State Auditor's charges that the Hawaiian Homes Commission and State Department of Hawaiian Home Lands are disorganized and "unauditable." The report makes 134 recommendations to improve the programs. The report says many people have been waiting for 30 years for a homestead, and the 7,900 people on a waiting list might have to wait 50 years. Past governors took 13,600 acres from the program to build game preserves, airports, parks and defense projects. As a result of the report, 2,500 lots are awarded to native Hawaiians in the 1980s.

September 21, 1983: Two residents and 16 supporters are arrested at Hale Mōhalu, a home for Hansen's Disease patients – ending 5 years of resistance. All the buildings are demolished. The residents are acquitted of any crime.

October 17, 1983: Honolulu Mayor Eileen Anderson signs a law to make fireworks illegal without a permit, except for cultural or religious purposes.

November 16, 1983: A 6.7 earthquake centered near Koiki, Hawai'i Island causes $6 million damage.

November 17, 1983: Carpenter Union leader and State AFL-CIO chief Walter Kupau is convicted of 6 counts of perjury in a labor dispute with Maui contractor Walter Mungovan. Kupau is sentenced to 2 years in federal prison and fined $10,000. Mungovan reported he had received death threats, and enters the federal witness protection program.

November 20, 1983: A two-day strike by UH faculty is their first ever. The strike intends to improve contract negotiations for better pay.

January 19, 1984: Francis Morgan buys the 35,000 acre Hāmākua Sugar Company from Theo Davies for $69 million. It is a "gutsy" buy because other sugar plantations are closing. On June 1, 1988, Governor John Waihe'e signs a $10 million state government loan for Hāmākua, plus a $2 million loan for small farmers, for 5 years at 3% interest. On June 8 it is the State Agriculture Department's largest loan ever.

February 4, 1984: By 59%-40%, Kaua'i voters approve a referendum to restore resort zoning at Nukoli'i Beach. After Hurricane 'Iwa struck in 1982, Kauai's economy plunged, hotels closed, and thousands of people lost their jobs. The developer-funded, pro-resort group, "Kauaians for Nukoli'i" gave the county $50,000 to pay for the special election.

March 1, 1984: A new $40 million, 455 room, Halekūlani Hotel opens. In 1999, readers of GOURMET Magazine vote Halekūlani Hotel as the world's best hotel.

March 12, 1984: U.S. Post Office issues a 20¢ stamp to honor the 25th anniversary of Hawai'i statehood.

March 25, 1984: Mauna Loa erupts for 22 days with a "curtain of fire" that sends lava to within 4 miles of Hilo.

March 30, 1984: When Kīlauea erupts with 700-foot fountains, it is the first time since 1868 that Kīlauea and Mauna Loa both erupt at the same time.

April 22, 1984: President Ronald Reagan arrives in Hawai'i for two days, en route to China. As a spokesman for General Electric, he came to Hawai'i in 1959 to speak against Communism.

May 4, 1984: House Speaker Henry Peters is selected as a Bishop Estate trustee. He says the Legislature is a part-time job, but many people complain his two jobs represent a conflict of interest. Peters is House Speaker from 1981-1986, and a Bishop Estate trustee from 1984-1999.

May 14, 1984: Protect Kaho'olawe 'Ohana persuades Japan, New Zealand and Australia not to bomb Kaho'olawe during the annual Pacific Rim (RIMPAC) military exercises. Canada agrees to use "puff" bombs. This is the largest RIMPAC war activity since 1971, with 80 ships and 50,000 military. Only the U.S. will bomb Kaho'olawe. Two years later, on May 16, 1986, Protect Kaho'olawe 'Ohana persuades Japan, England and Australia not to participate in RIMPAC's June bombing. Only the U.S. and Canada bomb the island.

May 14, 1984: Honolulu Advertiser publishes a story about the impact of tourism from an April 1983 state report. Tourism provides 25% of Hawaii's revenue and 33% of Hawaii's jobs.

May 20, 1984: Maui-born sumo wrestler Jesse Kuhaulua, who took the Japanese name Takamiyama, retires after 20 years. In 1972, he became the first Westerner to win a major tournament.

May 30, 1984: U.S. Supreme Court unanimously upholds Hawaii's 1967 Land Reform Act. The law is intended to break up large estates by forcing large landowners to sell leasehold land occupied by single-family residential lessees. Bishop Estate, which owns 20% of all private property on O'ahu, fought the state law, and didn't want to sell its land to its tenants at prices set by a judge or jury.

May 31, 1984: Governor George Ariyoshi signs a law to prohibit police officers from striking, and sends contract disputes to binding arbitration. Ariyoshi says, "I would hate to think of a policeman on strike when a crime victim needs help."

July 6, 1984: Capital District Jaycees of the Honolulu Jaycees defies its national organization and admits 3 women members for the first time in 65 years, and is suspended for it. On August 16, 30 women are admitted when the U.S. Supreme Court rules the national organization must admit women members.

July 18, 1984: MIDWEEK publishes its first issue. Publisher Ken Berry adopts a magazine style newspaper with syndicated national and local columns rather than news. It is free on O'ahu, circulation 270,000.

August 21, 1984: To celebrate Hawaii's 25th statehood anniversary, First Lady Jean Ariyoshi plants the first of "Million trees of Aloha." By December, 1986, about 1,370,000 trees are planted.

September 14, 1984: The ACLU of Hawai'i files suit against the State for overcrowding at men's and women's prisons, OCC and WCC. The prisons hold twice as many inmates as they are built to hold. The lawsuit says overcrowding creates "a harmful and intolerable environment" which falls "below standards of human decency..."

September 19, 1984: Three strikes hit Hawai'i, which cost the economy $122 million. 360 Concrete Union workers strike from July 17 to October 10; 1,000 electricians strike from September 10 to December 28; and 2,000 Carpenters Union workers are locked out 4 months from September 19 to January 16, 1985.

October 19, 1984: Puna Sugar Company, owned by Amfac, completes its last cane harvest after 85 years. The company is going out of business. Each of the 55 employees gets 5 acres.

November 6, 1984: Chuck Norwood is elected by voters to the Board of Education, and is re-elected until 1993. He was convicted of 2nd degree murder in 1971, paroled from prison in 1975, and later pardoned. On September 5, 1989, he settles with the U.S. Attorney after defaulting on a $22,873 state loan.

November 6, 1984: O'ahu voters approve the Date-La'au initiative to control excessive growth in Mō'ili'ili, and lowers the building height limit from 350 feet down to 40 feet.

December 1, 1984: PACIFIC BUSINESS NEWS is purchased by American City Business Journals.

December 20, 1984: U.S. defeats Japan in a "legends" baseball game on Maui, 10-7. Players include Willie Mays, Hank Aaron, Sandy Koufax, Don Drysdale, Ernie Banks, Frank Robinson, Lou Brock, and Willie McCovey. The most famous Japan player is Sadaharu Oh.

January 16, 1985: Six alleged Yakuza (Japan's organized crime) are fined and ordered to be deported by Federal Judge Martin Pence for lying to Immigration officials about their criminal records.

January 24, 1985: Lt. Colonel Ellison Onizuka is the first Hawai'i-born astronaut. His 3-day flight on the space shuttle, DISCOVERY, is America's first secret military mission. He was selected from 8,100 applicants on January 16, 1978.

May 8, 1985: HAWAI'I TIMES files for bankruptcy after 90 years. At its peak, the Japanese newspaper had 10,000 circulation.

May 13, 1985: The U.S. Supreme Court upholds the August 21, 1984 ruling of a Federal Appeals Court to stop H-3 construction.

May 17, 1985: Liquid ammonia spills from a 70,000 gallon Pier 1 tank in Kahului. As a safety precaution, 2,000 people are

Astronaut Ellison Onizuka

evacuated from homes, hotels, and shopping centers in a one-mile area.

May 17, 1985: United Airlines pilots strike until June 14. Hawai'i officials recognize our dependence on United Airlines, which brings one-half of our tourists here. Hawaii's tourist-dependent economy loses $155 million during the strike.

June 12, 1985: Hawaiian Airlines is Hawaii's first airline to fly daily round-trips to the mainland. The first flight is to Los Angeles.

July 2, 1985: California billionaire David Murdock purchases financially troubled Castle and Cooke, a 135-year old Hawai'i company. He announces plans to develop a luxury hotel on Lāna'i, and considers relocating the Iwilei Cannery to Central O'ahu.

July 19, 1985: National accreditors evaluating the University of Hawai'i, criticize Hawaii's "pattern of doing business" and "inappropriate intrusions" by politicians in UH affairs. On June 16, 1998, Governor Ben Cayetano signs a law to give UH responsibility for its legal, personnel, financial and purchasing matters.

August 13, 1985: Hawai'i Supreme Court Chief Justice Herman Lum appoints a citizens panel to investigate a variety of legal improprieties involving political and administrative lobbying by court employees.

August 19, 1985: Mayor Frank Fasi signs an ordinance to build an H-Power project that will convert garbage to energy at Campbell Industrial Park. The facility will be financed with a $195 million bond.

October 5, 1985: Three veteran City Councilmen – George Akahane, Toraki Matsumoto and Rudy Pacarro – are removed from office by voters in a special election, after they change political affiliation from Democrat to Republican.

October 21, 1985: Ronald Rewald is convicted on 94 counts of fraud, perjury and tax evasion after being accused of stealing $22 million from 400 investors. On December 9, he is sentenced to 80 years imprisonment, fined $325,000, and must pay restitution to 300 victims. On June 23, 1995, he is released on parole from a California federal prison, probably due to a back injury.

November 23, 1985: Chaminade brings the Hawaiian Air Silversword Invitational basketball tournament to Maui for the first time. The tourney will become the prestigious Maui Invitational Tournament, perhaps the nation's the top college basketball tourney.

November 27, 1985: Maui Mayor Hannibal Tavares approves a land swap with Seibu to result in closing part of the Old Mākena Road alongside the ocean, and give Seibu 1,100 beachfront acres for its $35 million Mākena Prince Hotel. A new mauka road will be built.

December 21, 1985: 1,000 Moloka'i residents attend a rally to support the construction of a West Moloka'i luxury hotel at Kaiaka Rock.

January 28, 1986: Ellison Onizuka, age 39, dies aboard the space shuttle, CHALLENGER, with 6 other astronauts in an explosion about one minute after launching.

National News

February 19, 1986: U.S. Senate ratifies a United Nations treaty to prohibit genocide. The U.S. had signed the treaty in 1948, but the U.S. Senate had never ratified it.

February 26, 1986: Former Philippines President Ferdinand Marcos and others arrive in Hawai'i as exiles, after he is overthrown by a peaceful revolt. During his exile, he is accused of stealing $10 billion from his nation, and there are many protests against his residency here.

March 1, 1986: Bank of Hawai'i economist Wali Osman says it costs 26% more than the national average to live in Hawai'i.

April 4, 1986: Mayor Frank Fasi's administration submits plans to the City Council for a fast-track, affordable housing project known as Waiola Estates. It would be one of the city's largest housing projects, with 1,535 homes on 269 acres. The city bought the land from Castle and Cooke for $7 million. The city buys a full-page newspaper ad on April 9 to attract homebuyers, and 6,000 people respond. The ads are premature because the project is on prime agriculture land. The project dies on June 5, 1987 when the State Land Use Commission votes to keep Waiola in agriculture zoning. An environmental group, Hawaii's Thousand Friends, files a lawsuit seeking $482,921 that the city spent on the project. On August 24, 1987 a Circuit Court jury convicts Mayor Frank Fasi, Managing Director Andy Anderson and Housing Director Alvin Pang of fraud and libel for the project. On February 16, 1989, the Hawai'i Supreme Court reverses the convictions.

April 22, 1986: Governor George Ariyoshi signs a law to repeal the Hawai'i Newspaper Agency and anti-trust exemption for the HONOLULU ADVERTISER and STAR-BULLETIN.

May 3, 1986: Hawaii's only serial killer murders the 5th and final young woman. The cases are unsolved.

May 19, 1986: Governor George Ariyoshi signs the "Aloha Spirit" law. The new law proclaims that expressing "warmth in caring with no obligation in return" as well as kindness, harmony, modesty, humility, pleasantness, and patience are the character traits of Hawaii's people.

May 20, 1986: Mary Pukui, age 91, dies. She composed 150 songs, and wrote 50 books including the HAWAIIAN DICTIONARY, PLACE NAMES OF HAWAI'I, and 'OLELO NO'EAU: HAWAIIAN PROVERBS AND POETICAL SAYINGS. She was Hawaii's foremost Hawaiiana scholar.

June 13, 1986: Governor George Ariyoshi signs a law to raise Hawaii's legal drinking age from age 18 to 21. The drinking age was reduced in 1972, but too many young drunk drivers were involved in accidents.

June 13, 1986: Governor George Ariyoshi signs a law to create a 5% hotel room tax to raise about $55 million a year. The Legislature had debated the room tax for 20 years.

June 26, 1986: U.S. Justice Department seizes 141 acres of land worth $2.2 million at Kīlauea, Kaua'i. A Hong Kong company had bought the property with drug money.

July 4, 1986: KGMB-TV news anchor Bob Sevey retires after 25 years. He began in 1959, and spent all but 4 years at KGMB.

July 14, 1986: Unsuccessful 1982 Lt. Governor candidate Bernaldo Bicoy, a former state legislator, is convicted of illegally accepting $23,430 in matching State Campaign Spending funds. On August 29, he is sentenced to 4 months in prison.

August 8, 1986: Honolulu Symphony musicians strike for 16 weeks until November 26. Musicians gain a 38% wage increase. It is the Symphony's first major strike in 86 years.

September 20, 1986: Lt. Governor John Waihe'e, the underdog, comes from behind to defeat Congressman Cecil Heftel as the Democratic Party nominee for Governor. A late, rumor-based smear campaign spread by unknown people may have contributed to Heftel's defeat.

October 13, 1986: 850 employees of Kaiser Hospital strike for 7 weeks until November 29.

October 18, 1986: President Ronald Reagan signs a law to make H-3 the nation's first freeway to be exempt from a federal transportation law. U.S. Senator Daniel Inouye and Congressman Daniel Akaka had attached amendments for the exemption to a major budget bill that allows the federal government to pay its bills and also limits weapons in space. When the bill passed the House on September 25 by 201-200, the tie-breaking vote was cast by Congressman Neil Abercrombie, who repeatedly said he opposed H-3 but favors arms control. Abercrombie became a member of Congress the previous day, after winning a special election.

November 4, 1986: Lt. Governor John Waihe'e, is elected governor. He is the first elected state governor of Hawaiian ancestry.

Governor John Waihe'e

November 4, 1986: Pat Saiki is the first Hawai'i Republican elected to Congress since Hiram Fong.

November 4, 1986: By a 2-1 margin, Hawai'i Island voters reject a referendum to exempt the military from a 1981 county law that bans nuclear materials. In 1984, activist James Albertini tried to apply the law to stop U.S. Navy ships from entering Hilo Harbor, so the county amended the law to exempt the military.

November 12, 1986: The British Airways supersonic jet, CONCORD, arrives in Hawai'i for the first time. The Concord flew from Oakland in 2 hours and 15 minutes, at 1,350 mph. A ticket costs $24,000.

November 26, 1986: Kīlauea eruption destroys many Kalapana homes.

December 2, 1986: Resort construction begins at West Beach, O'ahu. Plans for a $2 billion, 640-acre development include 8 hotels, 5,000 condos and homes, and 4 man-made lagoons in two years. The Horita-Kumegai Gumi project is about the same size as Waikīkī, and is renamed Ko 'Olina. When Japan's recession hits, financing became unavailable and little is done beyond building the golf course, one hotel and some townhouses. In 1999, the project is sold to developer Jeff Stone. The 387-room 'Ihilani Hotel opens on December 15, 1993. The State Land Commission had rezoned the former sugar land on June 15, 1977.

December 23, 1986: Honolulu Liquor Commission rules the Waikīkī Hyatt Regency Hotel is guilty of racial discrimination, and suspends its liquor license for 3 days.

December 31, 1986: Maui receives 2 million tourists in a year, for the first time.

January 7, 1987: U.S. Senator Daniel Inouye chairs the Senate Select Committee on Military Assistance to Iran and the Nicaraguan Opposition. The panel investigates the "Iran-Contra" scandal involving presidential aides who secretly arranged an illegal weapons sale to Iran, then used the money to help Nicaraguan rebels overthrow their government.

January 16, 1987: Thomas Jaggar Museum opens at the Hawai'i Volcanoes National Park.

February 4, 1987: Dole Plantation announces the end of a 20-year summer tradition. Off-island high school students won't be hired to pick pine-apple on Lāna'i because Dole is harvesting a new pineapple all year.

U.S. Congresswoman Pat Saiki

March 15, 1987: Ka Lahui is established, with 8,000 members to achieve a sovereign Hawaiian nation.

March 16, 1987: Honolulu City closes the popular Ha'ikū "Stairway to Heaven" because it needs $875,000 in repairs. The 2,800-foot site has a steel ladder "stairway" with 3,922 steps, built in 1955.

March 29, 1987: California oil millionaire Ed Pauley sells Coconut Island, Moku-O-Lo'e, for $8.5 million to Japanese developer Katsuhiro Kawaguchi, just a few hours after rejecting an $8 million state offer. On May 22, 1989, a federal Immigration judge bans Kawaguchi from the U.S. because he entered with a false visa, and fines him $100,000.

March 31, 1987: A lava flow destroys a popular lava-shaped, Kalapana swimming pond known as "Queens Bath."

April 16, 1987: Honolulu City Council approves a Kaiser Development plan to build a 192-unit residential subdivision across from Sandy Beach. Opponents seek a ballot initiative to downzone the property.

May 23, 1987: The Hōkūle'a returns to Hawai'i with a crew of 15 after a 2-year, 16,000 mile "Voyage of Discovery" without any modern navigation instruments, and sailing against prevailing winds. Nainoa Thompson is the first Hawaiian in 500 years to navigate a voyaging canoe. Hōkūle'a may have been the first Hawaiian canoe in 1,000 years to make the "Polynesian Triangle" voyage from Hawai'i to Society Islands, to Cook Islands, to New Zealand, to Tonga, to American Samoa, to Cook Islands, to Tahiti, to Rangiroa, to Hawai'i. 12,000 people welcome the HōKŪLE'A at Kualoa Beach.

May 28, 1987: Dillingham Corp., the nation's 15th largest construction company, is sold to Shimizu Construction. Dillingham Corp. was founded on December 29, 1961 with the merger of O'ahu Railway and Land Co. and Hawaiian Dredging and Construction. In 1986, Dillingham sells Young Brothers and Hawaiian Tug and Barge Co. to Hawaiian Electric Industries.

May 28, 1987: Japanese Cultural Center opens on Beretania Street.

June 13, 1987: U.S. Post Office issues a 22¢ stamp with a picture of an 'I'iwi, bird found only in Hawai'i, for a series honoring wildlife.

June 14, 1987: Tom "Fat Boy" Okuda, Deputy Court Administrator, head of the Traffic Violations Bureau and Sheriff's Office, is found guilty of 19 counts of fixing tickets and altering public records. Prosecutors had found police records alleging 14,000 cancelled tickets. On July 27, 1990 he is dismissed after 41 years on the job.

July 7, 1987: Governor John Waihe'e signs a Plant Closing Law to require businesses with 50 or more employees to give workers 45 days notice that the business is sold or closing. This law protects workers from sudden, unexpected layoffs. The law is adopted because Airport Holiday Inn was sold to Nimitz Partners, and 140 union workers were fired without advance notice on New Year's eve.

July 14, 1987: Hawai'i Supreme Court rules that geothermal development doesn't violate the constitutional rights of native Hawaiians to worship Pele, the volcano goddess. Campbell Estate begins a $40 million geothermal project to provide 235 megawatts of electricity.

July 15, 1987: The Alexander & Baldwin Sugar Museum opens in Pu'unēnē, Maui to exhibit the history of Maui's sugar industry and plantation life.

July 23, 1987: Board of Education approves a pilot project to teach K-1 students in the Hawaiian language. The first Hawaiian Language Immersion Program begins at two schools in September. The program seeks to prevent the extinction of the Hawaiian language. The program has expanded to nearly 20 K-12 schools.

August 11, 1987: Human skeletal remains of 900 Native Hawaiians begin to be removed from Maui's Honokahua sand dunes during site work for the future Kapālua Hotel. One-half of the burial site is excavated when statewide protests erupt and Governor John Waihe'e stops the digging. On June 13, 1988, Governor John Waihe'e signs an amendment to the state Historic Preservation Law to create Island Burial Councils, administered by DLNR through a burial sites program. On September 7, 1989, an agreement to rebury the skeletal remains is signed by Kapālua Land, OHA, the state, and Hui Alanui 'O Mākena. The State pays $6 million for conservation easement and to restore the burial site. Developer Colin Cameron changes the location of his hotel.

August 18, 1987: Hawaii's only professional baseball team, the Hawai'i Islanders leave after 27 years, and relocate to Colorado Springs. Lack of attendance is the primary reason.

September 13, 1987: Real Estate developer Chris Hemmeter announces he will buy Hawaiian Airlines for $100 million from John Magoon, but the deal dies a month later when the stock market drops.

September 17, 1987: State Board of Education votes to require students to use standard English and to discourage pidgin English in public schools. On the same day, the DOE releases an annual report of national reading scores, which again shows Hawai'i students scoring below the national average.

September 29, 1987: Russia fires two unarmed nuclear missiles, which land in the sea, 500 miles from Hawai'i. This is the closest any nuclear missiles have ever come to Hawai'i The U.S. military failed to notify Hawai'i officials. On August 16, 1989, Congresswoman Pat Saiki says the Pentagon told her that U.S. missiles have been flying over Maui for 20 years, and landing about 2,600 miles southwest of Hawai'i. In contrast, on August 11, 1989, an unarmed Russian missile landed only 1,250 miles southeast of O'ahu.

November, 1987: HONOLULU MAGAZINE celebrates its 100th anniversary. PARADISE OF THE PACIFIC was published from 1888-1966, and renamed as HONOLULU MAGAZINE in July, 1966.

November 1, 1987: Alice Llanos Busmente and Mary Llanos Cordero publish the first issue of FIL-AM COURIER.

November 23, 1987: Federal Judge Alan Kay rules the "Good Friday" state holiday is constitutional. It became a Hawai'i holiday in 1941 because government workers had no holiday from February 22 to May 30. Judge Kay says, "whatever its intended purpose, (it) has become a traditional...day of rest and relaxation."

December 8, 1987: The state-subsidized Moloka'i Ferry begins taking 70 workers to jobs on Maui, especially at the Westin Maui Hotel in Lahaina. Soon, 150 workers are taking the daily 90-minute ferry, operated by Sea Link Hawai'i. Moloka'i has 12% unemployment in 1987.

December 8, 1987: C. Brewer's Wailuku Agriculture announces it will replace sugar with pineapples. The company had been growing sugar since 1862. The company is also growing macadamia nut trees.

January 19, 1988: Mid-Pacific Airlines stops passenger flights and files for bankruptcy after 7 years of low budget fares. At its peak, the new airline got one-fourth of Hawaii's passenger business.

February 4, 1988: Former Christian evangelist Pat Robertson wins Hawaii's Republican presidential primary. When the "religious right" takes control of the Republican Party, several female Republican legislators and party leaders protest the anti-abortion platform by becoming Democrats. They are Rep. Virginia Isbell and former legislator Kina'u Kamali'i, Senator Donna Ikeda, and Senator Ann Kobayashi.

April 28, 1988: Just 20 minutes after an Aloha Airlines flight leaves Hilo, an 18-foot roof section between the cockpit and wings, rips off at 24,000-foot altitude. A flight attendant is sucked through the roof to her death, and 61 of the 95 passengers and crew are injured. Pilot Robert Schornstheimer guides the damaged, 19-year old airplane to a safe, emergency landing in Kahului 13 minutes later.

May 12, 1988: Federal Aviation Administration fines Hawaiian Airlines $1,169,000 for 5 years of violations. It is the second highest fine issued by the FAA to date.

June 17, 1988: Governor John Waihe'e signs a law to establish Bishop Museum as the State Museum of Natural and Cultural History.

July 16, 1988: Aaron Mahi conducts the Royal Hawaiian Band in a concert at New York's Carnegie Hall.

National News

July 3, 1988: U.S. Navy mistakenly shoots and destroys an Iran passenger jet. All 290 people aboard the airplane died.

August 10, 1988: President Ronald Reagan signs the Civil Liberties Act, which apologizes to AJAs for WW II internment and relocation, compensates about 60,000 AJAs with $20,000 for financial losses, and urges presidential pardons for those convicted of violating laws in protest of internment. President Reagan says, "We admit a wrong...It was based solely on race." No funding is provided until U.S. Senator Daniel Inouye amends a bill that President George Bush signs on November 21, 1989. Nationwide, Japanese people lost more than $200 million in property and assets in 1945 dollars or $1-$4 billion in 1983 dollars.

September 9, 1988: The $360 million, 1,242 room Hyatt Regency Waikōloa Hotel opens. Built by Chris Hemmeter, the 4-acre resort is Hawaii's second largest. Described as a "fantasy resort," it features a large art collection, a tramway, a lagoon, waterfalls, and an opportunity to swim with dolphins for $35.

October 12, 1988: Moloka'i Ranch is sold to a Hong Kong company, Industrial Equity, for $23 million. Moloka'i Ranch owns one-third of the island, and is Hawaii's second largest ranch.

October 13, 1988: The NBA champion Los Angeles Lakers basketball team finishes its first Hawai'i training camp with a sell-out pre-season game against the Golden State Warriors at Blaisdell Center. The Lakers had played NBA exhibition games here in the 1960s.

November 2, 1988: Del Monte closes its Moloka'i pineapple operations after 61 years.

November 8, 1988: Hawai'i Island voters approve a ballot measure to allow construction of a $329 million luxury resort at Hāpuna Beach.

November 8, 1988: A 9-time loser for public office, Bernard Akana, age 69, shocks everyone by defeating Hawai'i Island Mayor Dante Carpenter. Akana spent only $1,661 to Carpenter's $146,689.

November 8, 1988: By a 2-1 margin, the Save Sandy Beach initiative wins. Voters downzone the proposed development area from residential to preservation. The initiative backers are outspent by Kaiser Development Co., $325,000 to $61,000.

November 17, 1988: JMB Realty Corporation in Chicago buys Amfac, a 139-year old Hawai'i company, and its subsidiaries for $885 million.

December 1, 1988: A 65-foot tall religious cross that stood at Camp Smith for 22 years is removed, and replaced with a giant 20 x 38 foot U.S.

"Save Sandy Beach" committee says "thank you!"

flag. A Washington, D.C. federal judge ordered the cross removed because it is an unconstitutional endorsement of a religious symbol.

December 29, 1988: Hawaiian Airlines sells a 20% interest to a subsidiary of Japanese Airline investors for $20 million.

December 31, 1988: Hawai'i receives 6 million tourists in a year for the first time.

February 24, 1989: At 24,000 feet altitude, a huge hole is blown near the front of a United Airlines jet, just 9 minutes after leaving Honolulu. Nine people are swept away, and 20 of 336 passengers are injured. The airplane returns to Honolulu and lands safely.

March 16, 1989: Hawaii's largest gas company, PRI is sold to BHP, Australia's largest company, for $370 million. On May 29, 1998, the company is again sold to Tesoro.

April 11, 1989: First Hawaiian Bank's newsletter reports Japanese investments and tourist spending is $9 billion or 45% of Hawaii's $21 billion gross state product. Japanese investors are boosting Hawaii's economy by buying many hotels, homes and businesses. On April 14, a HONOLULU ADVERTISER story says Japanese visitors spend $600 a day compared with American visitors, who spend $120 a day.

May 17, 1989: After voters approve the Sandy Beach initiative, the State Supreme Court rules that land can't be rezoned by initiative. On May 23, 1989, the City Council responds to the 2-1 public vote, and downzones Sandy Beach from residential to preservation, which finally kills the proposed 171 home development.

May 19, 1989: Judge Philip Chun orders Bishop Estate to disclose trustee commissions. Trustees were paid $920,000 in 1987. The commissions were kept secret for two years, but federal law requires public disclosure. From 1987 through most of the 1990s, trustees are entitled to about $1 million or more in commissions for each year, but they waive 10%-60%, and receive less than $1 million each. After 1999, the new trustees receive about $100,000 a year.

June 22, 1989: A Kīlauea eruption destroys the Wahaʻula Visitors Center and covers several archeological sites. Wahaʻula heiau is surrounded by lava.

July 28, 1989: State Representative Roland Kotani is murdered by his wife at home. On the evening of July 31, she goes to the police station, confesses the murder, and kills herself with a gun in the bathroom on the early morning hours of August 1. The police didn't search her because she hadn't yet been charged with a crime.

September 22, 1989: Most prison guards call in sick to protest excessive vacant positions. The prison guards are concerned that they earn $400 a week less than police officers, yet their job qualifications are similar.

September 29, 1989: NASA Kōkeʻe Tracking Station closes, and is replaced by the satellites it launched. It opened in 1960 and provided a communications link with satellites and space shuttles. Astronauts stationed at Kōkeʻe talked with astronauts during space flights and during their re-entry to earth.

October 28, 1989: An Aloha Island Air plane crashes near Hālawa Valley, Molokaʻi, killing 20 people, including one-half of the high school volleyball team. It is Hawaii's 3rd worst air disaster.

December 14, 1989: During a "national day of outrage" against geothermal development, 39 of 75 protestors are arrested for trespassing on a geothermal site on Campbell Estate property.

December, 1989: Former Honolulu resident, Ron Takaki, a professor at the University of California at Berkeley is nominated for a Pulitzer Prize for his book, STRANGERS FROM A DISTANT SHORE.

1990-1999

February 5, 1990: The innovative A+ program begins. It is the first of its kind in the U.S. The program, suggested by Lt. Governor Ben Cayetano, provides subsidized after-school activities such as child care, tutoring and recreation – with learning opportunities – for 15,000 elementary school students at $1 day for most parents.

February 8, 1990: Governor John Waiheʻe announces the state will increase its annual payments to OHA from $1.3 million to $9 million for using former Hawaiʻi Kingdom land.

March 3, 1990: 7,500 hotel workers strike 11 Waikīkī hotels for 22 days until March 24. The settlement gives many workers a 35% pay raise over 5 years.

April 1, 1990: Federal census begins. Hawaiʻi has 1,108,229 population, a 15% increase since 1980 – 13% Hawaiian, 33% Caucasian, 6% Chinese, 22% Japanese, 15% Filipino, 2% Korean. About 15% is foreign-born.

April 1, 1990: Castle and Cooke owner David Murdock opens the Lodge at Kōʻele. The Mānele Bay Hotel opens on May 1, 1991. The two luxury hotels plus affordable housing for Lānaʻi workers cost about $160 million. The resorts transform the pineapple isle to the resort isle, as workers are retrained for tourism jobs. Lānaʻi now has about twice as many workers at the resorts as it had in pineapple.

April 16, 1990: U.S. Supreme Court refuses an appeal of a discrimination case filed by Manuel Fragante of Honolulu. Honolulu city denied him a job because his accent affected his ability to be understood.

May 4, 1990: The historic, 60-year old Star of the Sea Church in Kalapana, known as the Painted Church, is moved before it is destroyed by lava.

May 4, 1990: 65 of Miloliʻi's 125 residents come to Honolulu to protest a proposed $700 million "fantasy" resort to be called the Hawaiian Riviera. The resort would have three hotels, 1,050 rooms, and a marina in a quiet Hawaiʻi Island fishing village.

June 25, 1990: U.S. Air Force completes its first successful relay of a "Star Wars" laser beam from Haleakalā to a mirror on an orbiting satellite, and to a target near the Kīhei Research and Technology Park. On October 29, 1987, an Air Force Environmental Impact Statement says the lasers are safe.

August 13, 1990: A Kīlauea eruption destroys Kaimū Beach, known as "Black Sand Beach." The black sand was formed in the 1700s when lava cooled in the sea and was washed ashore by waves.

August 18, 1990: When a statute of Duke Kahanamoku is unveiled today on his 100th birthday, his friends complain it should face the ocean, not the hotels. On February 7, 1961, Hawai'i businessman Daniel Wallace displayed a design of a sculpture of Duke surfing on a wave, made several years earlier by sculptor Robert Wallace.

September, 1990: A special edition of MONEY MAGAZINE ranks UH as the nation's #10 public university for quality and cost. In 1996, U.S. NEWS AND WORLD REPORT says UH Mānoa is among the top 13% of American universities which provide best educational value and low cost.

October 15, 1990: A Hawai'i ceremony gives $20,000 reparation payments and a national apology to Hawai'i AJAs and permanent aliens who were interned during WW II. 560 Hawaii residents will get checks.

October 22, 1990: President George Bush orders a halt to the bombing of Kaho'olawe, which began in 1941, and creates a federal-state commission to plan the future of the island. The military has been using Kaho'olawe about 20 days a month for bombing and other training activities.

October 26, 1990: President George Bush visits Hawai'i for the weekend. He speaks to leaders of Pacific Island nations, and to 1,200 Republican Party supporters of Congresswoman Pat Saiki's U.S. Senate campaign.

November 4, 1990: Financier Harry Weinberg, age 82, dies. A self-made billionaire with a 6th grade education, he acquired substantial stock and real estate in Hawai'i while fighting the management of those corporations. He was one of America's richest people, worth $900 million at death. He bought the Honolulu Rapid Transit Company, then fought the Teamsters Union over wages, resulting in a worker strike, and the city bought the bus company, now called TheBus, in 1971. His will establishes the Harry and Jeannette Weinberg Foundation with

25 largest private foundations. The foundation gives tens of millions of dollars a year to charities.

November 6, 1990: Daniel Akaka is the first native Hawaiian elected to the U.S. Senate.

December, 1990: State Labor Department reports that Hawaii's 1.9% unemployment rate is the nation's lowest and the lowest ever for Hawai'i.

March 7, 1991: 1988 Democratic Presidential candidate and former Massachusetts Governor Michael Dukakis is a visiting UH professor of Political Science for half of the Spring semester.

U.S. Senator Daniel Akaka

April 1, 1991: Maui Mayor Linda Lingle signs a law to establish a 17-month ban on hotel construction in South and West Maui. This will give planners time to review infrastructure needs and development plans.

April 1, 1991: Former Congresswoman Pat Saiki is the director of the Small Business Administration. She is appointed by President George Bush.

April 9, 1991: All O'ahu is hit by a daytime electrical transmission failure, causing a daytime blackout, and a $60 million business loss.

April 9, 1991: A Honolulu Advertiser story reveals that many real estate hui (people pool their money to invest in property) skirt the law with secret ownership by not registering with the State Department of Commerce and Consumer Affairs.

April 28, 1991: Astronaut Charles Lacy Veach of Honolulu launches into space aboard the Space Shuttle Discovery for 8 days of a "Star Wars" military mission that returns on May 6. He makes his second space flight on October 22, 1992, aboard the Space Shuttle Columbia, a 10-day flight.

May 15, 1991: 10,000 job seekers attend a job fair sponsored by the State Labor Department. More than 100 employers offer 2,000 jobs. It is the largest-ever crowd for a single day event at Blaisdell.

May 15, 1991: A State Housing Agency says it will spend $39 million to build a 190-acre Kapolei Golf Course if the developer, Herbert Horita doesn't build it at the nearby Ko 'Olina resort. Some legislators are angry because the state funds are intended for affordable housing.

June 2, 1991: Former Hawai'i resident Lea Salonga wins a Tony Award for her acting and singing in the Broadway musical play, MISS SAIGON.

June 3, 1991: Maui Mayor Linda Lingle allows a 3-year property tax freeze to become law without her signature. She says the ordinance is unfair to new homeowners who will pay higher property taxes.

June 19, 1991: Governor John Waihe'e signs a law to establish the Hawai'i Technology Development Corporation, to encourage the high tech industry here, with loans up to $1 million.

July 17, 1991: HONOLULU WEEKLY begins publication as a free "alternative newspaper" published by Laurie Carlson.

July 30, 1991: Castle and Cooke changes its name to Dole Food Company. Ironically, the Dole name didn't appear on pineapples until James Dole left the company in 1932. Dole becomes the world's largest fruit and vegetable producer. On October 10, 1995, the 140-year old company name, Castle and Cooke survives as the manager of Dole Food Company's resort and real estate business.

September 9, 1991: A WALL STREET JOURNAL story criticizes the Hawaiian Home Lands program for mismanagement, and for leaving thousands of people on the waiting list for decades, while non-Hawaiians lease land at low rates.

November 1, 1991: Maui's largest hotel, the $600 million, Grand Hyatt Wailea Resort and Spa opens with 815 rooms on 18 acres.

November 1, 1991: The 1,389 acre Wheeler Air Force Base is transferred to the U.S. Army.

December 1, 1991: Dole Food Co. closes Lāna'i Plantation, but continues growing pineapples on 600 acres. Dole has been growing pineapples in Asia with Lāna'i crowns – since 1963 in the Philippines, since 1968 in the Dominican Republic and Honduras, and since 1974 in Thailand. Previously 80% of the world's pineapples came from Hawai'i, and about 50% were from Lāna'i. Dole closes the Iwilei Cannery on October 31, 1992.

December 7, 1991: President George Bush visits Hawai'i to commemorate the 50th anniversary of the Pearl Harbor attack. This huge event attracts 1,500 international journalists.

December 7, 1991: U.S. Post Office issues a 29¢ stamp to commemorate the 50th anniversary of the Pearl Harbor attack. It is part of a series of WW II stamps.

December 12, 1991: The Hawai'i Advisory Committee to the U.S. Civil Rights Commission says the U.S. government has failed in its trust obligation to Hawaiian Homelands and makes 12 recommendations to improve the Hawaiian Home Lands program.

December 14, 1991: Flooding at Anahola, Kaua'i kills 4 people and creates $5 million damage.

December 16, 1991: A law allowing lease-to-fee simple conversion at a "fair and reasonable price" is adopted when Mayor Frank Fasi refuses to sign an ordinance passed by the City Council. Large landowners had been reluctant to sell their land, and they were requiring people to sign long term leases. The law is patterned after the 1967 Hawai'i Land Reform Law. In 1998, the U.S. Supreme Court rejects Bishop Estate's challenge to the city law.

February 19, 1992: Former Honolulu resident Bette Midler, gets an Academy Award nomination for Best Actress, for the movie, FOR THE BOYS.

April 3, 1992: Maui Mayor Linda Lingle signs the state's first law to exempt Hawaiian Home Land lessees from paying property taxes, because they can't own or sell their property.

April 14, 1992: The world's largest optical infrared telescope, the $94 million W.M. Keck telescope atop Mauna Kea, begins operation. The telescope mirror is 33 feet in diameter. The telescope will "discover" many unknown planets located as far as 1,500 trillion miles from earth. The "Keck II" telescope is dedicated on May 8, 1996. These are the world's two largest telescopes.

July 24, 1992: U.S. Post Office issues a 29¢ stamp with a picture of a 'Ōhi'a Lehua, honoring wildflowers.

July 28, 1992: Hawai'i Pacific University (HPU) and Hawai'i Loa College merge to become HPU.

August 24, 1992: Universal Pictures begins filming the movie, JURASSIC PARK on Kaua'i. The movie wins an Academy Award for Best Visual Effects. The Steven Spielberg movie earns $900 million at the box office, the highest ever to date. Filming is delayed by Hurricane 'Iniki.

September 5, 1992: U.S. Government approves the State Transportation Department's plan to realign the H-3 freeway to save archeological sites, Luakini heiau and Hale 'O Papa in Hālawa Valley.

September 11, 1992: Hurricane 'Iniki is Hawaii's most destructive storm ever recorded. Its 160 mph winds devastate Kaua'i, killing 4, injuring more than 1,000 people, damaging 13,000 homes and businesses, and causing $2.5 billion in damage. It is the nation's 3rd most costly national disaster to date.

September 20, 1992: Hawaii's Plantation Village opens in Waipahu. It is a replica of sugar plantation homes representing 8 major ethnic groups.

September 22, 1992: Honolulu City Council votes 5-4 to kill the Rapid Transit program it approved on August 27, 1991 after criticism grew about questionable costs and efficiency. The program would have increased the excise tax a half-cent to fund the $1.76 billion, 15.6 mile rapid transit from Pearl City to UH.

October 22, 1992: Hawai'i Astronaut Charles Lacy Veach makes his second space flight on the Space Shuttle COLUMBIA. It is a 10-day flight.

October 28, 1992: An historic 3-way conversation includes astronaut Charles Veach from the COLUMBIA Space Shuttle, HōKūLE'A navigator Nainoa Thompson at sea near the Cook Islands, and 'Aikahi Elementary School students. Thompson says the space shuttle represents science and technology, and the HōKūLE'A represents history and culture.

October 30, 1992: U.S. Post Office issues a "Year of the Rooster" stamp, designed by Honolulu designer Clarence Lee. It is the first of several Lunar New Year stamps he designs.

November 3, 1992: Keiko Bonk-Abramson of the Green Party is elected to the Hawai'i Island County Council. She is the first 3rd-party candidate to win a Hawai'i election since the Home Rule Party in the early 1900s.

November 11, 1992: The Broadway play LES MISERABLES is presented at Blaisdell Center for 2 weeks to sold out crowds. As a result of this success, other off-Broadway musical plays such as PHANTOM OF THE OPERA, CATS, and MISS SAIGON come to Blaisdell in the next few years.

November 30, 1992: The Polynesian voyaging canoe Hōkūle'a returns to Hawai'i at Hōnaunau, from a 6-month, 5,500 mile-long voyage to Tahiti and the Cook Islands. It is the canoe's longest voyage. The Hōkūle'a returns to Kualoa Park on December 5. Students followed the canoe with daily, live radio reports.

January 13, 1993: 10,000 people attend 5 days of speeches and activities to commemorate the 100th anniversary of the overthrow of the Hawaiian Kingdom. A 3-day re-enactment of the overthrow is written by Victoria Kneubehl. On January 17, Ka Lahui leader and UH Professor Haunani Trask tells 15,000 people, "We are not American. We are not American. We are Hawaiian."

January 14, 1993: Governor John Waiheʻe orders the U.S. flag lowered from state buildings for the January 14-17 observance of the overthrow. Only the Hawaiian flag flies.

January 17, 1993: Rev. Paul Sherry, national president of the United Church of Christ, formally apologizes to Native Hawaiians for the church's role in overthrowing the Hawaiian monarchy. He says the church "repent(s) for the wrongs done to kanaka maoli..."

January 26, 1993: Chad Rowan of Waimānalo, known in Japan as Akebono, is the first foreigner to become a yukozuna or grand champion of the sumo wrestling sport.

January 30, 1993: Gannett Corporation sells the HONOLULU STAR-BULLETIN to Liberty Newspapers, and buys the HONOLULU ADVERTISER, news building and land from Persis Corp. for $250 million. The ADVERTISER has 105,000 circulation, and the STAR-BULLETIN has 88,000. The ADVERTISER passed the STAR-BULLETIN in circulation in 1971. Gannett bought the STAR-BULLETIN in 1971 for $12 million.

February 24, 1993: By a 17-7 vote, the State Senate rejects Governor John Waihee's nomination of Sharon Himeno to the State Supreme Court. The controversial nomination is described as "political cronyism" and "old boy politics." Himeno is the wife of a former Attorney General and the daughter of a prominent land developer. On the same day, the Senate approves Ronald Moon, a Republican, as Supreme Court Chief Justice. The only other Supreme Court nominee ever rejected by the Hawaiʻi Senate was Betty Vitousek, in 1974.

February 26, 1993: A "Star Wars" rocket is launched from Pacific Missile Range Facility at Barking Sands, which is located on ceded lands. It is the first of 40 Star Wars rockets. In the days prior to the launch, 19 protesters were arrested for trespassing. On March 17, 60 people protest the arraignment of Native Hawaiians and environmentalists. Another "Star Wars" test missile is launched from Kauaʻi on August 25, 1993.

March 22, 1993: HPU basketball team coached by Tony Sellitto wins the NAIA small college title, defeating Oklahoma Baptist, 88-83.

March 31, 1993: Hāmākua Sugar Company goes out of business, $100 million in debt. On April 29, 1993, Governor John Waiheʻe signs an $8 million loan for one last sugar harvest. Hāmākua finally closes on August 30, 1994.

April 13, 1993: Governor John Waiheʻe signs a law to establish September 2 annually as Queen Liliʻuokalani Day, not a state holiday. She was born on September 2, 1838.

April 22, 1993: Governor John Waiheʻe signs a law to begin paying OHA

$136 million for ceded lands the state is using and hadn't been compensating Hawaiians.

April 22, 1993: Honolulu City Council votes to grant a permit to allow the Hilton Hawaiian Village to demolish the geodesic dome and replace it with a 26-story, 400-room hotel. The resort now has 3,000 rooms.

April 26, 1993: Governor John Waiheʻe signs a law to repeal loyalty oaths.

April 28, 1993: State Senator Richard Matsuura begins a 7-month investigation of non-bid state contracts, government waste, fraud, abuse, and unethical practices. The investigation results in a law that Governor John Waiheʻe signs on October 4, 1993, to establish a Procurement Code to guide contracts and purchases.

April 30, 1993: A Puna geothermal power plant begins producing 25% of the island's energy. It is Hawaii's first commercial producing power plant. In June 1991, environmental and health concerns are raised when the power plant releases hydrogen sulfide and other gases.

May 5, 1993: Hawaiʻi Supreme Court rules that same-sex marriage is constitutional unless the state can justify the law banning it. Hawaiʻi would be the first state to allow it. On June 22, 1994, Governor John Waiheʻe signs a law to ban same-sex marriage, and voters approve a constitutional amendment in 1998.

May 17, 1993: House Speaker Joe Souki and Rep. Calvin Say reveal their State Capitol offices were "bugged" with 3 and 4 electronic listening devices. On June 15 it is revealed that bugs were found in the Governor's offices on May 8, but there is some doubt because the same person had found them all.

May 24, 1993: NEW YORK TIMES-CBS News poll ranks Hawaiʻi as the #1 dream vacation.

June 28, 1993: Governor John Waiheʻe signs a law to guarantee 90% of a private loan up to $12.6 million for Hawaiʻi airlines.

June 30, 1993: Governor John Waiheʻe signs a law to establish the Kahoʻolawe Island Reserve Commission to manage preservation.

July 11, 1993: President Bill Clinton is the 11th U.S. president to visit Hawaiʻi. He praises Hawaiʻi for its model health insurance program to a huge crowd of thousands at Waikīkī Beach.

July 26, 1993: The remains of Henry Opukahaia, the first Hawaiian to convert to Christianity, are returned in a koa box to Hawaiʻi from Cornwall, Connecticut, where he was buried in 1818. He is reburied in Kahikolu Cemetery in Nāpōʻopoʻo, Hawaiʻi Island.

July 30, 1993: Bishop Estate says it will sell the fee interest in 8,400 Honolulu condominiums and townhouses for $35,000-$200,000, but homeowners say these prices are too high. Bishop Estate also offers loans to help homebuyers.

September 5, 1993: The body of former Philippines President Ferdinand Marcos is flown from Hawai'i to the Philippines, four years after he died on September 28, 1989.

September 8, 1993: Facing a $1 million deficit, the Honolulu Symphony makes cuts, and musicians are locked out. The Symphony is replaced by the same musicians in a new Hawai'i Symphony. The Honolulu Symphony returns on December 15, 1995.

September 21, 1993: Hawaiian Airlines files for bankruptcy, $320 million in debt, but continues operations.

September 30, 1993: Maui High Performance Computing Center opens at the Maui Research and Technology Park. The U.S. Defense Department's "Supercomputer," now managed by the University of Hawai'i, provides 9 million hours of computing time annually for researchers, scientists and the military.

October 1, 1993: The State loses a jury trial, ending an 11-year effort to recover millions from U.S. Steel for the rust at Aloha Stadium. In a 1972 out-of-court settlement, the State agreed to a $27 million settlement with Bethlehem, Nippon and Kaiser Steel. It cost $32 million to build Aloha Stadium and $80 million to repair it.

October 3, 1993: Mahalo Airlines begins service. Their low fares start a price war with competitors.

October 5, 1993: Dole Cannery's 65-year old, 195-foot tall water tower at the Iwilei Cannery is dismantled for safety reasons.

October 19, 1993: Charlie Sonido publishes HAWAI'I FILIPINO CHRONICLE.

October 27, 1993: Doris Duke, age 80, dies. A long-time Hawai'i resident, she is the daughter of the founder of American Tobacco Company. She is one of the world's richest women. Her Hawai'i Kai home at

Dole Water Tower at Iwilei

Black Point, called Shangri-La, has a rare collection of Islamic art.

November 8, 1993: U.S. Supreme Court rejects an appeal from Bishop Estate, and upholds a March 31 Federal Appeals Court ruling that Kamehameha Schools can't discriminate against non-Protestant teachers, even though the will of Bernice Pauahi Bishop requires it.

November 11, 1993: President Bill Clinton signs a Defense Appropriation law with $400 million to clean Kaho'olawe, remove explosives, and transfer the island to Hawai'i jurisdiction in 6 months. The U.S. Navy will control access until November 11, 2003.

November 23, 1993: President Bill Clinton signs a Congressional Joint Resolution to formally apologize for the illegal actions of U.S. diplomat John Stevens and USS BOSTON Captain John Wiltse for their role in the 1893 overthrow of the Hawaiian Kingdom. The Resolution is introduced by U.S. Senators Daniel Akaka and Daniel Inouye.

1994: CONDE NAST travel magazine votes Maui the world's best island for the first of 11 consecutive years.

January 1, 1994: Lāna'i is closed to the news media for a day when Bill Gates, founder of Microsoft Corporation is married there. Some news reporters file complaints that public areas are closed. On April 12, 1995, Gates and Lāna'i owner David Murdock formally apologize to a Seattle news reporter who was illegally arrested on Lāna'i for covering Gates' wedding.

January 2, 1994: Former Honolulu resident, Bruce Yamashita, an attorney, finally becomes a Captain in the U.S. Marine Corps Reserves 5 years after being dismissed from Officer Candidate School. He sued and won, proving his case against racism.

January 16, 1994: The 'Ohana Council, a group with 7,000 supporters, proclaims the Independent Sovereign Nation of Hawai'i at 'Iolani Palace. On June 27, 1995, the Nation of Hawai'i charges state and federal judges with "war crimes against humanity" toward the Hawaiian people.

January 31, 1994: Keith Haugen presents the first regularly scheduled Hawaiian-language news broadcast on public radio KHPR and KKUA.

February 16, 1994: Hawai'i has the nation's highest auto insurance rates, according to the national Insurance Information Institute. Hawaii's average no fault claim is twice the national average.

February 20, 1994: 100 members of the 'Ohana Council distribute leaflets to Waikīkī tourists that say "Tourist go home" and "Your visit and stay in Hawai'i assists the illegal State of Hawai'i."

February 24, 1994: The bones of 15th century Hawaiian chiefs stored in two woven sennet caskets, kā'ai, are discovered stolen from Bishop

Museum. An anonymous phone call says the bones were returned to Waipi'o Valley, Hawai'i Island.

March 3, 1994: The new $10 million Hawai'i Film Studio opens. It is considered essential to attracting film productions to Hawai'i.

April 18, 1994: 16,000 HGEA state and county workers begin a 12-day strike until April 29. It is the first-ever HGEA strike. Many state services are substantially reduced during the strike

May 4, 1994: During routine maintenance, the USS LAKE ERIE accidentally shoots two missiles at the 'Aiea Hills. There are no injuries.

May 7, 1994: The U.S. government returns Kaho'olawe to the state of Hawai'i at a ceremony on Maui's Palauea Beach. 800 people witness the signing of two documents, in English and Hawaiian.

May 17, 1994: The movie, PICTURE BRIDE, receives its world premiere at the Cannes Film Festival. The movie is about a 1915 era Japanese picture bride who immigrates to live on a Hawai'i sugar plantation.

June 14, 1994: More than 30 Hawai'i missionary stamps sell at a Switzerland auction for $3.1 million to an anonymous buyer.

June 21, 1994: Governor John Waihe'e signs a law to set aside 1,100 Kapolei acres for affordable housing and public facilities. 500 acres are for a new UH West O'ahu campus. On February 9, 1973, UH Regents said a new school for 7,500 students will be built on Campbell Estate land in 1975.

June 21, 1994: Governor John Waihe'e signs a law to require the state to take control of fireworks from the counties. Users no longer need a permit for non-aerials.

June 29, 1994: Governor John Waihe'e signs the state budget which creates the Health Quest program, providing health insurance for more than 100,000 low income people.

July 29, 1994: The Persis collection of rare Hawai'i missionary stamps, valued at $8.5 million, is displayed for 2 months at the Smithsonian Institution in Washington, D.C. Also on display is the earliest known letter mailed from Hawai'i, in 1819, by Sybil Bingham.

August 12, 1994: Bank of Hawai'i reports Hawaii's cost of living is 39% higher than the mainland.

August 20, 1994: A 9,000 lb. Circus International elephant named Tyke, kills its trainer and runs wild on the streets near the Blaisdell Center. Police shoot and kill the elephant after 13 people are injured.

August 30, 1994: Hāmākua Sugar Co. closes.

September 2, 1994: Hilo Coast Processing Company closes.

October 3, 1994: U.S. Post Office issues four 29¢ stamps with colorful pictures of Hawai'i reefs. The stamps are the first to be "cancelled" 80 feet underwater at Waikīkī Beach.

October 21, 1994: The $32 million Special Events Arena at UH opens, with 10,000 seats. It is renamed Stan Sheriff Arena in 1998 for the Athletic Director of 10 years who died on January 16, 1993.

Governor Ben Cayetano

November 8, 1994: Lt. Governor Benjamin Cayetano is elected governor. He is the nation's first governor of Filipino heritage.

November 16, 1994: President Bill Clinton visits Hawai'i for a 3-day golf vacation after attending meetings in Asia.

November 19, 1994: Aloha Tower Marketplace opens.

November 28, 1994: Governor John Waihe'e signs rules to reduce Worker Compensation costs. Hawaii's rates are the second highest in the U.S.

December 31, 1994: Entertainer Danny Kaleikini gives his final performance after 28 years at the Kahala Hilton.

February 1, 1995: Two Hawaiian voyaging canoes, Hōkūle'a and Hawai'iloa leave Honolulu for a 5,000 mile round trip journey to Marquesas, without using modern instruments. Nainoa Thompson, Chad Babayan and Bruce Blankenfeld are captain-navigators for the voyage. The canoes return to Hawai'i on May 13.

February 9, 1995: Hawai'i Civil Rights Commission awards $2,500 to a worker who said someone called him a "haole" intended as a racial slur.

April 2, 1995: Arakawa's historic store in Waipahu closes after 86 years.

April 9, 1995: O'ahu Sugar, owned by Amfac/JMB, processes its last sugar cane after 98 years. It once employed 3,000 workers.

April 12, 1995: Two Kāne'ohe Marines are the first-ever to refuse to give mandatory DNA samples, claiming it violates their right to privacy. On May 23, a military judge dismisses the charges.

May 13, 1995: UH-Hilo Valedictorian, Rhonda Dudoit gives her speech in English and Hawaiian.

May 15, 1995: National Oceanic and Atmospheric Administration (NOAA) reports that the ozone layer over Hawai'i is the thinnest ever. This increases the possibility of getting skin cancer from sun rays.

May 21, 1995: Jack Gonzalez, chairman of the State Campaign Spending Commission for 18 years, is convicted of money laundering and $10 million fraud against Unity House, a labor organization. On November 3, a Tacoma federal judge sentences him to 15 years in prison.

May 30, 1995: The Department of Education tells the Kailua High School valedictorian that she can express her personal feelings in her June 3 commencement speech by saying "thank you God." In early May, the student was told that mentioning God may be considered praying or preaching religion, which violates the First Amendment.

June 4, 1995: Father Damien is "beatified" in Belgium, a Catholic ritual required for sainthood status, an effort first begun in 1936. It must be proven that Damien performed a miracle.

June 13, 1995: The Independent Nation of Hawai'i, led by Dennis "Bumpy" Kanahele, ends its 15-month occupation of Makapu'u Beach and Kaupō Beach Parks when the state gives the organization a lease for 69 acres of state-owned land in Waimānalo. The Makapu'u occupancy began on September 24, 1993.

June 27, 1995: Hawai'i Ecumenical Coalition buys a full-page ad in the western edition of the NEW YORK TIMES. The ad asks, "Is it time to give back Hawai'i?"

June 29, 1995: Governor Ben Cayetano signs a law to provide $600 million to settle land claims for Hawaiian Homelands, pending since 1959. 16,000 acres of state lands are to be transferred to the Hawaiian Home Land Trust.

July 6, 1995: Without the signature of Governor Ben Cayetano, a bill becomes law to prevent the public from knowing the names of police officers that have been discharged. The police union had objected to revealing this information to University of Hawai'i student journalists.

August 3, 1995: U.S. Senator Daniel Akaka introduces a Senate amendment to determine if America's Asian-Pacific military qualify for the Congressional Medal of Honor and other medals for WW II deeds. This results in 12 Hawai'i veterans receiving the Medal of Honor, including Senator Daniel Inouye.

August 31, 1995: President Bill Clinton arrives in Honolulu for two days to observe the 50th anniversary of Victory over Japan day.

September 2, 1995: U.S. Post Office issues 32¢ stamps aboard the USS CARL VINSON in Pearl Harbor to commemorate the 50th anniversary of the Japan's formal surrender on the USS MISSOURI, ending WW II.

November 2, 1995: The Federal Hawaiian Home Lands Recovery Act resolves the long-term claims against the federal government, when Hawaiian Home Lands are removed during Hawaii's Territorial years. DHHL will have first preference to receive any excess federal lands, such as 500 acres at Kalaeloa.

November 7, 1995: Thurston Twigg-Smith sells rare Hawaiian missionary stamps at a public auction. The stamps sell for $10 million, including a major sale to the Smithsonian Institution.

December 28, 1995: To relieve prison overcrowding, the state sends 300 inmates to Texas, at an annual cost of $15,000 per inmate.

1995: To help reduce a $200 million state budget deficit, 1,300 state workers are laid off this year.

March 26, 1996: Hung Wo Ching, age 83, dies. An immigrant, he served on the board of directors of Bank of Hawai'i and A&B, become a trustee of Bishop Estate, and saved Aloha Airlines from bankruptcy. He said, "The haole community does not realize that by not...integrating their companies, they are forcing the young Orientals to go into business for themselves. (We) are going to give them a hard time. It's shortsighted."

March 27, 1996: C. Brewer closes Ka'ū Sugar, which opened in 1868 as Nā'ālehu Plantation, and became Hutchinson Sugar in 1884. It is one of Hawaii's oldest, and Hawai'i Island's last sugar plantation.

April 28, 1996: Hawai'i Theatre opens after a $22 million restoration.

July 1, 1996: 80,000 native Hawaiians receive ballots for a Hawaiian sovereignty vote by mail from July 1-August 15. On September 11, it is announced that 33,000 people or 38% voted, and their vote is 3-1 to elect delegates to a proposed Native Hawaiian government. The Hawaiian Sovereignty Elections Council dissolves on December 31, 1996, and is replaced by Hā Hawai'i, a non-profit organization. On January 17, 1999, 78 convention delegates are elected by just 9% of the possible voters. The first meeting of Aha Hawai'i 'Ōiwi is July 31, 1999, to create a government. Many Hawaiians opposed the July 1 elections because of state involvement.

September 3, 1996: Kamehameha Schools opens elementary schools on Hawai'i Island and Maui. A new grade is added every year until reaching the 12th grade.

September 13, 1996: A&B's McBryde Sugar Mill closes on Kaua'i, and 275 workers lose jobs. McBryde was founded in 1899.

October 4, 1996: Waialua Sugar Company closes. It is Oahu's last sugar plantation. The 12,000 acre plantation, established in 1898 by Castle and Cooke, had been one of Hawaii's largest sugar plantations. In 1920, it was the first plantation to build a hydro-electric plant.

October 18, 1996: Hawaii's tallest building, First Hawaiian Center, which houses First Hawaiian Bank, is dedicated. The $175 million building is nearly 429 feet tall.

November 1, 1996: An airplane crash kills Maui Councilman Tom Morrow and 4 others on Moloka'i. Morrow is re-elected on November 5.

November 5, 1996: Voters reject holding a constitutional convention.

November 15, 1996: President Bill Clinton arrives in Hawai'i for a 4-day visit. It is his 4th visit to Hawai'i.

January 18, 1997: UH Regents establish the Hawaiian Studies Department at Mānoa. Regents establish a B.A. and M.A. program at UH Hilo on September 11, 1998.

February 28, 1997: Hawai'i Supreme Court rules that state and county governments can't privatize services that are "traditionally" provided by government. The case involves a Hawai'i County attempt to privatize a landfill, and save money by not using county workers. When several mayors complain that hundreds of contracts might be illegal, the court rules on May 13, that privatization must follow civil service laws and be "consistent with practical and public interest concerns."

March 17, 1997: Governor Ben Cayetano signs a law to rename the Hawai'i Visitors Bureau as Hawai'i Visitors and Convention Bureau.

April 19, 1997: Hawaii's first Major League Baseball game features the National League's St. Louis Cardinals and San Diego Padres. 81,000 people attend the two-day, three game series at Aloha Stadium.

May 5, 1997: Governor Ben Cayetano marries Vicky Liu, owner of United Laundry, at Washington Place. He is Hawaii's first governor to marry while in office.

May 15, 1997: 700-1,000 people protest how Bishop Estate trustees manage Kamehameha Schools, a $10 billion trust.

May 15, 1997: Astronauts Ed Lu and Carlos Noriega, with Hawai'i ties, make their first space flight aboard the Space Shuttle ATLANTIS, which docks at the Russian Space Station MIR for 9 days. The Space Shuttle travels 3.6 million miles and orbits earth 144 times. Lu takes Kona coffee, macadamia nuts, Hawaiian bird feathers and a fishhook on his space flight. From 1992-1995, Lu was a post-doctoral fellow at the University of Hawaii's Institute for Astronomy. Noriega was stationed at Kāne'ohe Marine Corps Base from 1983-1985.

June 5, 1997: Governor Ben Cayetano signs a law to give a tax credit for movies and TV producers that promote Hawai'i.

June 26, 1997: Musician Israel Kamakawiwi'ole, age 38, dies. He was considered a "living treasure" of Hawai'i. The state flag is flown at half-staff, and his body lay in state at the State Capitol, perhaps the first time for a non-public official.

July 8, 1997: The State Reciprocal Benefits law takes effect without Governor Ben Cayetano's signature. The law allows non-married people, such as people of the same gender who are prohibited to marry, to receive some of the same benefits that married people get. It is the first such law in the nation.

July 21, 1997: Hawai'i car insurance companies earn the nation's biggest profits for two consecutive years, 1995 and 1996, according to a national publication, Auto Insurance Report.

August 9, 1997: The HONOLULU STAR-BULLETIN publishes a "Broken Trust" essay, written by Randy Roth, Gladys Brandt, Walter Heen, Charles Kekumano, and Samuel King. They urge the state to investigate Bishop Estate's management of Kamehameha Schools and other issues. On August 21, the HONOLULU STAR-BULLETIN publishes a letter from all 5 Hawai'i Supreme Court Justices. They reject the "Broken Trust" essay as "irresponsible (and) inaccurate" and criticize the newspaper for questioning the court's honesty and integrity.

August 11, 1997: Lava covers the 800-year old Waha'ula heiau.

September 2, 1997: Mahalo Airlines flies for the last time after 4 years.

December 12, 1997: The controversial 16-mile, $1.3 billion H-3 Freeway opens. It connects Kāne'ohe to Hālawa after 37 years of court hearings, protests, realignment and construction. In Kāne'ohe, construction destroyed the Kukuiokani heiau, possibly Oahu's largest heiau.

December 15, 1997: Federal Office of Management and Budget creates a

new census category of "Native Hawaiians or other Pacific Islanders."
The new category takes effect in the 2000 census.

December 20, 1997: Yielding to public protest, Hawai'i Supreme Court
Justices say they will end the 114-year practice of appointing Bishop
Estate trustees. The appointments appear to be a conflict of interest,
but Bernice Pauahi Bishop's 1884 will requires it. Trustees are now
appointed by Probate Court judges, the same as other charity estates.

March 13, 1998: Maui Ocean Center opens. It features a 750,000 gallon
ocean tunnel to view sea life.

March 28, 1998: Dole Plantation opens the world's largest maze, with
11,000 plants and a path length of 1.7 miles in Wahiawā.

June 5, 1998: Governor Ben Cayetano signs a law to buy the Waiāhole
water system to help small farmers and support diversified agriculture.

June 17, 1998: A federal judge sentences former House of Representatives Speaker Daniel Kihano to 2 years in prison for money laundering, obstructing justice, and filing a false income tax return. This is
Hawaii's first federal case involving campaign law violations. Kihano
was a state legislator for 22 years, and House Speaker from 1987-1992.

June 21, 1998: USS MISSOURI arrives at Pearl Harbor for
homeporting as a museum, near the USS ARIZONA. Japan surrendered to the U.S. on this battleship, ending WW II.

July 1, 1998: The $350 million Hawai'i Convention Center opens
with 1 million square feet. It can host 15,000-20,000 people.

July 9, 1998: Governor Ben Cayetano signs a law to establish the
Hawai'i Tourism Authority to manage tourism plans and mar-
keting, and provide more consistent state funding, with a 7.25%
hotel room tax.

July 10, 1998: Governor Ben Cayetano signs a $750 million, 4-
year income tax cut – one of the nation's largest state tax cuts.

July 22, 1998: UH scientists led by Prof. Ryuzo Yanagimachi,
Teruhiko Wakayama and Tony Perry announce that they have
cloned three generations of 50 mice from a single cell. The
mice have a green glow.

August 10, 1998: A photographic display of 1897 petitions signed
by 21,000 Hawaiians protesting annexation, are viewed at the
State Capitol. The actual petitions are kept in the National
Archives in Washington, D.C.

August 10, 1998: A&B sells a majority of California and Hawai'i (C&H) Sugar Co. for $80 million to Citibank Venture Capitol of New York.

August 12, 1998: In federal court, the Department of Education agrees to pay $80,000 for a racially-insensitive photo caption that appeared in the 1997 Kalaheo High School yearbook.

August 12, 1998: On the 100th anniversary of annexation, 5,000 Hawaiians raise the Hawaiian flag at 'Iolani Palace.

October 5, 1998: U.S. Supreme Court upholds Honolulu's lease-to-fee conversion law for condominiums.

November 1, 1998: A $1 billion stock deal is Hawaii's biggest stock transaction. First Hawaiian Bank is renamed BancWest Corporation after merging with San Francisco's Bank of the West. First Hawaiian was founded as Bishop and Co. in 1858 by William Aldrich and Charles Bishop. It is the nation's 2nd oldest bank west of the Rockies.

November 3, 1998: Voters overwhelmingly approve a constitutional amendment limiting marriage to opposite-sex couples.

November 19, 1998: Pacific Tsunami Museum opens in Hilo. It exhibits information about Hilo's devastating tsunami.

May 7, 1999: Probate Court Judge Kevin Chang ousts 4 Bishop Estate trustees, and accepts a resignation from the 5th trustee. The trustees administer the 115-year old, $6 billion Bishop Estate. The Internal Revenue Service and State Attorney General had been investigating questionable management practices of the trustees. The 5 trustees were the only all-Hawaiian trustee board in the history of Bishop Estate.

May 9, 1999: A rockslide at Sacred Falls Park kills 8 and injures 50 people. The park is closed after the slide.

May 15, 1999: A Pūnana Leo school, Ke Kula 'Ohina 'O Nāwahī'okalani 'Ō Pu'u High School in Kea'au, Hawai'i Island graduates 5 students who were taught the Hawaiian language in every grade since pre-school in 1985. Pūnana Leo School was established because of concerns that the Hawaiian language is nearing extinction, and students should learn the language.

May 25, 1999: U.S. Senate votes 52-47 to clear Admiral Husband Kimmel and General Walter Short, the scapegoats of the December 7, 1941 attack on Pearl Harbor. The Senate resolution says the losses were "not the result of dereliction of duty" because they were "denied vital intelligence available in Washington" and didn't they receive decoded Japanese messages. They are pardoned and restored to their rank before December 7, 1941.

June 15, 1999: Hōkūle'a sails from Hilo to begin a 9,000 mile voyage to

Rapa Nui. This HŌKŪLE'A voyage "closes the Polynesian Triangle" by visiting every Polynesian Island group during the past 25 years.

June 22, 1999: General Eric Shinseki, a former Kaua'i resident, becomes the U.S. Army Chief of Staff. He is appointed by President Bill Clinton, and he is Hawaii's only 4-star General.

July 2, 1999: The Pentagon closes Barber's Point Naval Air Station after 55 years. It is again called Kalaeloa. Most of the 3,700 acres are given to the state and city for an airport for small airplanes, for business and recreation, as well as military purposes.

July 9, 1999: A hotel renovation tax credit, worth up to $1 million through 2006 becomes law without the signature of Governor Ben Cayetano.

July 22, 1999: Governor Ben Cayetano signs a law to declare hula as Hawaii's official state dance. The first oral accounts of hula are from the 7th century.

September 8, 1999: Amfac's Pioneer Mill in Lahaina closes.

September 16, 1999: The HONOLULU STAR-BULLETIN announces it will end 117 years of publication on October 30. Circulation of this and many mainland afternoon newspapers have declined.

November 2, 1999: A Xerox Corp. worker, Bryan Uyesuki shoots and kills 7 workers at the office. It is Hawaii's worst mass-murder.

December 23, 1999: MAUI NEWS announces it's sale to Ogden Newspapers of West Virginia. Since 1940, the MAUI NEWS had been locally and family-owned by J. Walter Cameron and his Trust.

December 30, 1999: Wailuku Agribusiness closes its macadamia nut business after 12 years.

December 31, 1999: Honolulu's Consumer Price Index for cost-of-living in 1999 is 76% higher than in 1982, the highest to date, announces the U.S. Department of Labor.

December 31, 1999: Thousands of residents break the law while celebrating the Millennium, launching illegal aerial fireworks that create a densely polluted haze. The noise reminds residents of what a war zone must be like. One person is killed by fireworks. Residents can see aerials from just about anywhere. Despite hundreds of telephone complaints to the Honolulu Police Department on New Years eve, Honolulu police officers cite no one because they claim they didn't see anyone in the act of shooting fireworks.

National Magazines Say Hawai'i
Needs a Business Boost

HONOLULU MAGAZINE, September 1, 1998, says national business magazine stories have been complaining about the poor state of doing business in Hawai'i for 20 years, and "the writing is on the wall."

BUSINESS WEEK, May 9, 1977, says sugar and pineapple are dying, and "Hawaii's trouble is that it has few alternatives to spark the economy."

INC. MAGAZINE, October 1, 1981, gives Hawai'i a failing grade. "Poor marks for capital resources."

FORBES MAGAZINE, January 31, 1983, reports, "The 'paradise' state is a veritable purgatory for business with a stagnant agricultural economy and a powerful political and labor union bureaucracy that has smothered attempts at industrial development. (Hawai'i) could compete with the Soviet Union's bureaucrats in their rigid regulation of every facet of the islands' economic life."

U.S. NEWS AND WORLD REPORT, September 14, 1992, lists Hawai'i #51 for economic health.

FORTUNE MAGAZINE, November 15, 1993, reports "Executives say innovation is dead." Honolulu is ranked in the bottom 10 in most survey issues and "dead last for pro business attitude, cost of living..."

FORBES MAGAZINE, June 16, 1997, entitles its story, "The People's Republic of Hawai'i."

THE ECONOMIST (a British magazine), June 20, 1998, says "This is an expensive, highly taxed, highly regulated little dot on the Pacific...It is also a lousy place to do business...The Aloha State thinks of itself as on Asia's doorstep....(Its reforms are) "not painful enough to jolt Hawai'i out if its love of the status quo."

"I Couldn't Resist"

February 23, 1901: Territorial House votes to eject Secretary of Territory Henry Cooper for "occupying a seat" on the House floor. House members said he was taking notes of the proceedings, which violates the separation of powers and independence of the Legislature.

April 18, 1901: The Legislature overrides Governor Sanford Dole's veto of a bill to reduce the tax on female dogs from $3 to $1, the same as male dogs. The first Territorial Legislature is known as the "Lady Dog" Legislature because a lot of time is devoted to dog taxes.

May 22, 1902: U.S. Agriculture Secretary James Wilson adopts a regulation to prohibit snakes in Hawai'i.

November 28, 1902: Hawai'i Senate votes to remove W. Austin as Territorial Auditor because of negligence, misconduct and financial irregularities. The treasury is $18,000 short. Governor Sanford Dole had suspended him on September 25.

August 1, 1903: Mrs. Samuel Parker is robbed of $80,000 in jewelry from her home. She wore the jewelry the previous night at the Alexander Young Hotel opening.

February 18, 1907: Hawai'i Governor George Carter gets a front-page headline when he says he wouldn't mind if his daughter marries a Japanese man...if she wants to. He explains that some Japanese men with white wives "make better husbands than many white men." He says Japanese have not been give an opportunity to integrate into society. This admission shocks Hawaii's legislators. A February 26 story in the HAWAIIAN STAR reports legislators saying, "We are Americans now and we do not care for any Jap sons-in law." A bill to outlaw marriage of Caucasians or Hawaiians to Japanese is prepared for the Territorial House, but wasn't introduced because it lacked the support of 2/3 of the Legislature to override a Governor's veto.

August 27, 1910: MAUI NEWS reports that 18-year old Kalua Kaaihue was stranded on Kahoʻolawe for 3 months, from May to August, until rescued by a fisherman. His foreman forgot to return for him.

December 20, 1910: Oʻahu Board of Supervisors adopts a law to prohibit anyone from spitting on a building floor. On January 8, 1911, the first arrest is made for violating this law. The law may have been intended for people who spit while chewing tobacco.

April 11, 1911: A bill to allow teaching the Hawaiian language in public schools passes the House, but dies in the Senate. Opponents of the bill ask why not teach Chinese or Japanese.

October 2, 1916: Maui County Fair Committee votes unanimously to prohibit hula entertainers at the Maui County Fair.

October 20, 1916: The Hawaiʻi Promotions Committee says a proposed aerial tramway up the Pali would be "unsightly."

June 12, 1917: A 14-year old Hawaiian girl, Kaneau of Hoʻokena, Hawaiʻi Island, leads 26 other Hawaiians of all ages to Kīlauea, with the intention of sacrificing themselves. Newspapers call Kaneau the Hawaiʻi "Joan of Arc." She dreamed that the spirit of Pele told her that Hawaiʻi would be destroyed on Kamehameha's birthday on June 11. To satisfy the gods and prevent a catastrophe, Kaneau convinces others to join her, but they are exhausted and starving after a long hike, and rescued before anyone gets near the volcano.

July 6, 1918: HONOLULU ADVERTISER reports that swimmer Duke Kahanamoku insured his feet for $50,000.

July 12, 1918: A front-page HONOLULU ADVERTISER story reads in entirety – "All loafers are being rounded up in Hilo and given the alternative of getting busy or going to jail. Fifty caught in the police net are today ordered to work or serve a jail term."

July 12, 1918: Everton Conger, who led the capture of President Abraham Lincoln's assassin John Wilkes Booth, dies of a stroke in Honolulu. He is the father-in-law of future Governor Joseph Poindexter.

October 2, 1918: For purposes of the WW I Selective Service draft, native Hawaiians are considered as white, announced Captain H. Gooding Field, in charge of the draft.

January 4, 1919: An arson-caused fire burns many Lahaina stores, creating $150,000 damage. Firefighters lacked a hose connection, and the entire town almost burned.

February 8, 1919: Hawai'i Judge Clarence Ashford says he would be happy to be known as the judge who advocates whipping husbands who beat their wives. He says, "A jail sentence is only a picnic for them."

May 6, 1920: Education Superintendent Vaughan MacCaughey gives a speech at a Rotary Club luncheon and asks if anyone has a child attending a public school. No one responds.

April 11, 1921: Governor Charles McCarthy signs a law to prohibit speaking obscene language on the telephone, punishable by $100 fine or 3 months in jail.

April 25, 1921: Governor Charles McCarthy signs the Desha Bathing Suit law to prohibit any person older than age 14 on a Honolulu street or highway from wearing a bathing suit without an outer garment that does not cover the knees. The penalty is a $50 fine. The law is repealed by Governor Ingram Stainback on April 6, 1949.

September 22, 1922: Hawaiian Civic Club condemns the modern hula as "indecent" because it appeals to tourists by "degrad(ing) women" and "exploit(ing) Hawai'i" in the disguise of "ancient hula."

January 13, 1923: George Peka, a night watchman in the Territorial Treasurer's Office foils two masked robbers at 1 a.m. Peka unmasks one and the other drops his gun as he runs out. The office had $750,000 cash and $7.5 million in securities.

March 27, 1923: Kaanana Mahikoa is freed from Iwilei jail after spending 18 months waiting for his trial. He is "the man the law forgot." On June 7, 1922, he finished a 25 day misdemeanor sentence and was supposed to go on trial for a robbery charge, but his case got lost and no one could "find him."

August 22, 1924: More than 20 city officials pay overdue taxes only after 80 officials were told yesterday that their wages would be withheld. Among the delinquents are Mayor John Wilson, and elected Supervisors William Ahia and W.K. Bassett.

August 5, 1924: Honolulu Mayor John Wilson punches Supervisor Ben Hollinger inside City Hall. They had been arguing 7 months over political issues. Wilson is arrested, pleads guilty to assault on August 14, and pays a $20 fine. Wilson said Hollinger accused him of "shielding grafters and crooks."

April 27, 1925: Governor Wallace Farrington signs a Joint Resolution making Thomas Square a public park, to be "maintained as a sacred ground." The intent is to prohibit the city from extending Young Street through the park. During WW II, the park is surrounded by barbed wire, and littered with jeeps and barracks.

April 26, 1928: Hawai'i Supreme Court rules that Territorial Representative Norman Lyman, an attorney, is guilty of professional misconduct and disbarred from practicing law.

July 18, 1928: HONOLULU STAR-BULLETIN reports small pieces of gold are found on Sierra Ave. The next day, William Castle says a California miner found gold in the Ko'olau mountains 60 years earlier, and the gold was displayed at Bishop Bank.

May 18, 1931: The Territorial Supreme Court rules that whipping a prisoner is not "cruel or unusual punishment." Two years earlier, on August 19, 1929, 12 prisoners had escaped, and 11 were quickly captured. The Prison Board ordered 24 lashings with a "cat o' nine tails." After 9 lashes they cried "enough." Three weeks later, the 12th escapee, Lucas Candido, was captured but not whipped due to public outcry.

October 31, 1931: Orieman Fujihara, age 68, is sentenced to life in prison for setting fire to a man's home. He is the only man sentenced twice to life in prison for two different crimes, decades apart. On June 27, 1901, he was convicted of first degree murder on Hawai'i Island, and sentenced to hang. On November 15, 1909, his sentence was commuted to life in prison, and Governor Charles McCarthy pardoned him on December 24, 1919.

June 2, 1932: A man shoots and kills his girlfriend at the volcano rim because she refused to marry him. He clutches her dead body and jumps into the Halema'uma'u fire pit.

July 2, 1932: Joseph Medeiros, age 52, dies. He is known as "The Statue Worshipper" because from age 16, he stood in front of the Kamehameha statue every day for 34 years.

May 10, 1935: Governor Joseph Poindexter signs a Joint Resolution to establish a Bureau of Leisure Activities and Self Help – to help "idle youth" live constructive, useful lives, and become good citizens.

July 10, 1935: Mutual Telephone Co. says it will install 300-400 pay telephones and charge 5¢ per call. The phone company says people are canceling their home phones and making free calls at nearby stores.

August 10, 1935: From the balcony of 'Iolani Palace, 6-year old actress Shirley Temple sings "Good Ship Lollipop" to 16,000 admiring young fans.

May 6, 1937: Governor Joseph Poindexter signs a law to establish a "Pauper's Oath." A convict with less than $20 assets can take this oath and be released from prison if he can't pay the fine.

August 3, 1937: The most unusual death of a police officer occurs when Detective Wah Choon Lee is electrocuted and thrown 7 feet by electric volts after touching a "wired" door knob at a Wahiawā brothel.

December 28, 1940: Maui Subcommittee of the Citizens Committee on Public Finance suggests that the County Board of Supervisors should be paid $1 a year.

May 2, 1941: Police Commissioner Alexander Castro offers $100 for the best citizen suggestion to control prostitution.

December 7, 1941: During the Japanese attack, Pearl Harbor Marine Chaplain Lt. Howell Forgy, utters the words, "Praise the Lord and pass the ammunition" – soon popularized into a top-selling national song.

April 28, 1943: Governor Ingram Stainback signs a law to allow police to arrest a child under age 15 on the street without a parent after 8 p.m.

January 3, 1945: Soon after inauguration ceremonies, Maui County Chairman Eddie Tam and Supervisor John Bulgo scuffle in Tam's office. Other Supervisors have to separate them.

October 17, 1945: Hawaii's 55 lb. formal proposal to host the new United Nations headquarters in Waimānalo is received in London. It has the full support of Governor Ingram Stainback, a business committee, and is backed with $10,000 for publicity. Honolulu is one of 8 cities to submit a proposal.

February 1, 1949: Honolulu Mayor John Wilson wants the city to buy Waikīkī beachfront property to prevent hotel construction near Diamond Head. In a letter to the editor of the HONOLULU ADVERTISER, "R.M." writes – "I think I shall never see a building lovely as Waikīkī. Come to think of it, unless a building fall, I shall never see Waikīkī at all."

September 25, 1951: Six Oʻahu prison inmates die after drinking a bottle of poison that they stole from a locked locker. They dilute the poison and share the bottle, even though the bottle is clearly marked as poison with a big X.

October 26, 1952: The Honolulu Water Board predicts Honolulu will have 400,000 population in the year 2000. The study is "based on math calculations."

November 2, 1958: E.C. Quinn, a Chrysler Vice President announces that

Hawai'i has the nation's most cars per population. Hawai'i has one car for every 3 residents or 30 cars per square mile compared with 22 cars per square mile on the mainland.

April 10, 1959: Governor William Quinn withdraws his re-appointment of Harry Kronick to the O'ahu Liquor Commission a day after Kronick tells news reporters that Filipinos are "bound to be trouble" when they drink alcohol.

July 25, 1959: After the last Territorial Legislature ends, thousands of dollars worth of supplies and equipment are reported missing. Many legislators admit taking small supplies as a "tradition." Soon after news stories expose the problem, expensive equipment such as rugs and chairs reappear. The Attorney General investigates but says there is insufficient evidence to indict anyone. Senate purchase practices are revised.

November 24, 1959: 25,000 bronze and gold Hawai'i State medallions go on sale as statehood souvenir coins, but O'ahu is misspelled. Another 75,000 medallions will be printed correctly. The sale is sponsored by the Maui Chamber of Commerce.

August 24, 1960: Bishop Estate announces plans to build a $12 million "Disneyland of the Pacific," featuring ethnic and cultural themes in Hale'iwa.

August 6, 1961: National TV personality Arthur Godfrey tells the HONO-LULU STAR-BULLETIN that Duke Kahanamoku is getting "shabby treatment" and is underpaid as Honolulu's official greeter, a job that pays $688 a month. Duke admits, "I am barely getting along..." especially "after I put all my life selling Hawai'i without pay." For decades, Duke promoted Hawai'i on the mainland as an unpaid spokesman.

May 1, 1962: Gubernatorial-candidate John Burns rejects a $25,000 offer to appoint a State Land Director from a list submitted by a campaign contributor.

July 27, 1962: U.S. National Park Service rejects Diamond Head as a National Monument because it is "notable" but not "historic." Diamond Head is a state park known as Diamond Head State Monument.

September 24, 1963: The Maui Planning Commission receives a proposal for an aerial tramway to an 800-foot level above Olowalu.

December 14, 1963: Several days of newspaper stories reveal complaints from realtors that Bishop Estate is responsible for unwritten "gentlemen's agreements" that prevent non-Caucasians from buying homes in Kahala. Bishop Estate denies the charge. Realtors say there is a special desk in Bishop Estate's office where realtors must bring home buyers, allegedly for an "ethnic check." If a spouse is absent, the buyer must bring a photo of the spouse or a wedding photo. In 1963, author James Michener said he left Hawai'i, because he couldn't buy a home in Kahala, and his AJA wife experienced discrimination here.

March 26, 1964: Hawai'i sends and receives its first fax. On the 93rd birthday of Jonah Kūhiō, his photo is faxed from the U.S. Navy ship KINGSPORT at Pier 39 to a SYCOM 2 satellite above South America. The image is sent to Honolulu, and printed by a fax machine in 6 minutes.

June 20, 1964: President Lyndon Johnson's daughter, Lynda Bird, is forced to extend a 10-day visit to Hawai'i an extra day when a jealous man threatens to shoot his ex-girlfriend and her husband in the airplane lobby. They are all on the same flight as Johnson, so the Secret Service cancels her return flight, just in case.

January 26, 1965: Hotel owner Roy Kelley opposes increasing parking space in Waikīkī. He says, "We should put a wall around Waikīkī and not let anyone in except tourists." Kelley's idea is ridiculed in a Harry Lyons' cartoon, depicting Waikīkī as "Kelleyland" in the January 29 HONOLULU ADVERTISER.

May 6, 1965: The City Planning Commission ignores public protests and votes 5-0 to rezone Diamond Head for apartment-hotel construction, yet several Commissioners fail to disclose conflicts of interest. News stories reveal that some Commissioners hadn't filed conflict of interest reports for 7 years, which violates the City Charter. Mayor Blaisdell later admits his administration had been "lax" in enforcement.

May 7, 1965: A former WW II fighter pilot, James Ashdown, steals a B-25 airplane and takes a half-hour "aerial joy ride" over most of O'ahu at 1:30 a.m. He scares residents by flying near hotels, and at tree top heights. His airplane grazes a radio tower, and he returns to the airport.

October 13, 1965: As a Hawai'i State Prison inmate is interviewing Warden Ishmael Manus in the Warden's Office, the inmate shows his knife and takes Manus hostage for an escape. Manus grabs the inmate's knife and receives minor cuts.

October 30, 1965: A HONOLULU STAR-BULLETIN investigation reveals 28 children and relatives of state and federal officials got summer Post Office jobs. The jobs were intended for poor and needy students with a federal Youth Opportunity Program. The names of job seekers were submitted by Hawai'i Congressmen. This problem occurs nationally, and the U.S. Postmaster General resigns.

December 15, 1966: The diary of Undersecretary of State Edward Stettinius is made public – revealing President Franklin Roosevelt's desire to locate the United Nations in places with a "fine climate," such as Ni'ihau and the Azores. Roosevelt didn't recall Ni'ihau by name, but he told Stettinius on August 24, 1944 that Ni'ihau is "the most interesting and heavenly spot he knew on earth." Roosevelt never visited Ni'ihau, but he said the island is northwest of O'ahu and owned by a sugar family.

February 9, 1967: Seven royal palm trees, each 40 feet tall, surrounding the Kamehameha Statue fronting Ali'iōlani Hale are cut down as the result of a prank. A man posing as a state official tells a private contractor to cut the trees at 6 a.m., and he does.

April 5, 1967: Governor John Burns signs a law to remove an 1860 requirement that parents give their children a Christian name. The requirement was approved by King Kamehameha IV on August 24, 1860.

October 3, 1968: E.K. Fernandez announces plans to build a $1.5 million aerial tramway and restaurant in Koko Crater.

November 13, 1968: Maui Police Commission fires Police Chief Edward Hitchcock for being "disrespect(ful)" for arguing with commissioners. Hitchcock says it is "political" because he told police to stop political campaigning, and told the vice squad to raid gambling. On November 26, the Commission changes its mind, but Hitchcock is fired again on April 25, 1969 for being "emotionally unfit" and lacking administrative ability – 3 days after accusing two county officials of gambling.

October 7, 1969: The HONOLULU STAR-BULLETIN reports that Admiral Donald Davis bans cars with peace symbols from the Pearl Harbor Naval base, but allows cars having decals with the word "peace." Davis fears peace symbols might create violence on the base.

October 5, 1970: UH microbiologist, Dr. Kaare Gundersen, says Kaho'olawe is a good place for a nuclear power plant and an aqauculture center.

February 15, 1972: State Ethics Commission says all 17 Senate Democrats are in "probable violation" of state law for requiring staff to donate two days of pay to political campaigns. On January 20, 1973, two workers in Senator Mason Altiery's office are fired for not giving two days of pay to the Democratic Senate campaign fund. Democrats say their "donation" is mandatory, and Republicans say theirs is voluntary.

December 19, 1972: Termites are found in Hawaii's 4-year old, $30 million State Capitol building. The ground wasn't treated first.

May 14, 1974: Mayor Frank Fasi offers to give the City a $365,046.66 check from money left over from his last campaign. The City Council approves, then rejects the money over concerns that Fasi may have violated campaign spending laws. On May 29, Fasi's attorney says the mayor would have had to pay taxes on some of the money if he hadn't donated it. On August 8, the Campaign Spending Commission rules that Fasi's gift is a political expense, and the mayor must reveal his donors. Fasi refuses to reveal the names because he doesn't have a complete list back to 1969. On September 23, 1977, the Hawai'i Supreme Court rules that the Campaign Spending Commission was wrong to censure Fasi on September 26, 1974 and to retroactively investigate his campaign finances. Fasi blamed the investigation on his 5,000 vote loss in the October 5, 1974 Democratic primary for Governor.

September 14, 1974: HONOLULU ADVERTISER reports the State Agriculture Board recently reviewed a proposal to produce 10,000 monkeys a year on Moloka'i, free of disease – and sell them to scientific institutions for research. There is a world shortage of disease-free monkeys.

April 18, 1975: Governor George Ariyoshi vetoes a bill to give state legislators a 250% pension hike. The public was not allowed to testify at hearings, and many Democratic legislators said they made a mistake by passing the generous bill. "I am aware of the legal questions, but I am more concerned about the public outcry," Ariyoshi says.

November 24, 1975: Castle and Cooke tells the U.S. Securities and Exchange Commission it paid an average $80,000 a year in bribes to Latin American government officials. Castle and Cooke owns plantations in Latin America, and says payoffs are "fairly standard practices."

May 1, 1976: A 14-year business, Trader Halls' Giftshop in He'eia closes. The store lost business because its owners refused to pay $20 per busload kickbacks for tour buses to stop there. A HONOLULU ADVERTISER story alleges the bus drivers also get 10% of sales above $80. Tour bus companies deny the charge.

April 15, 1978: 1,200 people enter a drawing for 148 Wailea, Maui condominiums. All 148 condos are sold today for $25 million total. "Condomania" brings many speculators to Maui with suitcases full of cash to buy condos.

September 28, 1980: Stephen Craven, district director of the U.S. Commerce Department's International Trade Office tells the Hawai'i Economic Association — "The world view of Hawai'i is that it's a place to play, and such a place is not a place to do business."

December 11, 1986: C. Brewer Company proposes to establish a space launching center on Hawai'i Island. A spaceport would be built on 500 isolated acres at Kāhilipali Point, near South Point.

May 27, 1987: Returning from a Japan trip, former Governor George Ariyoshi and wife Jean fail to declare $44,000 in jewelry with Honolulu Airport customs. They pay a $11,389 fine in November, which is 5 times more than if they had declared their jewelry.

December 21, 1987: MAUI NEWS reports that Rose Fisher of Kīhei received a "thank-you" letter from President Ronald Reagan, in response to her sending the government a $12,771 check to help balance the federal budget. An immigrant, Fisher owns Rainbow Mall.

March 13, 1989: State Senator Steve Cobb pleads no contest to a charge of soliciting sex from an undercover policewoman posing as a prostitute. He is fined $500. The Senate censures him on August 31 for "unacceptable conduct," requires him to make a public apology, and takes his committee chairmanship.

December 14, 1989: 600 people attend a $50 per person fundraiser to help Deputy Court Administrator Tom Okuda pay his legal bills after lengthy trials. Legislators, a Supreme Court justice, politicians and labor leaders attend his party. For many years, Okuda organized Judiciary employees to cook food at Democratic Party fundraisers. On June 14, 1987, he was found guilty of fixing tickets and altering public records.

September 5, 1990: A letter from a UH student, Joey Carter, published in the student newspaper KA LEO says, "racism is not an exclusively white endeavor." On September 19, UH Professor Haunani Trask responds in KA LEO, "If Mr. Carter does not like being called a haole he can return to Louisiana. Hawaiians would certainly benefit from one less haole on our land." After receiving threats and facing financial problems, Carter leaves Hawai'i on October 8. The UH Philosophy Department faculty vote to censure Trask, and she replies on November 16 in the HONOLULU ADVERTISER, "My open letter to a 32-year old student educating him about haole supremacy, and instructing him that his behavior is both disrespectful and dangerous to Hawaiians, is met by a campaign against me by the Philosophy Department that this is nothing short of McCarthyism." On November 5, Dr. Trask clarifies that she is against "haole supremacy" not haoles.

December 26, 1995: Haleakalā National Park renames "7 Sacred Pools" as 'Ohe'o gulch and stream. There are 22 pools, not 7. In 1979, the Lt. Governor ordered the state to stop using the name "7 Sacred Pools," created in 1946 to attract visitors.

"Power in the Hands of a Few"

How a few people in a few big companies controlled Hawaii's economy through Interlocking Directorates

adapted from: Labor in the Territory of Hawai'i, 1939, by James Shoemaker, U.S. Bureau of Labor Statistics, Washington, D.C., June 1939, p. 197

Agents
Alexander & Baldwin
C. Brewer
Castle & Cooke

Banks
Bank of Hawai'i
Bishop Trust Co.
Hawaiian Trust Co.

Public Utilities
Hawai'i Consolidated Railway
Hawaiian Electric
Honolulu Rapid Transit
O'ahu Railway & Land

Pineapples
Baldwin Packers
Hawaiian Canneries Co.
Hawaiian Pineapple Co.
Kaua'i Pineapple Co.

Steam Navigation
Inter-Island Steam Navigation
Matson Navigation

Newspapers
Advertiser Publishing Co.
Honolulu Star-Bulletin

Insurance & Financial Agents
B.F. Dillingham Co.
Home Insurance Co. of Hawai'i

Miscellaneous
Lewers & Cooke, Ltd
Von Hamm Young Co.
Hawaiian Hotels Ltd.
Inter-Island Airways
Pacific Guano & Fertilizer

President
Vice President
Vice President
Vice President
Vice President
Vice President
Treasurer
Assistant Treasurer
Secretary
Assistant Secretary
Director
Director
Director
Director
Director

Sugar
American Sugar Co.
'Ewa Plantation
Hawaiian Agricultural Co.
Hawaiian Cane Products
HC&S
Hawaiian Sugar Co.
Hilo Sugar Co.
Honomu Sugar Co.
Hutchinson Sugar Plantation
Kaleku Sugar Co.
Kahuku Plantation
Kekaha Sugar Co.
Kohala Sugar Co.
Koloa Sugar Co.
Lihu'e Plantation
Maui Agricultural Co.
McBryde Sugar Co.
O'ahu Sugar Co.
Ola'a Sugar Co.
Onomea Sugar Co.
Paauhau Sugar Co.
Pepe'ekeo Sugar Co.
Pioneer Mill Co.
Sugar Factors Co.
Waialua Agricultural Co.
Wai'anae Co.
Wailuku Sugar Co.
Waimanalo Sugar Co.

Irrigation & Water
East Kaua'i Water Co.
East Maui Irrigation Co.
Waiahole Water Co.

Bibliography

Adelman, William. History of the U.S. Army in Hawai'i, 1849-1939. Schofield Barracks, Territory of Hawai'i.

A History of Fort Shafter 1898-1974. Office of the Deputy Installation Commander, Fort Shafter. December 31, 1974.

Albertini, Jim. The Dark Side of Paradise: Hawai'i in a Nuclear World. Catholic Action of Hawai'i, 1980.

Alexander and Baldwin: 90 Years a Corporation, 1900-1990. Honolulu: A&B, June 30, 1990.

Allen, Gwenfred. Hawaii's War Years, 1941-1945. Honolulu: University of Hawai'i Press, 1950.

Allen, Helena. Betrayal of Lili'uokalani: Last Queen of Hawai'i, 1838-1917. Glendale, California: Arthur Clark Co., 1982.

_____. Sanford Ballard Dole: Hawaii's Only President, 1844-1926. Glendale, California: Arthur Clark Company, 1988.

Allen, Robert. Creating Hawai'i Tourism: A Memoir. Honolulu: Bess Press, 2004.

Alvarez, Patricia. A History of Schofield Barracks Military Reservation. Department of the Army, Fort Shafter, March 1982.

Ames, Kenneth. On Bishop Street: Avenue of Hawai'i Pioneers. Honolulu: First Hawaiian Bank, 1996.

Anthony, J. Garner. Hawai'i Under Army Rule. Honolulu: University of Hawai'i Press, 1955.

A Report of the Governor, 1974-1985. Honolulu: Governor's Office, 1985.

Ariyoshi, Jean. Washington Place: A First Lady's Story. Honolulu: Japanese Cultural Center of Hawai'i, 2004.

Ariyoshi, Koji. From Kona to Yenan: The Political Memoirs of Koji Ariyoshi. Edited by Alice and Edward Beechert. Honolulu: Biographical Research Center, University of Hawai'i Press, 2000.

Arnold, Frank, Michael Booth and Gilah Langner. Economic Losses of Ethnic Japanese as a Result of Exclusion and Detention, 1942-1946. Prepared for the Commission on Wartime Relocation and Internment of Civilians. ICF Inc., June 1943.

Ashford, Marguerite. Lāna'i: A Narrative History. Unpublished report, Stanford University, January 1974.

A Short History of Schofield Barracks. Tropic Lightning Museum, October 1999.

Auchter, E.C. People, Research and Social Significance of the Pineapple Industry of Hawai'i. Unpublished manuscript, May 1951.

Baker, Ray Jerome. Odessey of a Cameraman.

Bandy, David. The History of the Royal Hawaiian Band 1836-1980. Masters Thesis for Music. University of Hawai'i, 1989.

Bank of Hawai'i. Business Trends. A Report on Economic Conditions in Hawai'i. Economic Department of Bank of Hawai'i, July/August 1994.

Barber, Joseph. Hawai'i: Restless Rampart. New York: Bobbs-Merrill, 1941.

Barnard, Walther. Kaho'olawe. Fredonia, NY, 1996.

Baro, Agnes. Effective Political Control of Bureaucracy: The Case of Hawaii's Prison System. A Dissertation presented to the College of Criminal Justice, Sam Houston State University, December 1990.

Beechert, Edward. Aupuni I Lā'au: A History of Hawaii's Carpenters Union Local 745. Honolulu: University of Hawai'i Center for Labor Education and Research, 1993.

_____. Honolulu: Crossroads of the Pacific. Columbia: University of South Carolina Press, 1991.

_____. Working in Hawai'i: A Labor History. Honolulu: University of Hawai'i Press, 1985.

Beekman, Allan. The Ni'ihau Incident. Honolulu: Heritage Press of the Pacific, 1982.

Bell, Roger. Last Among Equals: Hawai'i Statehood and American Politics. Honolulu: University of Hawai'i Press, 1984.

Benham, Maenette and Heck, Ronald. Culture and Educational Policy in Hawai'i: The Silencing of Native Voices. Mahwah, New Jersey: Lawrence Erlbaum Associates, Publishers, 1998.

Bergin, Billy. Loyal to the Land: The Legendary Parker Ranch, 750-1950. Honolulu: University of Hawai'i Press, 2004.

Bishop Estate. Annual Report. 1953-1964, 1990-1995.

Black, A. Duane. Lāna'i: The Elusive Hawaiian Island. New York: Vantage Press, 2001.

Black, Cobey. Hawai'i Scandal. Waipahu: Island Heritage, 2002.

Blackford, Mansel. Fragile Paradise: The Impact of Tourism on Maui, 1959-2000. Lawrence, Kansas: University of Kansas Press, 2001.

Brennan, Joseph. Duke: The Life Story of Hawaii's Duke Kahanamoku. Honolulu: Ku Pa'a Publishing, 1994.

Brieske, Phillip. A Study of the development of public elementary and secondary education in the Territory of Hawai'i, Ph.D. thesis, University of Washington, 1961.

Brown, DeSoto. Hawai'i Goes to War. Honolulu: Editions Limited, 1989.

Buck, Elizabeth. Paradise Remade: The Politics of Culture and History in Hawai'i. Philadelphia: Temple University Press, 1993.

Budnick, Rich. Stolen Kingdom. Honolulu: Aloha Press, 1992.

Cahill, Emmett. Hawaiian Stamps. Volcano: Orchid Isle Publishers, September 1996.

Carayannis, George. Catalog of Tsunamis in the Hawaiian Islands. May 1969, World Data Center A: Tsunami. U.S. Department of Commerce Environmental Science Services Administration, Coast and Geodetic Survey

Carr, Norma. The Puerto Ricans in Hawai'i: 1900-1958. Ph.D. Dissertation, American Studies, UH, 1989.

Carruth, Gorton. The Encyclopedia of American Facts and Dates. 9th edition. New York: HarperCollins, 1993.

Chang, Carol. Straub: Four Generations of Excellence. Straub Clinic and Hospital, 1996.

Chang, Thelma. "I Can Never Forget": Men of the 100th/442nd. Honolulu: SIGI Productions, 1991.

Chapin, Helen. Guide to Newspapers in Hawai'i 1834-2000. Honolulu: Hawaiian Historical Society, 2000.

_____. Shaping History: The Role of Newspapers in Hawai'i. Honolulu: University of Hawai'i Press, 1996.

Chun-Lum, Sharlene and Agard, Lesley. Legacy: A Portrait of the Youg Men and Women of Kamehameha Schools, 1887-1987. Honolulu: Kamehameha Schools Press, 1987.

Cisco, Dan. Hawai'i Sports: History, Facts and Statistics. Honolulu: University of Hawai'i Press, 1999.

Code of Federal Registers. Title 3–The President. National Archives and Records Service, General Service Administration. Office of Federal Register, 2000. Washington, D.C. Government Printing Office.

Coffman, Tom. Catch a Wave. Honolulu: University of Hawai'i Press, 1973.

_____. The Island Edge of America: A Political History of Hawai'i. Honolulu: University of Hawai'i Press, 2003.

_____. Nation Within. Kāne'ohe: Epicenter Press, 1998.

Cohen, Daniel. Hiram Bingham and the Dream of Gold. New York: M. Evans and Co., 1984.

Cohen, Stan. Hawaiian Airlines: A Pictorial History of the Pioneer Carrier in the Pacific. Missoula, Montana: Pictorial Histories Publishing Co., 1986.

_____. First Lady of Waikīkī: A Pictorial History of the Sheraton Moana Surfrider. Missoula, MT: Pictorial Histories Publishing Co., 1995.

_____. Princess Victoria Kai'ulani and the Princess Kai'ulani Hotel in Waikīkī. Missoula, MT: Pictorial Histories Publishing Co., 1997.

_____. The Pink Palace: Royal Hawaiian Waikīkī. Missoula, MT: Pictorial Histories Publishing Co., 1986.

Coletta, Paolo. United States Navy and Marine Corps Bases, Domestic. Wesport, CT.: Greenwood Press, 1985.

Congressional Record.

Cook, Chris. A Kaua'i Reader: The exotic literary heritage of the Garden Island. Honolulu: Mutual Publishing, 1995.

Cooke, George. Mo'olelo 'O Moloka'i: A Ranch Story of Moloka'i. Honolulu: Honolulu Star-Bulletin, 1949.

Cooper, George and Daws, Gavan. Land and Power in Hawai'i: the Democratic Years. Honolulu: Benchmark Books, 1985.

Crawford, David. Paradox in Hawai'i: An examination of industry and education and the paradox they represent. Boston: Stratforts Co., 1933.

Crost, Lynn. Honor by Fire: Japanese Americans at War in Europe and the Pacific. Novato, CA: Presidio Press, 1994.

Day, A. Grove. History Makers of Hawai'i. Honolulu: Mutual Publishing, 1984.

Dean, Arthur. Alexander and Baldwin, Ltd. and the Predecessor Partnerships. Honolulu: Alexander and Baldwin, Ltd., 1950.

Dedmon, Donald. An Analysis of the arguments in the debate in Congress on the admission of Hawai'i to the Union. Ph.D. Dissertation in Speech, State University of Iowa, 1961.

Dodd, Carol. The Richardson Years, 1966-1982. Honolulu: UH Foundation, 1985.

Dorita, Sister Mary. Filipino Imigration to Hawai'i, 1975. M.A. Thesis, University of Hawai'i, 1954.

Dole, Richard and Porteus, Elizabeth Dole. The Story of James Dole. Honolulu: Island Heritage, 1990.

Dorrance, William. Oahu's Hidden History. Honolulu: Mutual Publishing Co., 1998.

_____, and Morgan, Francis. Sugar Islands: The 165-year story of sugar in Hawai'i. Honolulu: Mutual Publishing, 2000.

Dudley, Michael Kioni and Agard, Keoni. A Call for Hawaiian Sovereignty. Na Kāne 'O Ka Malo Press, 1990.

Duus, Masayo. Unlikely Liberators: The Men of the 100th and 442nd. Honolulu: University of Hawai'i Press, 1987.

_____. The Japanese Conspiracy: The O'ahu Sugar Strike of 1920. Berkeley: University of California Press, 1999.

Ethnic Studies Program. Uchinanchu: A History of Okinawans in Hawai'i. 1981, University of Hawai'i.

Ewanchuk, Michael. Hawaiian Ordeal: Ukranian Contract Workers 1897-1910. Winnepeg, Canada, 1986

Felix, John Henry and Senecal, Peter. The Portuguese in Hawai'i. Centennial Edition, 1978.

_____, Nunes, Leslie, and Senecal, Peter. The 'Ukulele: A Portuguese Gift to Hawai'i. Kailua, Hawai'i, 1963.

Forden, Lesley. Glory Gamblers: The Story of the Dole Race. Alameda, CA.: Nottingham Press, 1986.

Foster, Mark. Henry J. Kaiser: Builder in the Modern American West. Austin: University of Texas Press, 1989.

Foster, Nelson. Punahou: The History and Promise of a School of the Islands. 1991, Punahou School.

_____. Bishop Museum and the Changing World of Hawai'i. Honolulu: Bishop Museum Press, 1993.

Free, David. Vignettes of Old Hawai'i. Honolulu: Crossroads Press, 1994.

_____. More Vignettes of Old Hawai'i. Honolulu: Crossroads Press, 1994.

Fuchs, Lawrence. Hawai'i Pono. New York: Harcourt Brace Jovanovich, 1961.

Gall, Susan, Managing Editor. The Asian American Almanac. Detroit: Gale Research, 1995.

Garden Island newspaper.

Go For Broke: 442nd Regimental Combat Team. brochure.

Fairfax, Geoffrey. The Architecture of Honolulu. Honolulu: Island Heritage, 1971.

Gugliotta, Bobette. Nolle Smith. Cornwall, New York: Cornwall Press, 1971.

Hackler, Rhonda, editor. The Story of Scots in Hawai'i. The Caledonian Society of Hawai'i, 2000

Hagino, David. Palaka Power. Undated.

Hall, Dale. The Honolulu Symphony: A Century of Music. Honolulu: Goodale Publishing, 2002

Halloran, Richard. My Name is Shinseki…and I am a Soldier. Honolulu: Hawai'i Army Museum Society, 2004.

_____. Sparky: Warrior, Peacemaker, Poet, Patriot. Honolulu: Watermark Publishing Co., 2002.

Hancock, Lambreth. Hawai'i Kai: The First 20 Years. Honolulu, 1983.

Hardy, Thornton. Wallace Rider Farrington. Honolulu: Honolulu Star-Bulletin, Ltd., 1935.

Hausman, Ruth. Hawai'i: Music in its History. Rutland, Vermont: Charles E. Tuttle Co., 1968.

Hawai'i Department of Public Instruction and Department of Education. Annual Report, 1900-1994.

_____. Minutes of board meetings, 1920-1936.

Hawai'i Education Review. September 1935, p. 21.

Hawai'i Employers Council. Strikes and Work Stoppages in Hawai'i. Research Department. Special Publication Number 115. October, 1974.

_____. Strikes and Work Stoppages in Hawai'i. 1975-1997. Research Department. Unpublished manuscript. 1999.

Hawai'i Filipino News Specialty Publication. The Filipinos in Hawai'i: The first 75 years. Honolulu, 1981.

Hawai'i State Archives.

Hawai'i State Department of Labor and Industrial Relations. Records of Hawai'i Plant Closing Law.

Hawai'i Statehood Commission. Hawai'i, USA and Statehood. Honolulu, 1951.

_____. Statehood for Hawai'i. Honolulu, 1959.

Hawaiian Evening Bulletin.

Hawaiian Journal of History.

Hawaiian Sovereignty Advisory Commission: Final Report, February 18, 1994.

Hawaiian Sovereignty Elections Council: Final Report, December 1996.

Hawaiian Star.

Hawaiian Sugar Planters' Association. Memo dated June 6, 1924 from J. Butler, HSPA Executive Secretary to Hawai'i and Maui Plantation Managers.

Hawaii's English Standard Schools. Report No. 3-1948. Honolulu: Legislative Reference Bureau, University of Hawai'i, 1948.

Hearings before the House Committee on Labor Board and Wagner Act. Report of Elwyn Eagen on the Hawaiian Islands, May 3, 1940. Known as the Eagen Report.

Hilo Tribune, Hilo Tribune-Herald, Hawai'i Tribune-Herald.

Hodge, Clarence, and Ferris, Peggy. Building Honolulu: A Century of Community Service. Honolulu: Chamber of Commerce of Honolulu, 1950.

Holmes, T. Michael. The Specter of Communism in Hawai'i. Honolulu: University of Hawai'i Press, 1994.

Honolulu Advertiser.

Honolulu Evening Bulletin.

Honolulu Fire Department. Pride, Service, Dedication: 150 Years of Service. Honolulu: 2001.

Honolulu Magazine and Paradise of the Pacific.

Honolulu Star-Bulletin.

Hoover, J. Edgar. Alien Enemy Control. Iowa Law Review, pages 396-408, Vol. 29, 1994.

Horman, Bernhard. The Germans in Hawai'i. 1989, German Benevolent Society. UH M.A. Thesis, 1931.

Horvat, William. Above the Pacific. Fallbrook, CA: Aero Publishers, 1966.

Hoyt, Edwin. Davies: The inside story of a British-American family in the Pacific and its business enterprise. Honolulu: Topgallant, 1983.

Hutchinson, Edward. Legislative History of American Immigration Policy, 1798-1965. Philadelphia: University of Pensylvania Press, 1981.

Hyams, Ben and E. Curtis Cluff Jr. Two Half-Centuries and then Some: A History of the Pacific Club, 1851-1991. Honolulu: Pacific Club, 1991.

ILWU Story: Three Decades of Militant Unionism. San Francisco. ILWU. Second edition, 1979.

Jackson, Miles. And They Came: A Brief History and Annotated Bibliography of Blacks in Hawai'i. Durham, NC: Four-G Publishers, 2000.

Jennings, Helen. Chronology and Documentary Handbook of the State of Hawai'i. Dobbs Ferry, NY, Oceana Publications, 1978.

Joesting, Edward. Tides of Commerce. Honolulu: First Hawaiian Bank, 1983.

_____. Kaua'i: The Separate Kingdom. Honolulu: University of Hawai'i Press, 1984.

Johannssen, Edward: The Hawaiian Labor Movement: A Brief History. Boston: Bruce Humphriver Publishers, 1956.

Johnson, Donald. The City and County of Honolulu. Honolulu: UH Press and Honolulu City Council, 1991.

_____ and Miller, Michael. Hawaii's Own: A History of the Hawai'i Government Employees Association. Honolulu: 1986.

Jones, Charles. Hawaii's World War II Military Sites. Honolulu: Mutual Publishing, 2002.

Judd, Bernice. Voyages to Hawai'i before 1860. Honolulu: Hawaiian Mission Children's Society, 1974.

Judd, Lawrence. Lawrence M. Judd and Hawai'i: An Autobiography. Rutland, Vermont: Charles E. Tuttle Co., 1971.

Judd, Walter. Palaces and Forts of the Hawaiian Kingdom. Palo Alto, CA: Pacific Books, 1975.

Judiciary History Center. Hawai'i under Martial Law: 1941-1944. Judiciary, State of Hawai'i, 2003.

Kaho'olawe island Conveyance Commission: Kaho'olawe Island: Restoring a Cultural Treausre. Final Report of the Kaho'olawe Island Conveyance Commission to the Congress of the United States. March 31, 1993.

Kamae, Lori. The Empty Throne: A Biography of Hawaii's Prince Cupid. Honolulu: Topgallant Publishing Co, 1980.

Kamins, Robert and Potter, Robert. Mālamalama: A History of the University of Hawai'i. Honolulu: University of Hawai'i Press, 1998.

Kanahele, George. Hawaiian Music and Musicians. Honolulu: University of Hawai'i Press, 1979.

Kashima, Tetsuden. Judgment Without Trial: Japanese American Imprisonment during World War II. Seattle: University of Washington Press, 2003.

Kelly, Marjorie. Memory Banks and Political Ranks: Looking at Culture at Hawaii's Bishop Museum. UCLA Anthropology Ph.D. dissertation, 1993.

Kent, Noel. Hawai'i: Islands Under the Influence. New York: Monthly Review Press, 1983.

Kerkvliet, Melinda. Unbending Cane: Pablo Manlapit: A Filipino Labor Leader in Hawai'i. Honolulu: University of Hawai'i Press, 2002.

Kinnaman, William and Swift, David. Hawaii's Telecommuications 1872-1990. Honolulu: Pacific Telecommunications Council, 1993.

Klass, Tim. World War II on Kaua'i. Līhu'e: Kaua'i Historical Society, 1970.

Kotani, Roland. The Japanese in Hawai'i. Honolulu: Hawai'i Hochi, 1985.

Kramer, Raymond. Hawaiian Land Mammals. Rutland, VT: Charles E. Tuttle Co., 1971.

Krauss, Bob, edited, John Jardine and Edward Rohrbough. Detective Jardine: Crimes in Honolulu. Honolulu: University of Hawai'i Press, 1984.

_____. Johnny Wilson: First Hawaiian Democrat. Honolulu: University of Hawai'i Press, 1994.

Kuykendall, Ralph. Hawaiian Kingdom, 3 volumes. Honolulu: University of Hawai'i Press, 1938-1967.

_____. Hawai'i in the World War. Honolulu: The Historical Commission, 1928.

Labor in the Territory of Hawai'i. Bulletin No. 47, 2nd Report on Hawai'i by the Commissioner of Labor on Hawai'i. Gerald Wright, editor. Transmitted to the U.S. Senate on February 26, 1903. Washington, D.C.: Government Printing Office, 1903.

Laird, D. USARPAC Historian. Fact Sheet, 442nd Regimental Combat Team, June 1998.

_____. Fact Sheet, 100th Infantry Battalion. June 1998.

Landauer, Lyndall and Donald. Pearl: The History of the United States Navy in Pearl Harbor. South Lake Tahoe, California: Flying Cloud Press, 1999.

Lander, James. United Sates Tsunamis 1690-1988. U.S. Department of Commerce, National Oceanic and Atmospheric Administration, Publication 41-2, Boulder, Colorado, August 1989.

Lee, Harlan. The Waikīkī Reclamation Report. Unpublished report for History 424, Summer 1975, University of Hawai'i.

Linn, Brian. Guardians of Empire: The U.S. Army and the Pacific, 1902-1940. Chapel Hill, University of North Carolina Press, 1997.

Lind, Andrew: Hawai'i: The Last of the Magic Isles. London: Oxford University Press, 1969.

Lord, Clifford, editor. Presidential Executive Orders. Congressional Record. Hastings House, NY, 1944.

Love, Dean. The Lighthouses of Hawai'i. Honolulu: University of Hawai'i Press, 1991.

Lowe, Chuan-hua. Chinese in Hawai'i. Tapei: China Print, 1972.

Lum, Yansheng Ma and Lum, Raymond Mun Kong. Sun Yat-Sen in Hawai'i. Honolulu: Hawai'i Chinese History Center and Dr. Sun Yat-Sen Foundation, 1999.

MacDonald, Alexander. Revolt in Paradise. New York: Stephen Daye, Inc., 1944.

Macdonald, Gordon, Abbott, Agatin, and Peterson, Frank. Volcanoes in the Sea: The Geology of Hawai'i. Honolulu: University of Hawai'i Press, 1983.

Mackenzie, Jean. Tandy. Honolulu: Island Heritage Ltd., 1975.

McDermott, John. Kelleys of the Outrigger. Honolulu: ORAFA Publishing Company, 1990.

_____, Tseng, Wen-Shing, and Maretzki, Thomas, editors: People and Cultures of Hawai'i: A Psychocultural Profile. Honolulu: University of Hawai'i Press, 1980.

McKenzie, Roderick. Oriental Exclusion: The Effect of American Immigration Laws, Regulations and Judicial Decisions upon the Chinese and Japanese on the American Pacific Coast. New York: American Group Institute of Public Relations, 1927 and 1971.

McMillan, Susan and Moris, Nancy. Hawai'i Newspapers: A Union List. 1987.

Makiki: A Memorial Publication for the 75th Anniverary of Makiki Japanese Langauge School. 1983.

Mardfin, Jean. Hawai'i Legislators' Handbook. Honolulu: Legislative Reference Bureau, March, 1997.

Maretzki, Thomas: "The Hawaiians of Hawai'i" in People and Cultures in Hawai'i, Wen-Shing Tseng, John McDermott, Jr. and Thomas Maretzki, editors, pages 44-55, University of Hawai'i School of Medicine, Department of Psychiatry, 1974.

Mast, Robert and Mast, Anne. Autobiography of Protest in Hawai'i. Honolulu: University of Hawai'i Press, 1996.

Matsuo, Dorothy. Boyhood to War: History and Anecdotes of the 442nd Regimental Combat Team. Honolulu: Mutual Publishing, 1992.

Maui News.

Melendy, H. Brett. Walter Francis Dillingham, 1875-1963: Hawaiian Entrepreneur and Statesman. Lewiston, New York: Edwin Mell Press, 1996.

Memorandum on the History of Labor and the Law in the Territory of Hawai'i. ILWU vs. Walter Ackerman, in the U.S. District Court for the District of Hawai'i, Civil No. 828 and 836, August 24, 1948.

Midkiff, Frank. The Economic Determinants of Education in Hawai'i. Ph.D. Dissertation, Yale University, April 1, 1935

Military Intelligence Service Veterans Club of Hawai'i. Secret Valor: M.I.S. Personnel World War II Pacific Theater: Pre-Pearl Harbor to September 8, 1951. 50th Anniversary Reunion, July 8-10, 1993.

Mitchell, Donald Kilolani. Resource Units in Hawaiian Culture. Honolulu: Kamehameha Press, 1992.

Mitchell, Donald Kilolani. Ku Kilakila 'O Kamehameha: A Historical Account of the Campuses of the Kamehaeha Schools. 1993, Kamehameha Schools Bishop Estate.

_____. A Brief History of the Bernice Pauahi Bishop Museum, Honolulu, Hawai'i. Ph.D. dissertation, University of California, Berkeley, 1963.

Modavi, Neghin. "Land, Environment and Power: State, Captial and Community Forces in Environmental Disputes in Hawai'i." Ph.D Dissertation, Sociology, University of Hawai'i, May, 1992.

Mohr, James. Plague and Fire: Battling Black Death and the 1900 Burning of Honolulu's Chinatown. New York: Oxford University Press, 2005.

Morales, Rodney, editor. Ho'iho'iho: A Tribute to George Helm and Kimo Mitchell. Honolulu: Bamboo Ridge Press, 1984.

Murphy, Thomas. Ambassadors in Arms: The Story of Hawaii's 100th Battalion. Honolulu: University of Hawai'i Press, 1954, 1982.

Myatt, Carl. Hawai'i, the Electric Century. A Special Edition for Hawaiian Electric Company. Honolulu: Signature Pubishing, 1991.

Nakamura, Barry. The Story of Waikīkī and The "Reclamation" Project. M.A. Thesis, History, University of Hawai'i, May, 1979.

New York Times.

National Park Service, U.S. Department of the Interior. USS Arizona

Niiya, Brian, editor. Encyclopedia of Japanese American History: An A-to-Z Reference from 1868 to the Present. New York: Japanese American National Museum, 2001.

Oaks, Robert: Hawai'i: A History of the Big Island. Charleston: Arcadia Publishing, 2003.

Odo, Franklin, editor. The Columbia Documentary History of the Asian American Experience. New York: Columbia University Press, 2002.

_____. No Sword to Bury: Japanese Americans in Hawai'i During World War II. Philadelphia: Temple University Press, 2004.

Often, James. Tripler History. Unpublished manuscript, 1995.

Okahata, James, editor. A History of Japaese in Hawai'i. 1971, United Japanese Society of Hawai'i.

Okamura, Jonathan, Guest Editor. Social Process in Hawai'i: Filipino American history, Identity and Community in Hawai'i, Sociology Department, University of Hawai'i, volume 57, 1996.

Okihara, Gary. Cane Fires: The Anti-Japanese Movement in Hawai'i, 1865-1945. Philadelphia: Temple University Press, 1991.

Okumura, Rev. Takie and Umetaro Okumura. Hawaii's American-Japanese Problem: A Campaign to Remove Causes of Friction Between the American People and Japanese. Report of the Campaign, January 1921 to January 1927. Honolulu: 1927.

_____. Seventy Years of Divine Blessings. Honolulu: 1939.

Oliver, Anthony Michael. Hawai'i Fact and Reference Book. Honolulu: Mutual Publishing, 1995

Olson, Gunder. The Story of the Volcano House. Hilo: Bookfinders of Hawai'i, 1984.

Outline of the History of the Catholic Church in Hawai'i, June 3, 1999.

Owens, Harry. Sweet Leilani: The story behind the song. Pacific Palisades, CA: Hula House, 1970.

Pacific Business News.

Parker, Linda. Native American Estate: The Struggle over Indian and Hawaiian Lands. Honolulu: University of Hawai'i Press, 1989.

Peek, Jeannette. Stepping Into Time: A Guide to Honolulu's Historic Landmarks. Honolulu: Mutual Publishing, 1994.

Perlman, Mark. Organized Labor in Hawai'i. Hawai'i Employers Council reprint of April 1952 CCH Labor Law Journal, volume 3, number 4.

Phillips, Paul. Hawaii's Democrats: Chasing the American Dream. Washington, D.C.: University Press of America, 1982.

Pinklam, Lucius. Reclamation of the Waikīkī District of the City of Honolulu Territory of Hawai'i. Honolulu: Hawaiian Gazette, 1906.

Prange, Gordon. At Dawn We Slept. New York: Penguin Books, 1981.

Public Affairs Division: Hickam: The First Fifty Years. Hickam AFB, 1985.

Public Archives. Roster of Legislatures of Hawai'i 1841-1918. Honolulu: Hawaiian Gazette, 1918.

Puette, William. The Hilo Massacre: Hawaii's Bloody Monday. Honolulu: University of Hawai'i Center for Labor Education and Research, 1988.

_____. CLEAR Guide to Hawai'i Labor History. Pearl City: Center for Labor Education and Research, University of Hawai'i, West Oahu, 2003.

Pukui, Mary, Samuel Elbert and Esther Mo'okini. Place Names of Hawai'i. Honolulu: University of Hawai'i Press, 1989.

Ramil, Antonio. Kalai 'Āina County of Maui. Wailuku: Anvil-Maui Press, 1984.

Reed, Francis. Prince Jonah Kūhiō Kalanianaole 1871-1922. Honolulu: Hawai'i State Library System, Centralized Processing Center, 1974.

Reinecke, John. A History of Local 5, Hotel and Restaurant Employees and Bartenders International Union AFL-CIO. Edited by Edward Beechert. Honolulu: University of Hawai'i, College of Business Administration, Labor-Management Education Program, 1970.

_____. The Filipino Piecemeal Sugar Strike of 1924-1925. Honolulu: Social Science Research Institute, University of Hawai'i Press, 1996.

_____. Labor Unions of Hawai'i: A Chronological Checklist. Honolulu: Industrial Relations Center, University of Hawai'i, October 1966.

_____. A Man Must Stand Up: The Autobiography of a Gentle Activist. Edited by Alice and Edward Beechert. Honolulu: Biographical Research Center, University of Hawai'i Press, 1993.

Report of the Commission on Wartime Relocation and Internment of Civilians. Personal Justice Denied. Foreword by Tetsuden Kashima. A reprint of the two-volume, 1982-1983 Commission report. Washington, D.C.: Civil Liberties Public Education Fund and University of Washington Press, 1997.

Report of the Joint Committee on the Investigation of the Pearl Harbor Attack. New York: Da Capo Press, 1972. U.S. 79th Congress, 2nd Session, July 16, 1946 (also known as the Barkley Report).

Report: Kohala Task Force. February 26, 1980.

Reyes, Luis. Made in Paradise. Honolulu: Mutual Publishing, 1995.

Richards, Mary. No Ordinary Man: William Francis Quinn, His Role in Hawaii's History. Honolulu: Hawai'i Education Association, 1998.

Ritte, Walter and Sawyer, Richard. Na Mana'o Aloha O Kaho'olawe. Honolulu: Aloha 'O 'Āina 'O Na Kupuna, 1978.

Saiki, Patsy. Ganbare! An Example of Japanese Spirit. Honolulu: Mutual Publishing, 1982.

Sakamaki, Shunzo. A History of the Japanese Press in Hawai'i. M.A. Thesis in History and Political Science, University of Hawai'i, January 24, 1928.

Scheppler, Robert: Pacific Air Race. Washington, D.C.: Smithsonian Institution Press, 1988.

Schmitt, Robert. Firsts and Almost Firsts in Hawai'i. Honolulu: University of Hawai'i Press, 1995.

_____. Demographic Statistics of Hawai'i, 1778-1965. Honolulu: University of Hawai'i Press, 1968.

_____. Hawai'i Data Book. Hawai'i State Department of Business Economic Development and Tourism.

_____. The Missionary Censuses of Hawai'i. Honolulu: Department of Anthropology, Bernice Pauahi Bishop Museum, 1973.

Schofield Barracks Cultural Resource Management Plan. Prepared for the U.S. Army by Belt Collins Hawai'i. April 2000.

Shoemaker, James. Labor in the Territory of Hawai'i, 1939. U.S. Department of Labor, Bureau of Labor Statistics, June 1939. Transmitted to Congress on June 5, 1940. Washington, D.C.: Government Printing Office, 1940.

_____. The Economy of Hawai'i in 1947. U.S. Departmentof Labor, Bureau of Labor Statistics, 1948. Transmitted to Congress on June 29, 1948. Washington, D.C.: Government Printing Office, 1948.

Sigall, Bob. The Companies We Keep: Amazing Stories About 450 of Hawaii's Best Known Companies. Honolulu: Small Business Hawai'i, 2004.

Silva, Noenoe. Aloha Betrayed: Native Hawaiian Resistance to American Colonialsm. Durham: Duke University Press, 2004.

Simprich Jr., Frederick. Dynasty in the Pacific: Amfac. New York: McGraw Hill, 1974.

Simpson, MacKinnon and Brizdle, John. Streetcar Days in Honolulu. Honolulu: JBL Press, 2000.

Slackman, Michael. Target: Pearl Harbor. Honolulu: University of Hawai'i Press and Arizona Memorial Museum Association, 1990.

Social Process in Hawai'i.

Stathis, Stephen. Landmark Legislation 1774-2002: Major U.S. Acts and Treaties. Washington, D.C.: Congressional Quarterly Press, 2003.

Stern, Bernard and edited by William Puette. Rutledge Unionism: Labor Relations in the Honolulu Transit Industry. Honolulu: University of Hawai'i Center for Labor Education and Research, 1986.

Stern, Bernard. The Aloha Trade: Labor Relations in Hawaii's Hotel Industry 1941-1987. Honolulu: University of Hawai'i Center for Labor Education and Research, 1988.

Stone, Scott. The Royal Hawaiian Band: Its Legacy. Honolulu: Hawaiian Heritage Publishing, 2004.

_____. The Story of C. Brewer and Co., Ltd. 'Aiea: Island Heritage, 1991.

Strauss, Leon. The Honolulu Police Department: A Brief History. Honolulu: The 200 Club, 1978.

Stueber, Ralph. Hawai'i: "A Case Study in the Development in Education, 1778-1960." Ph.D. Dissertation in Education, University of Wisconsin, 1964.

Stump, Jane and Raven, Donald. Our Hawai'i Kai. Honolulu: 1981.

Sullam, Brian. Bishop Estate, the Misused Trust. Honolulu: Hawai'i Observer, 1976.

Takabuki, Matsuo. An Unlikely Revolutionary: Matsuo Takabuki and the Making of Modern Hawai'i. Honolulu: University of Hawai'i Press, 1998.

Tamura, Eileen. Americanization, Acculturation, and Ethnic Identity: The Nisei Generation in Hawai'i. Urbana, Il: University of Illinois Press, 1994

Taylor, Frank, Welty, Earl, and Eyre, David. From Land and Sea: The Story of Castle and Cooke of Hawai'i. San Francisco: Chronicle Books, 1976.

TenBruggencate, Jan. Hawaii's Pineapple Century: A History of the Crowned Fruit in the Hawaiian Islands. Honolulu: Mutual Publishing Co., 2004.

Thiele, Ray. Kennedy's Hawaiian Air. Honolulu: Olomana Publishers, 1994.

Thompson, Pacific Ocean Engineers. History of the U.S. Army Corps of Engineers in the Pacific, 1905-1980.

Thrum, Thomas. Hawaiian Annual: All About Hawai'i.

Tillich, Linda. Crossroads Sanctuary. August 1987.

Todaro, Tony. The Golden Years of Hawaiian Entertainment. Honolulu: Tony Todaro Publishing Co., 1974.

Trask, Haunani-Kay. From a Native Daughter: Colonialism and Sovereignty in Hawai'i, University of Hawai'i Press, Honolulu, 1999.

_____ and Ed Greevy. Kū'ē: Thirty Years of Land Struggles in Hawai'i. Honolulu: Mutual Publishing, 2004.

Tsukiyama, Ted. A Salute to "the One Puka Puka."
_____. Go For Broke 1943-1993.
United States Code, 1900-2000. Washington, D.C.: U.S. Government Printing Office.
U.S. Department of the Interior, Bureau of Education. A Survey of Education in Hawai'i. Made under the direction of the Commissioner of Education. Bulletin, 1920, No. 16. Washington, D.C.: Government Printing Office, 1920.
U.S.G.S. Professional Paper 1350. Volcanism in Hawaii. Bob Decker, editor.
U.S. Postal Service. "People and Places of the Pacific: A Celebration on Stamps." Publication 153. May 2002.
U.S. Statutes at Large, 1901-2000. Washington, D.C.: U.S. Government Printing Office.
Uyehara, Mitsue. Almanac of Hawaiiana 1970-1972. Honolulu: Hawaiiana Almanac Publishing Company, 1971.
Waihe'e, Lynn and the Docents of Washington Pace. Her Royal Highness Queen Lili'uokalani: Poet, Composer, Musician.
Wang, Jim. Hawai'i State and Local Politics. Hilo: Wang Associates, 1998.
Warfield, Charles. History of the Hawai'i National Guard, from feudal times to June 30, 1935. Masters Thesis in History, University of Hawai'i, 1935
Weingarten, Victor. Raising Cane: A Brief History of Labor in Hawai'i. Honolulu, ILWU, September 1946.
West Hawai'i Today.
Wilcox, Carol. Sugar Water: Hawaii's Plantation Ditches. Honolulu: University of Hawai'i Press, 1966.
Williams, Edith. Ka Hae Hawai'i: The Story of the Hawaiian Flag. 1963.
Wisniewski, Richard. Hawai'i, the Territorial Years, 1900-1959. Honolulu: Pacific Basin Enterprises, 1984.
Wong, Barbara and Daryl Aiwohi. The Legacy of Kapu Kanawai, 1750-2000. Honolulu.
Wood, Bill. Fifty Years of Aloha: The Story of Aloha Airlines. Honolulu: Aloha Airlines, 1996.
Worden, William. Cargoes: Matson's First Century in the Pacific. Honolulu: University of Hawai'i Press, 1981.
Wright, Thomas, Takahashi, Takeo, Griggs, J. Hawai'i Volcano Watch. Honolulu: University of Hawai'i Press, 1992.
Yardley, Maili and Rogers, Miriam. The History of Kapi'olani Hospital. Honolulu: Topgallant Publishing Company, 1984.
Yardley, Paul. Millstones and Milestones: The Career of Benjamin Franklin Dillingham, 1944-1918. Honolulu: University of Hawai'i Press, 1981.
Yost, Harold. The Outrigger: A History of the Outrigger Canoe Club 1908-1971. 1971.
Zalburg, Sanford. A Spark is Struck! Jack Hall and the ILWU in Hawai'i. Honolulu: University of Hawai'i Press, 1979.

About the Author

Rich Budnick received his B.A. Degree in History and Political Science from U.C.L.A. and a M.A. Degree in Government from California State University, Sacramento.

He has worked for Governor Ben Cayetano and Maui Mayor Hannibal Tavares, and has been a government Public Information Officer, Legislative Assistant, and a history teacher.

He is the author of three other Hawaiiana books – HAWAIIAN STREET NAMES, MAUI STREET NAMES, and STOLEN KINGDOM. He has written freelance articles for local and national magazines, and completed research assignments for Hawai'i businesses.

Budnick is the founder of the HONOLULU WRITERS CONFERENCE, which has helped aspiring writers meet national and local book editors, literary agents, and authors, as they learn the business of writing and publishing. As a book consultant and editor, Budnick has helped many people publish their books. He also gives workshops on book publishing.